Mrs Beeton's
BEST
OF
BRITISH
HOME
COOKING

MRS Beeton's
BEST
OF
BRITISH
HOME
COOKING

CONSULTANT EDITOR

Bridget Jones

TED SMART

A WARD LOCK BOOK

First published in the UK 1997 by Ward Lock,
A Cassell Imprint, Wellington House, 125 Strand,
London WC2R 0BB

This edition produced for
The Book People Ltd,
Hall Wood Avenue,
Haydock,
St Helens WA11 9UL

**Mrs Beeton's is a registered trademark
of Ward Lock Ltd**

EDITED BY *Jenni Fleetwood*
DESIGNED BY *Balley Design Associates*
Simon Balley and Joanna Hill
PHOTOGRAPHY BY *Tim Hill*
STYLING BY *Zoë Hill*
BLACK & WHITE ILLUSTRATIONS BY *Vana*
COLOUR ILLUSTRATIONS BY *Sarah Symonds*

British Cataloguing-in-Publication Data

A catalogue record of this book is available from the
British Library

ISBN 0-7063-7620-X

Printed and bound in Spain

FOLLOWING THE RECIPES

Use either metric or Imperial measures, never
a combination of both from any one recipe.
Spoon measures are always level and refer to
standard measuring spoons.

tbsp = tablespoon (15 ml spoon)

tsp = teaspoon (5 ml spoon)

*Items marked with a star are included
in the A–Z of Basic Recipes, see page 214.

CONTENTS

A HERITAGE OF HOME

The tradition of eating well in Britain is founded on good home cooking and the simple preparation of fine produce. Chefs' passions and elaborate culinary philosophies have long been dismissed in a country where, historically, meals are centred on the family table rather than a restaurant menu. As a nation, we may be eating out more now than ever before, but the domestic kitchen is still the place to discover British food at its very best.

In keeping with the character of the British people, food is seldom masked with complicated sauces nor finished with flounces of elaborate garnishes. Regional specialities, passed down through generations of cooks, highlight the local nature of many recipes – indeed even the names of dishes vary according to the area from which they originate. For example, a crumpet in some kitchens would be called a pikelet in others. The same term – pikelet – would be used to describe a drop scone in another part of the country.

With its temperate climate, fertile soil and extensive coastline, the British Isles offer an unbeatable choice of high-quality ingredients accessible to home cooks who traditionally match meals to the seasons and the weather. From reassuring main dishes, like steaming-hot suet puddings packed with succulent beef and kidneys, to unforgettable summer desserts, such as strawberries with Devonshire cream, many British specialities are seasonal treats.

Every week, on market stalls and in village halls, tables are laid with home baking and seasonal preserves that reflect local skills and tastes. Home-grown produce, local cheeses, Bath chaps, black puddings, brawn and other traditional butchers' products are among the bounty to be discovered in country markets, while quayside fishmongers still sell shrimps, crabs, cockles and mussels along with mackerel and other fish. Exhausted shoppers who know where to buy the best, rest in tea rooms, roadside cafés and cosy pubs, where adventurous home cooks often extend their repertoires to provide unbeatable small-scale catering, including favourite homely snacks or heart-warming pies and stews.

Meals have changed with the generations, but many traditional treats survive as weekend indulgences, if not as the essential part of daily routine they once were. The irresistible aroma of breakfast bacon rashers, curling as they cook to crisp perfection to accompany golden-yolked eggs, slices of spicy black pudding and crunchy fried potatoes, still tempts the tastebuds on cold winter mornings. North of the border, in Scotland, high tea satisfies raging appetites after a day at work or play. A meal to suit all tastes, this includes savouries, like Scotch eggs or tempting fish cakes, and sweet specialities ranging from lightly toasted muffins or teacakes to fruit tarts or seed cake. Teatime in city drawing rooms once heralded the arrival of trays of dainty cucumber sandwiches, fruity jam tarts and large or small cakes, and such rituals endure to this day.

COOKING

When it comes to high days and holidays, the British are united in their culinary expectations. Britain is known for its fine roasts and a joint of meat, with crisp roast potatoes, garden-fresh vegetables and lashings of gravy, is still the firm favourite for traditional Sunday lunch. Yorkshire pudding always complements beef, roast pork without apple sauce is unthinkable and mint sauce invariably balances the richness of lamb. In some homes a baked savoury suet pudding may still be served with the roast, but it is today more likely to be a treat than a filling accompaniment to stretch the joint. During the Christmas season, on Shrove Tuesday, over the Easter weekend and on Bonfire Night in chilly November, in homes from north to south, millions enjoy the same favourite foods: festive roast turkeys, spicy hot cross buns and sizzling grilled sausages.

From simple favourites, like warm soda bread, golden fish pie, kedgeree, comforting toad-in-the-hole or steamed sponge pudding with creamy custard to poached salmon, raised pies, syllabubs and trifles, the tradition of British home cooking is one to preserve and celebrate.

We owe a huge debt of gratitude to those wonderful home cooks of the past, whose recipes were handed down, first by word-of-mouth and example, and later in treasured notebooks. It took an exceptional woman, Isabella Beeton, to collect and collate those recipes and present them in a simple and systematic way. The enduring popularity of her famous cookbook is a testament to her success and to that treasurehouse that is British home cooking.

This collection of her recipes required remarkably few adjustments when tested in a modern kitchen, and proved to be every bit as delicious as when they were written over a century ago.

MRS BEETON - a woman

'I have striven, too, to make my work something more than a Cookery Book, and have, therefore, on the best authority that I could obtain, given an account of the natural history of the animals and vegetables which we use as food.'

When she wrote her book on household management, Isabella Beeton set about her work with a professional approach that distinguished her from any of her predecessors; however, she could never have foreseen the impact it would make on generations of women.

Isabella Mayson, as she was known before her marriage to Sam Beeton, had an unusual family background. After the death of her father, her mother remarried. The outcome was a household of twenty-one children. Her stepfather was clerk to the racecourse at Epsom and their family home was underneath the grandstand. As the eldest girl in the family, Isabella played a key role in looking after the younger children. She was well educated, particularly for a young lady of her day, having been sent to a girls' school in Germany, where she followed academic studies in French and German. Isabella was said to be an accomplished pianist and expressed an interest in cooking, which featured in only a small way in the education of young ladies of the period as it was not considered to be genteel. Having learnt to bake traditional cakes and breads in Germany, she became sufficiently fascinated by the subject to approach a pastry chef in Epsom for further instruction on her return to England.

The publisher Sam Beeton was a family friend. She eventually married the young man who was making such a name for himself during what was a boom period for publishing. Both Isabella and Sam invested much time, effort and enthusiasm in preparing their first home at Pinner. With her family and future husband, Isabella planned and discussed the details of equipping and furnishing the home. She and Sam regularly wrote to each other sharing ideas and plotting the progress of the practical work on the house. They moved into a home which was fitted out with all modern conveniences, including many stoves instead of open fires and plumbed-in bathroom facilities.

After all the work involved in planning a wedding and moving into her new home, Isabella found her life rather quiet after the activity she had experienced in the midst of the family at Epsom. The Beetons had a modest staff of cook, kitchen maid and housemaid. Sam travelled to London every day and worked long hours publishing, among other things, the *Englishwoman's Domestic Magazine*. It was inevitable that, after a few months of marriage, Isabella would become involved in her husband's work. Following a rather stilted début, she soon found her own style and her involvement increased until she eventually played a main role in editing the magazine. Apart from various written contributions, she researched and developed ideas for articles, including fashion features from Paris, and translated short stories from French.

Her success fuelled her enthusiasm for writing and the rapport she had developed with the readers proved to be the inspiration for her most famous work, *Beeton's Book of Household Management*.

Mrs Beeton was a creative, inspired editor and writer who was efficient, enthusiastic and professional. She was only twenty-one when she began the task of compiling *Household Management* but her energy and thoroughness compensated entirely for any experience she forfeited to youth. She spent four years testing, accepting or rejecting, collating and organising recipes and information for the book. Friends, family and acquaintances contributed recipes to add to Isabella's own and those sent in by readers of the *Englishwoman's Domestic Magazine*. Isabella also did considerable research on the subject of food and cooking.

The Beeton's approach to the work was vital in ensuring its success: they researched opinion on the type of book that was needed, then set out to provide practical, useful information and the level of detail required by the average home reader. In doing so, they often offended chefs and cooks who were willing to advise or contribute, but who would only have offered information relevant to the grand households of the day. Mrs Beeton was determined to make this a book for women of average means, not the incredibly rich, nor those who were experienced in running a household. She wanted her book to be a friend to other young women who were setting up home, commissioning staff for the first time and dealing with the daily economies of organising a household. She certainly succeeded.

Beeton's Book of Household Management was published in 1861 after four years' hard work. Sections had been issued with the *Englishwoman's Domestic Magazine* and the response to these had provided the reassurance the Beetons needed to keep the work going. Eventually, in the foreword to the first edition, Isabella acknowledged that she had not fully realised the extent of her undertaking until she was entirely committed to it:

'I must frankly own, that if I had known, beforehand, that this book would have cost me the labour which it has, I should never have been courageous enough to commence it.'

Mrs Beeton was an amazing young woman – an editor, journalist and, in realising the importance of testing recipes in a modest domestic kitchen, the forerunner of today's home economists. Sadly, Isabella Beeton did not survive to complete another major best seller. She was in the process of updating her existing publication, preparing a dictionary of cookery and writing a book on needlework when she died of puerperal fever following the birth of her fourth child. Although she was only twenty-nine years old when she died, Isabella Beeton was already a successful career woman, wife and mother. She proved herself, and her name has endured because of her unbounded energy and talent.

SOUPS

OYSTER SOUP

20 oysters

600 ml (1 pint) chicken stock*,

   fish stock* or white stock*

15 g (½ oz) butter

15 ml (1 tbsp) plain flour

salt

cayenne pepper

ground mace

300 m (1½ pint) single cream

a little chopped parsley

Open the oysters and tip them into a small saucepan with the liquid from their shells. Heat them gently in their liquor until almost simmering, then poach them for 1–2 minutes, until the oysters are opaque and just firm. Do not allow the liquor to boil and do not overcook the oysters or they will become tough.

Use a slotted spoon to remove the oysters from the pan. Cut off any dark edges which remain on the oysters (these black or dark brown slightly frilly rims may have been removed when the oysters were released from their shells). Set the oysters aside. Add the stock to the liquor remaining in the pan and heat until simmering. Cover the pan and cook gently for 15 minutes.

Meanwhile, mix the butter and flour to a smooth paste. Strain the stock through a muslin-lined sieve or a coffee filter to remove any tiny pieces of oyster shell. Rinse the pan and replace the stock. Add salt and a small pinch each of cayenne and mace, to taste. Bring the liquid to simmering point, then gradually whisk in the butter and flour paste until the soup thickens slightly. Continue simmering the soup for about 5 minutes.

Finally, stir in the reserved oysters and cream and heat the soup gently without boiling. Taste and adjust the seasoning, as necessary, then stir in a little parsley. Serve immediately.

COOK'S NOTES

This soup is rich and smooth, with a very delicate oyster flavour which will appeal to those who love these shellfish. Serve modest portions and offer crisp Melba toast* to balance the texture and flavour.

OPENING OYSTERS

Use an oyster knife to open the oysters. This is a short-bladed, blunt but sturdy knife with a guard to prevent your hand from slipping down over the blade.

1 Wear an oven glove and hold the oyster with the cupped shell down in the palm of your hand. Insert the knife in the hinged end of the shell and twist it to prise the shell open.

2 Slide the knife around the rim between the upper and lower parts of the shell to separate them, then slide it across under the top shell to free the oyster. Keep the knife as close to the top shell as possible to keep the oyster intact.

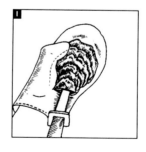
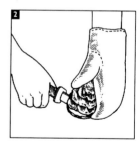

PRAWN SOUP

SERVES 4

450 g (1 lb) cooked prawns in shells

75 ml (3 fl oz) cider vinegar

1 blade of mace

25 g (1 oz) butter

25 g (1 oz) plain flour

50 g (2 oz) fresh white breadcrumbs

900 ml (1½ pints) fish stock★

5 ml (1 tsp) anchovy essence
  (optional)

salt and pepper

Peel the prawns, placing the shells in a saucepan and reserving the tail meat. Add the cider vinegar, mace and 250 ml (8 fl oz) water to the shells. Bring to the boil, cover the pan and cook steadily for 15 minutes.

Meanwhile, mix the butter and flour to a smooth paste. Purée the peeled prawns with the breadcrumbs in a blender or food processor, adding some of the fish stock to moisten the mixture. Strain the liquor off the shells and return it to the rinsed saucepan. Add the remaining fish stock and gradually stir in the puréed prawns.

Bring the soup to the boil. Whisk in the butter and flour paste until the soup thickens slightly. Reduce the heat, cover the pan with a lid and simmer the soup for 15 minutes. Add the anchovy essence (if liked) and salt and pepper to taste.

COOK'S NOTES

This soup is excellent! It is well worth tasting it before adding the anchovy essence as the prawns provide plenty of flavour which is evident when the soup is well seasoned with salt and pepper.

The original recipe (from the first edition of Mrs Beeton's work) was not thickened with beurre manié, which meant the puréed prawns and breadcrumbs gave it an unappetizing appearance. When tasted, the puréed ingredients did not combine as well with the liquid as when a little thickening was whisked in to marry the different elements in the soup.

The result is quite delicious and an ideal dinner-party first course. The soup can be prepared several hours in advance, cooled quickly and chilled, then reheated just before it is served.

GARNISHING PRAWN SOUP

The soup, which is a beige-pink colour, looks much better when garnished. It is a shame to add more ingredients to complicate the flavour unnecessarily, so try to resist the temptation to sprinkle chopped herbs over the soup. If the soup is served in small deep bowls on saucers or small plates, rest a couple of whole cooked prawns on the rim of each bowl, or arrange them on the saucer or plate, and add a sprig or dill or flat-leafed parsley. Alternatively, float a couple of peeled cooked small tiger prawns and a sprig of dill on the soup.

WHITE SOUP

50 g (2 oz) almonds

75 g (3 oz) skinned, boneless cooked
    chicken

1.1 litres (2 pints) chicken stock*
    or white stock*

25 g (1 oz) fresh white breadcrumbs

grated rind of ½ small lemon

1 blade of mace

salt and pepper

175 ml (6 fl oz) single cream

Blanch the almonds by pouring freshly boiling water over them and leaving them to stand for 1 minute. Drain the nuts and slip off their skins. Grind the blanched almonds coarsely in a food processor or blender, then add the cooked chicken. Continue to process the mixture, adding a little of the stock to make a smooth purée. Add the breadcrumbs and lemon rind to the purée, with more stock, and process the mixture until smooth.

Bring the rest of the stock to the boil in a saucepan. Add some of the stock to the purée, then pour it into the pan. Stir in the mace with a little seasoning. Cover the soup and simmer for 40 minutes.

Remove the blade of mace and stir in the cream. Taste for seasoning. Heat the soup gently, without boiling, before serving.

COOK'S NOTES

This simple, thin soup has the most wonderful flavour of chicken and almond, spiked with a hint of lemon and mace. It is ideal as a dinner party starter, when a little finely chopped parsley can be sprinkled over the surface to contrast with the pale soup; however, it is a mistake to introduce a strongly flavoured herb or other garnish. Toasted flaked almonds are often used as a garnish, but in this case they tend to interfere with the excellent flavour of the soup and are best avoided. Offer warm dinner rolls as an accompaniment.

THICKENING THE SOUP

The purée of chicken, almonds and breadcrumbs gives the soup a slightly grainy texture. It is not necessary to sieve the soup, but, before serving, it is a good idea to taste it and perhaps thicken it slightly.

A paste of 25 g (1 oz) each of flour and butter (beurre manié*) can be whisked into the simmering soup at the end of the cooking time. Add the beurre manié a little at a time, stirring or whisking after each addition, and cook the soup for about 3 minutes more. This brings the ingredients together, making the grainy texture less obvious.

MULLIGATAWNY SOUP

SERVES   8

25 g (1 oz) butter

1 chicken, jointed, or 4 chicken
   quarters

6 onions, sliced

4 rindless bacon rashers

1 garlic clove, crushed

2.25 litres (4 pints) chicken stock*,
   white stock* or water

salt and pepper

100 g (4 oz) long-grain rice

30 ml (2 tbsp) curry powder

25 g (1 oz) ground almonds

15 ml (1 tbsp) chopped Indian lemon
   pickle, mango juice or lemon juice

chopped fresh coriander leaves to
   garnish

Melt the butter in a large saucepan. Brown the chicken portions, then remove them from the pan. Fry the onions in the remaining fat until lightly browned, stirring occasionally. Remove the onions from the pan and turn off the heat.

Line the base of the pan with the bacon rashers, then replace the chicken and onions. Add the garlic and pour in the stock or water. Add a little seasoning and bring the soup just to the boil. Skim off any scum that rises to the surface of the soup in the next minute or so, then reduce the heat, cover and simmer for 1 hour.

Meanwhile, simmer the rice in salted water for 15 minutes. Drain the rice in a sieve and set it aside. Lift the chicken and bacon from the soup. Skin the chicken portions, then cut the flesh into chunks, discarding the bones. Cut the bacon into small pieces and replace it in the soup with the chicken. Mix the curry powder and almonds to a smooth paste with a little of the soup, then stir the mixture into the soup and bring it to the boil, stirring. Reduce the heat; simmer the soup, without a lid, for a further 15 minutes.

Finally, stir in the lemon pickle or a little mango or lemon juice to taste. Adjust the seasoning and stir in the rice. Cook briefly, to heat the rice, then serve the soup, garnished with a little chopped coriander.

VEGETABLE MULLIGATAWNY

Full-flavoured stock is essential for vegetable mulligatawny. Mrs Beeton suggested veal stock, but a good vegetable or chicken stock can be used. Leave out the bacon for a vegetarian soup; otherwise dice it and fry it with the onions. Use 450 g (1 lb) trimmed and sliced courgettes and 1 peeled and diced cucumber instead of the chicken and add them to the browned onions. Cook the vegetables for 5 minutes before adding the garlic, stock and 900 g (2 lb) roughly chopped tomatoes. Cook the soup for 30 minutes instead of 1 hour, then purée it in a blender or food processor and rub it through a sieve before adding the curry powder and almonds.

COOK'S NOTES

You will need a very large saucepan or stockpot for this soup, which is a meal in itself. The vegetable variation is less substantial than classic Mulligatawny, but the unusual combination of vegetables tastes extremely good. With the volume of vegetables, and the liquid they yield, the variation makes enough soup for about a dozen people. It is so delicious that it is worth making, even when you only want to serve two or four, as any surplus will freeze well.

SPICED LENTIL SOUP

Fry 2 chopped onions, 1 chopped celery stick, 1 bay leaf, 15 ml (1 tbsp) chopped fresh root ginger and 1 crushed garlic clove in 25 g (1 oz) butter until softened. Stir in 5 ml (1 tsp) turmeric and 15 ml (1 tbsp) each of ground coriander and cumin. Stir in 175 g (6 oz) red lentils, 1.1 litres (2 pints) stock and a little seasoning. Bring to the boil, reduce the heat and cover the pan. Simmer for 1 hour, stirring occasionally. Taste for seasoning and serve topped with a little yogurt or soured cream.

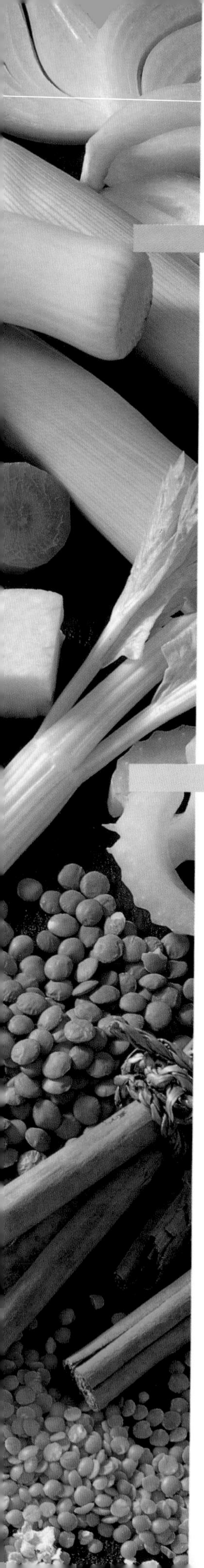

HODGE-PODGE

SERVES 6

25 g (1 oz) beef dripping or suet

450 g (1 lb) shin of beef or stewing
   beef, finely diced

2 onions, chopped

2 carrots, diced

2 turnips (or 1 large turnip), diced

1 head of celery, diced

300 ml (½ pint) pale ale or bitter

salt and pepper

40 g (1½ oz) butter

25 g (1 oz) plain flour

450 g (1 lb) spinach, trimmed and
   shredded (optional)

Melt the dripping or suet in a large saucepan. Add the beef to the hot fat and brown the pieces all over, stirring occasionally. Stir in the onions, carrots, turnips and celery, then cook for 2–3 minutes.

Pour in 1.75 litres (3 pints) water and the pale ale or bitter; heat until the liquid is just simmering. Simmer for a few minutes, skimming off the scum that rises to the surface of the liquid. Add plenty of seasoning. Cover the pan and continue to simmer the soup for 3 hours, stirring occasionally, until the beef is completely tender.

Mix the butter and flour to a smooth paste; stir knobs of this beurre manié into the simmering soup. Add the spinach (if using) and simmer, uncovered, for about 5 minutes. Taste and adjust the seasoning before serving.

COOK'S NOTES

Soups of this type have always been a popular feature of British home cooking as they turn a meagre portion of meat into a delicious, nourishing meal for all the family. Boiling bacon, gammon or lamb can be used instead of the beef, if preferred.

Look out for bags of washed, ready-to-cook baby spinach, often displayed alongside the prepared salads in the supermarket. Baby kale is also sold in this form and is excellent in soup.

BREAD AND CHEESE
TO MAKE A MEAL

Generous wedges of cheese and chunks of bread are traditional farmhouse accompaniments for hearty soups. Warm Irish Soda Bread (page 187), or its wholemeal and mixed grain variation is an ideal choice with mild-flavoured Wensleydale or creamy Double Gloucester cheese.

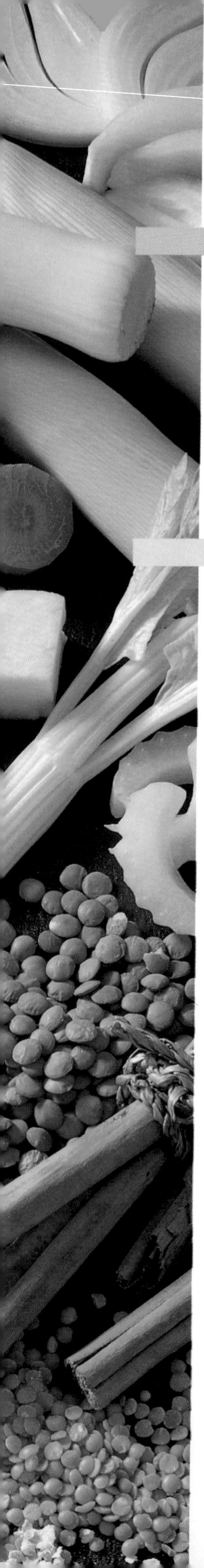

CREAM OF TURNIP SOUP

SERVES 4

40 g (1½ oz) butter

4 large turnips, thinly sliced

2 onions, thinly sliced

salt and pepper

900 ml (1½ pints) chicken stock★

150 ml (¼ pint) single cream

Melt the butter in a saucepan. Add the turnips, onions and a little seasoning. Cook the vegetables in the butter for 10 minutes, stirring often, then add the stock and bring to the boil. Reduce the heat, cover the pan and simmer the soup for about 30 minutes, until the turnips are tender.

Rub the soup through a fine sieve or purée it in a blender or food processor. Reheat the soup in the clean saucepan. Check the seasoning, then add the cream and heat the soup briefly without boiling. Serve at once.

COOK'S NOTES

This basic recipe can be used as the basis for making other simple vegetable soups. The following examples of similar soups come from the first edition of Mrs Beeton's work.

Chantilly Soup Cook the onions in butter as in the main recipe, but leave out the turnips. Add 450 g (1 lb) shelled fresh or frozen peas – about 900 g (2 lb) peas in pods – and a handful of roughly chopped parsley with the stock. Finish as above to make a delicious pea soup.

Cream of Onion Soup Increase the number of onions to 6. Add 1 large or 2 medium diced potatoes instead of the turnips.

Parsnip Soup Use 675 g (1½ lb) sliced parsnips instead of the turnips.

Potato Soup Use 900 g (2 lb) potatoes instead of the turnips. Add a generous sprinkling of chopped dill or fennel to the soup before serving

ACCOMPANIMENTS FOR PLAIN VEGETABLE SOUPS

Crunchy croûtons★ or sippets of fried bread★ offer a pleasing contrast in texture. Alternatively, diced crisp-fried bacon or crumbled blue cheese can be sprinkled over the soup. Bacon is particularly good with turnip soup; Stilton or Danish blue cheese go well with turnip or potato soup.

JERUSALEM ARTICHOKE SOUP

25 g (1 oz) butter

2 rindless bacon rashers, diced (optional)

3 celery sticks, sliced

1 small turnip, diced

1 small onion, chopped

450 g (1 lb) Jerusalem artichokes, sliced

900 ml (1½ pints) white stock★ or chicken stock★

300 ml (½ pint) milk

salt

cayenne pepper

sippets★ of fried bread to garnish

Melt the butter in a large saucepan. Add the bacon (if used), celery, turnip and onion and cook for 15 minutes, stirring often. Stir in the artichokes, then pour in the stock and milk.

Season the soup lightly with salt and a pinch of cayenne, bring it to the boil then reduce the heat. Cover the pan and simmer the soup for 20 minutes, or until the vegetables are tender.

Purée the soup in a blender or food processor, or rub it through a fine sieve. Reheat the soup and taste it for seasoning before serving, garnished with sippets of fried bread.

COOK'S NOTES

Jerusalem artichokes are knobbly root vegetables that resemble potatoes. They were first cultivated by American Indians. Related to the sunflower, they are easy to grow. Modern cultivars are smoother than old and wild varieties, which were very knobbly, trapping the dirt and making them notoriously difficult to peel. Jerusalem artichokes have a delicate, yet distinct, taste. They make a delicious, nutty soup with a flavour quite delicate enough for a dinner-party first course, but also sufficiently interesting to ensure that substantial portions are suitable for lunch or supper. Although the bacon adds its own inimitable flavour, the soup is well flavoured without it. If you grow artichokes, freezing a batch of soup is an excellent way of preserving a glut for future enjoyment. Jerusalem artichokes are also delicious tossed in butter, mashed or coated in Béchamel sauce.

SIPPETS

Sippets were a favourite garnish in Mrs Beeton's day and featured widely in her cook book – they were served with soups, casseroles and sauced dishes, and were often called into service for bringing texture to reheated foods and Monday meals traditionally made from the leftovers of the Sunday roast.

CARROT SOUP

S E R V E S 6

40 g (1½ oz) butter

1 onion, chopped

450 g (1 lb) carrots, sliced

1.1 litres (2 pints) chicken stock★

salt

cayenne pepper (optional)

Melt the butter in a large saucepan. Stir in the onion and carrots, cover the pan and cook gently for 30 minutes, stirring occasionally.

Pour in the stock, add a little salt and bring the soup to the boil. Reduce the heat, cover the pan and simmer the soup for 30 minutes. Purée the soup in a blender or food processor, or press it through a fine sieve.

Reheat the soup and check the seasoning, adding a little cayenne (if liked), before serving.

COOK'S NOTES

This simple soup has a delicious, uncomplicated flavour. It is thin and smooth with a buttery taste, pepped up by a hint of cayenne. The recipe serves as an excellent reminder not to mask simple ingredients in all cooking as the result of combining only a few everyday ingredients is surprisingly good. If you want to add visual interest and a hint of flavour contrast, garnish the soup with a little soured cream and snipped chives.

CHOICE OF STOCK

A good stock is important as a strong stock cube would introduce herbs and spices that tend to dominate straightforward flavours. Bought chilled chicken stock is an excellent substitute for the home-made version. Vegetable stock can be used, but take care to avoid very strong ingredients if you want to preserve the identity of the carrots.

WINTER PEA SOUP

225 g (8 oz) yellow split peas, soaked
   overnight in cold water

2.25 litres (4 pints) ham stock* or
   chicken stock*

225 g (8 oz) piece of bacon or
   gammon for boiling (optional, see
   method)

450 g (1 lb) onions, sliced

2 large carrots, diced

2 small turnips, diced

1 head of celery

1 bouquet garni

2 large sprigs of fresh sage

salt and pepper

Drain the peas and place them in a large saucepan. Add all the remaining ingredients, except the seasoning, and bring the stock to the boil. Reduce the heat and cover the pan, then simmer the soup for 2 hours or until the peas are completely tender and beginning to break up.

Remove the bacon or gammon (if used), the bouquet garni and the remains of the sage sprigs, then purée the soup in a blender or food processor. Alternatively, press the soup through a fine sieve. Reheat the soup and add seasoning to taste before serving. Remove any rind or fat from the bacon or gammon, then dice it and add it to the soup, if you like.

COOK'S NOTES

Peppery sage is superb with the onions and celery that flavour the floury split peas in this wholesome soup. Ideal comfort food for a wintry day, the soup should be made in substantial quantities as second helpings will undoubtedly be called for.

The split peas should be soaked in plenty of water and any discoloured peas should be discarded. Ham stock obtained from boiling a joint of gammon or bacon gives the soup by far the best flavour, but chicken stock can be used – or even water. If water is used, it is essential to add the bacon or gammon.

BOILING UP A LARGE BATCH OF SOUP

If you have a batch of ham stock it is worthwhile to prepare a large quantity of yellow split pea soup. Leftover soup will keep for 2–3 days in the refrigerator if cooled and chilled as quickly as possible. If appropriate, reheat portions as required rather than reheating and cooling the whole batch more than once. The soup can be frozen for up to 6 weeks if made with ham stock or for several months if chicken stock is used and the piece of bacon or gammon is left out.

LENTIL SOUP

Red lentils make a substantial soup. Like split peas, they are delicious cooked in ham stock and are even easier to use as they do not need soaking. They cook quickly, so if you use them instead of peas in the main recipe, reduce the cooking time to 1 hour.

BOUQUET GARNI

A bouquet garni is a bunch of herbs, sometimes with flavouring ingredients such as celery, fennel (Florence fennel, not the herb), carrot tops or a cinnamon stick added. A basic bouquet garni should include a bay leaf, a few parsley sprigs (including good long stalks for their flavour) and a couple of thyme sprigs. Celery leaves or a short piece of celery can be added. Other herbs can be included according to the flavour required – rosemary, sage, marjoram, savory and mint are all suitable. Tie the herbs together with a length of cooking string.

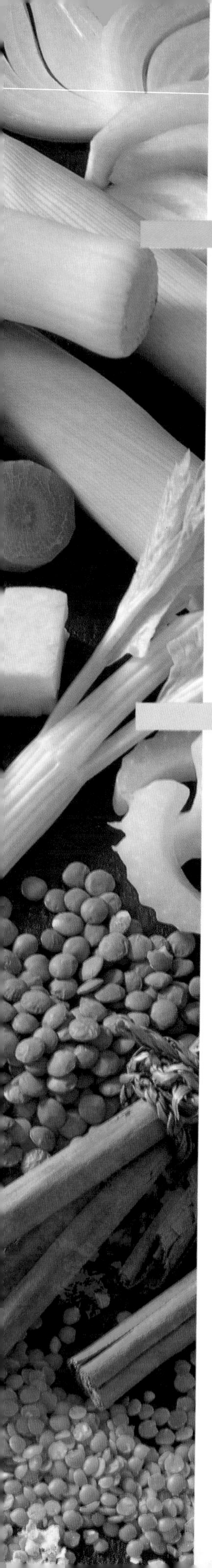

ASPARAGUS SOUP

SERVES 6

1.1 litres (2 pints) chicken stock*

1 round lettuce, coarsely shredded

handful of spinach leaves, shredded

4–6 fresh sorrel leaves (optional)

2–3 sprigs each of fresh mint and
marjoram

450 g (1 lb) asparagus

salt and pepper

25 g (1 oz) butter

25 g (1 oz) plain flour

200 ml (7 fl oz) milk

Pour the stock into a large saucepan. Add the lettuce, spinach, sorrel (if available), mint and marjoram. Trim the tips off the asparagus and set them aside, then slice the rest of the spears and add them to the soup. Sprinkle in a little seasoning.

Bring the soup to the boil, reduce the heat and cover the pan. Simmer the soup for 20–30 minutes, until the asparagus is tender. Remove the herb sprigs and purée the soup in a blender or food processor, then rub it through a fine sieve.

Return the soup to the rinsed saucepan and heat it. Meanwhile, mix the butter and flour to a smooth paste. As soon as the soup boils, whisk in the butter and flour paste. When the paste has melted and the soup thickened slightly, add the reserved asparagus tips, lower the heat and cover the pan. Simmer the thickened soup for 10–15 minutes, or until the asparagus tips are just tender.

Stir in the milk and heat the soup briefly. Taste the soup. Adjust the seasoning, if necessary, before serving it.

COOK'S NOTES

Mrs Beeton's original soup was made with beef stock. The butter and flour thickening, and the milk have been added to this version to balance the flavour and texture. The result is a smooth and rich, deep-green coloured soup with a superb flavour. It is quite different from the usual simple, creamy soup, but the asparagus flavour is neither lost nor wasted when combined with the lettuce and herbs.

SIEVING SOUPS
A blender or food processor can be used to reduce soups and sauces to a smooth consistency, but these appliances do not break down fibres or seeds. Rub the puréed asparagus soup through a fine sieve or it will have an unpleasant, slightly fibrous texture.

LEEK AND OAT BROTH

1 litre (1¾ pints) white stock★ or

    chicken stock★

3 large leeks, sliced

1 bay leaf

salt and pepper

60 ml (4 tbsp) fine or medium

    oatmeal

150 ml (¼ pint) single cream

Pour the stock into a large saucepan and add the leeks, bay leaf and seasoning. Bring the stock to the boil, then reduce the heat and cover the pan. Simmer the soup for 20 minutes.

   Sprinkle the oatmeal evenly into the leek soup, whisking all the time, then simmer, uncovered, for 5 minutes more. Cover the pan and cook the soup gently for 15–20 minutes more, stirring once or twice, until it has thickened. Taste and add more salt and pepper, if needed, then stir in the cream. Warm through gently and serve at once.

COOK'S NOTES

In terms of taste, the oatmeal is not as evident in the soup as the recipe title might suggest; however, any cook unaccustomed to using oatmeal as a soup thickening may be surprised to discover how well it works, giving a pleasing texture and contributing a slightly nutty flavour.

ACCOMPANIMENTS

Emphasize the oatmeal content of the soup by offering warmed coarse oatcakes as an accompaniment. Sprinkle a little crumbled Stilton or other blue cheese into the soup, if you like.

KALE BROSE

SERVES 6

40 g (1½ oz) medium oatmeal

1.4 litres (2½ pints) chicken stock*,
   beef stock* or white stock*

450 g (1 lb) kale or cabbage, shredded

1 leek, thinly sliced

salt and pepper

Sprinkle the oatmeal on a baking sheet or double-thick piece of cooking foil on a grill rack. Toast it under a moderately hot grill until lightly browned. Use a spoon or metal spatula to turn the oatmeal, drawing it together into a pile, then spreading it out again, so that it toasts evenly. Tip the toasted oatmeal into a small bowl.

Bring the stock to the boil in a large saucepan. Add the kale or cabbage, leek and seasoning to taste. Bring the soup back to the boil, reduce the heat so that the soup boils, but does not bubble too rapidly, and partly cover the pan. Cook the soup for 15 minutes.

Take the lid off the pan and have a whisk ready. Quickly whisk the toasted oatmeal into the soup. Still stirring, bring the soup to a full boil. Taste for seasoning, then serve at once.

COOK'S NOTES

Hot and healthy, this good, basic soup tastes wonderful. For everyday cooking, bought stock works quite well as the kale or cabbage are full-flavoured vegetables, but poor-quality, highly seasoned stock cubes should always be avoided. Try some of the concentrated stocks and bouillon cubes instead.

In her original recipe, Mrs Beeton mixed the toasted oatmeal with a little water before adding it to the soup, but this does not work particularly well as the toasted oatmeal does not blend with the water. It is easier simply to whisk it into the soup. This method of thickening is well worth remembering for other soups, and will prove to be an excellent rescue remedy if you have a potful which turns out to be rather thinner than you first expected.

KALE

This is a cabbage which forms neither heart nor head. Curly kale is dark green and, as its name suggests, has particularly curly leaves. Other forms of kale can be lightly curled, slightly spiky, or deeply dimpled, like an exaggerated form of Savoy cabbage leaf. The leaves may also be blue-green in colour. Kale is crisp in texture and it has a strong cabbage flavour. Young kale is sold prepared ready for cooking.

Ornamental kale is also popular as an autumn and winter bedding plant, valued for its pink or white tinged leaves. These types of kale are commonly referred to as ornamental cabbages. Kale is also the name sometimes applied to cabbage in Scotland.

CABBAGE SOUP

½ large cabbage, cut into wedges

a little meat dripping, fat skimmed
     from stock or butter

4 lean rindless bacon rashers

I onion, chopped

2 carrots, diced

salt and pepper

1.1 litres (2 pints) chicken stock*
     or beef stock*

Bring a large saucepan of water to the boil, add the cabbage and bring the water back to the boil as quickly as possible. Immediately drain the cabbage well in a colander, then shred it, discarding any tough stalk.

Grease the base of the dry pan with a little dripping, fat or butter and line it with the bacon rashers. Top with the onion, carrots and cabbage. Cover the saucepan tightly and cook the mixture over high heat for 5 minutes, until the bacon sizzles and cooks with the onion under the carrots and cabbage.

Meanwhile, bring the stock to the boil in a separate saucepan. Season the vegetables to taste, then pour in the stock without stirring the vegetables. Cover the pan and simmer the soup gently for 20 minutes. Skim off any fat, stir and taste the soup for seasoning before serving.

COOK'S NOTES

Much of the bacon we buy today bears little resemblance to the product Mrs Beeton would have known. Both breeds of pig and rearing methods have been changed to produce leaner carcasses, while new curing techniques have tended to create products with a higher water content and less flavour.

SOURCES OF TRADITIONAL BACON

It is well worth finding a source of bacon which is produced from traditional breeds, by old-fashioned rearing methods and traditional curing. Some independent butchers have access to a supply of 'proper' bacon and there are many mail-order sources of meat, all high quality and usually delivered efficiently by next-day service. In the case of bacon, it is most definitely worth paying a little more, even if only for the occasional breakfast treat of really good bacon and eggs.

LINING A PAN WITH BACON

Lining a pan with bacon was a standard technique in Mrs Beeton's day. Rashers of streaky bacon or the thin end of long back rashers would have been used for their good proportion of fat, which would melt to grease the base of the pan and provide a cooking medium to flavour the foods placed on top.

The technique has been retained in the above recipe because the bacon is essential for a good flavour and it prevents the vegetables from scorching on the bottom of the pan.

BARLEY SOUP

SERVES 8

25 g (1 oz) butter or beef dripping

450 g (1 lb) shin of beef or stewing
beef, finely diced

2 onions, chopped

75 g (3 oz) pearl barley

3 large potatoes, cut into eighths or
large chunks

salt and pepper

large bunch of parsley, chopped,
stalks reserved

Melt the butter or beef dripping in a large saucepan. Add the beef and onions, and brown them all over in the fat. Stir in the barley and potatoes. Pour in 2.25 litres/ 4 pints water and add plenty of salt and pepper. Tie the parsley stalks together and add them to the pan.

Bring the soup to the boil, skimming off any scum that rises to the surface as it starts to simmer. Reduce the heat immediately so that the soup barely simmers, cover the pan and cook for 3 hours, stirring occasionally.

Taste and adjust the seasoning, then remove the bunch of parsley stalks and stir in the chopped parsley before serving the soup.

COOK'S NOTES

The recipe from the first edition of Mrs Beeton's book was very simple and all the ingredients were placed in the pan, then boiled together. Browning the meat and onions before adding the water does enrich the soup and improve the flavour. There is no need to fuss over adding stock – water is perfectly adequate with plenty of seasoning.

SKIMMING SOUPS

When poultry and meat are brought to the boil in cold liquid, a scum rises to the surface as the protein begins to coagulate and some separates out. The scum should be skimmed off as it forms to prevent it from boiling back into the stock or soup. If it is allowed to cook back into the liquid, the result is a cloudy stock or soup. The flavour can be spoilt when boiling a large piece of meat or meat on the bone which produces a significant amount of scum.

Any chopped herbs or small whole spices, such as peppercorns, which are added loose to the liquid will rise to the surface with any scum, and it will be difficult to leave them in the pan when skimming the soup. Add these flavouring ingredients once the liquid has been skimmed or tie spices in a piece of muslin.

BARLEY

Barley is a hardy crop which was once very popular in Britain. Although it is traditionally favoured in Wales and Cornwall as a culinary grain, its main use throughout England is for preparing malt used in brewing.

Pot barley is the coarse grain, from which only the outer husk has been removed. It requires lengthy boiling. Pearl barley is the polished grain, which has long been used as a thickening for soup and to make barley water, a drink flavoured with lemon.

Barley also tastes good when simply boiled until tender (but with a bit of bite). Serve it in the same way as rice.

STARTERS

& SAVOURIES

POTTED SALMON

SERVES 6

900 g (2 lb) salmon fillet, skinned

salt and pepper

pinch of ground cloves

1.25 ml (¼ tsp) ground mace

3 bay leaves

100 g (4 oz) butter

100 g (4 oz) clarified butter* for
sealing the potted salmon
(optional)

Pick out any stray bones from the salmon, then cut the fillet into two or three pieces and lay it, skinned side down, in a shallow dish. Sprinkle the fish fairly generously with salt, cover it with cling film and weight it lightly with a plate or another dish. Leave the fish to stand for 2–3 hours in a cool place.

Set the oven at 180°C (350°F/gas 4). Drain the salmon and pat it dry with absorbent kitchen paper to remove the salt. Place it in an ovenproof dish and sprinkle with pepper, ground cloves and mace. Top with the bay leaves and dot with the butter. Cover tightly with foil and/or a close-fitting lid.

Bake the salmon for 20–30 minutes, until the flakes are firm and separate easily. Thicker fillets take longer to cook than thinner portions of fish. Leave the fish, covered, to cool in its cooking liquid for 30 minutes.

Drain the salmon, reserving the cooking liquid. Process it until smooth in a food processor or press it through a sieve. Stir in the reserved cooking liquid. Divide the salmon between small pots or press it into one large pot or dish. Leave to cool. If you like, cover the potted salmon with a layer of clarified butter.

Serve with thin bread and butter, Melba toast or hot toast fingers. Warm bread rolls or finger rolls also go well with the potted salmon, especially when it is accompanied by a cucumber salad.

POTTED LOBSTER

Remove the tail meat from 2 lobsters in one piece, if possible, or in large portions. Set the oven at the lower temperature of 160°C (325°F/gas 3). Cook the meat in the same way as the salmon, with the seasonings and butter. Cut the cooled lobster into slices, place in small pots, then pour over the cooking juices and chill.

COOK'S NOTES

This smooth, buttery potted salmon is the perfect starter for a summer dinner party, or would make a splendid light lunch. Spread between slim slices of bread and butter which are then trimmed of crusts and cut into triangles, the potted salmon will make irresistible sandwiches for afternoon tea.

If you prefer not to pot the salmon, it is absolutely delicious just as it is, baked with spices and served hot, with the cooking liquor poured over as a rich buttery sauce. It tastes wonderful with small new potatoes and slightly crunchy sugar snap peas. Use slightly less butter if cooking the salmon for serving hot.

POTTED SHRIMPS

SERVES 4

225 g (8 oz) butter

175 g (6 oz) peeled cooked shrimps

ground mace

grated nutmeg (optional)

cayenne pepper

Melt half the butter in a small saucepan over low heat. Add the shrimps and heat them very gently for 15 minutes. Do not allow the butter to become too hot or the shrimps will be overcooked.

Season the shrimps with a good pinch of mace, a sprinkling of freshly grated nutmeg (if liked) and a small pinch of cayenne. Divide the shrimp and butter mixture between small pots or place it in one large pot and leave to cool.

Clarify the remaining butter in a small, clean saucepan: heat it gently (do not let it get too hot or it will brown) until it stops bubbling and a white sediment forms on the base of the pan. Gently pour the clear yellow butter into a jug, leaving the sediment behind; the last of the butter may be strained through fine muslin if necessary.

Pour a thin layer of clarified butter over the potted shrimps and chill until the butter has set. Serve the potted shrimps with hot fresh toast, thin Melba toast★ or thin slices of wholemeal bread and butter.

COOK'S NOTES

Shrimps are seldom available in supermarkets, but can be found in specialist fishmongers or sold by local fishermen in regions where they are fished. They are sold cooked.

There are two types, one which turns pink on cooking and the other which turns brown. Brown shrimps are superior, with a delicious flavour – they are fiddly to peel, but worth the effort. Buy double the weight to allow for wastage by shell. As a practical alternative, pot prawns instead of the shrimps.

PEELING PRAWNS OR SHRIMPS

Break off and discard the head. Pull the shell apart from underneath and slip it all off. If the shell is parted all along the underside of a large prawn it will usually come off in one piece, but if it breaks, simply remove the shell in two or more sections. This will leave the tail intact.

THE SHRIMP

In the first edition of her work, Mrs Beeton declared that 'this shell-fish is smaller than the prawn, and is greatly relished in London as a delicacy'. In her day, the Isle of Wight was famous for shrimps. They are also netted on the East Coast around the Thames estuary and further north in The Wash. On the West coast, in Lancashire, Morecambe Bay is renowned for its shrimps.

Shrimping is an old-fashioned pastime, associated with Sunday afternoons spent pottering around shallow rock pools. The prize – a child-size bucket of shrimps, to be gently simmered, peeled and potted with butter.

Commercially, shrimps are cooked in huge pots of seawater on board the fishing boats.

Shrimps are also cooked in vast vats in some trade fish markets, then sold while still steaming hot.

HOT CRAB

SERVES 4

1 dressed crab or about 150 g (5 oz)
  crab meat

100 g (4 oz) fresh white breadcrumbs

grated nutmeg

salt and pepper

75 g (3 oz) butter

30 ml (2 tbsp) cider vinegar

Flake the crab meat and mix it with the breadcrumbs. Season the mixture with freshly grated nutmeg, salt and pepper. Dice the butter and mix it into the crab with the cider vinegar.

Divide the mixture between four shells or gratin dishes. Place the dishes under the grill, keeping them well away from the heat source, then turn the grill to a medium setting. Grill the crab mixture from cold, until it has heated through and is crisp and brown on top. Serve at once.

COOK'S NOTES

Cider vinegar is best for this type of mixture: malt vinegar would certainly be too harsh and many types of wine vinegar are also very tart. When cooking the mixture, do not have the grill too hot or the top will brown before the crab has heated through thoroughly and the breadcrumbs are crisp. When grilled slowly, the result is a moist and buttery, delicately flavoured mixture. Hot Crab makes a simple first course. Bread is not a suitable accompaniment, but a small salad of watercress mixed with mustard and cress would complement the crab.

CRAB-FILLED MUSHROOMS

The hot crab can be served as a filling for open cup mushrooms. Remove the stalks from four large mushroom caps and brush the curved tops with a little melted butter. Grill the tops for about 3 minutes, then turn them over and divide the crab mixture between them. Continue grilling them slowly, as in the main recipe, until the filling is crisp and browned on top and the mushrooms cooked. A little warm crusty bread may be served to mop up the juices from the mushrooms.

POTTED PARTRIDGE

SERVES 4–6

5 ml (1 tsp) ground allspice

2.5 ml (½ tsp) ground mace

1.25 ml (¼ tsp) ground white pepper

2.5 ml (½ tsp) salt (or to taste)

2 oven-ready partridges

225 g (8 oz) butter

Set the oven at 180°C (350°F/gas 4). Mix the allspice, mace, pepper and salt. Rub the seasoning mixture all over the partridges and place them in a small ovenproof casserole. Sprinkle any remaining seasoning over the partridges.

Set aside 50 g (2 oz) of the butter. Cut the remainder into pieces, then dot these over and around the partridges in the casserole. Fold a long piece of cooking foil into a strip about two or three layers thick and fold this over the rim of the casserole so that it hangs over the edge. Put the lid on the casserole, then crumple the foil up over the edge of the lid, pressing it on tightly to make an effective seal. Bake the partridges for 1½ hours.

Leave the partridges to cool in the unopened casserole, then remove them and pick all the meat off the bones, discarding the skin and any small bits of yellow fat or membrane. Look out for any shot which may still be lodged in the flesh. Chop the meat and place it in a small pot or dish, or six ramekins. Strain the cooking juices through a fine sieve. Pour them over the diced partridge meat, then chill the potted partridge. Clarify the remaining butter (see Potted Shrimps, page 31) and pour it over the potted partridge. Chill until set.

Serve the potted partridge with light rye bread or hot, crisp toast, and crab apple, rowanberry or redcurrant jelly.

COOK'S NOTES

The spices are perfect with the light gamey taste of partridge and they give the potted meat an almost festive flavour, making this an ideal first course for December dinner parties. Partridge is in season from September 1st to February 1st and the best birds are obtained in October and November.

CHOPPING THE PARTRIDGE

The cooked partridge meat is easily chopped by hand but a food processor can be used; however, take care not to reduce the partridge to a pulp.

PORK CHEESE

SERVES 10–12

1.4 kg (3 lb) belly of pork, boned

salt and pepper

40 g (1½ oz) plain flour

600 ml (1 pint) chicken stock*, white
stock* or vegetable stock*

30 ml (2 tbsp) chopped parsley

5 ml (1 tsp) chopped fresh thyme

2.5 ml (½ tsp) chopped fresh
rosemary

4 large fresh sage leaves, chopped

2.5 ml (½ tsp) ground mace

grated nutmeg

grated rind of ½ lemon

butter for greasing

Set the oven at 180°C (350°F/gas 4). Place the pork in a roasting tin, sprinkle it with a little seasoning, then roast for 1½ hours, until cooked through. Transfer the cooked meat to a plate, cover and set aside for about 30 minutes or until it is cool enough to handle.

Meanwhile, drain off any excess fat from the roasting tin. Stir the flour into the residue and cook it over medium heat, stirring continuously, until the paste begins to brown slightly and the residue on the pan darkens. Pour in the stock, stirring or whisking continuously, then bring the gravy to the boil. Reduce the heat and simmer steadily for 5 minutes, stirring occasionally and scraping in any sediment from the base of the roasting tin. The gravy should be quite thick.

Set the oven at 180°C (350°F/gas 4) again. Cut the rind off the pork, then chop the meat and fat either by hand or in batches in a food processor. Take care not to overprocess the meat and reduce it to a paste; the pieces should be about the size of small dice. Tip the pork into a bowl, season well and stir in the herbs, mace, a little nutmeg and the lemon rind. Pound the mixture with the back of a wooden spoon to combine the meat thoroughly with the flavouring ingredients. Gradually stir in 300 ml (½ pint) of the gravy – the mixture may take a little extra, which can only improve the flavour, but do not make it too sloppy or it will be too moist when it is baked.

Grease a 1.1 litre (2 pint) ovenproof dish (a soufflé dish or terrine) with a little butter and pour in the meat mixture. Smooth the top of the mixture and cover the dish with foil. Bake for 1¼ hours, then leave the mixture to cool completely.

Chill the pork cheese overnight. Use a dessertspoon to scoop it out in neat ovals and serve it with hot toast or warm Bath Oliver biscuits as a first course.

COOK'S NOTES

The pork cheese is a delicious alternative to pâté for a first course or light lunch. It can also be used as a canapé topping.

ACCOMPANIMENTS
A small salad garnish of watercress and herbs, such as parsley, basil and rocket, with finely diced, full-flavoured eating apple makes an attractive accompaniment. The crisp texture complements the pork and a slightly tangy dressing of olive oil and cider vinegar balances the rich flavour. Don't drown the salad in dressing, however; trickle over only a tiny amount, simply to surprise the palate occasionally as the starter is eaten.

POTTED BEEF

SERVES 6-8

900 g (2 lb) lean braising steak

salt and black pepper

pinch of cayenne pepper

2.5 ml (½ tsp) ground mace

100 g (4 oz) clarified butter*

Cut the steak into cubes and place them in a large pudding basin which is suitable for boiling. Sprinkle with plenty of salt and pepper, a good pinch of cayenne and the mace. Add a quarter of the butter to the meat with 15 ml (1 tbsp) water.

Cover the basin with double-thick foil, folding it firmly around the rim to make a good seal. Stand the basin in a large saucepan and pour in boiling water from a kettle to come about two-thirds of the way up the outside of the basin. Bring the water to the boil, then reduce the heat so that the water boils steadily, but not so vigorously that it knocks the basin off balance. Cover the pan. Cook the beef for 3½ hours, topping up the water as necessary.

Remove the basin from the pan and set it aside to cool for a while, without removing the cover. After about 30 minutes, the meat should be cool enough to mince or process in a food processor until very fine. Add the cooking juices that have formed in the bowl as you process the meat.

Melt the remaining clarified butter and stir it into the beef. Taste the mixture for seasoning before dividing it between ramekins or small pots, or turning it into a single dish. Press the meat down well with a palette knife or the back of a spoon, then cover and leave to cool. Chill overnight before using.

COOK'S NOTES

Originally, Mrs Beeton cooked the meat in one piece. The butter and seasonings were added to the pounded or minced and sieved cooked meat, with sufficient cooking liquor to give the required texture. Cooking the seasonings with the meat gives it an excellent flavour as they can otherwise taste rather harsh.

Before the days of refrigerators, a potted meat was something of a preserve, with a high proportion of clarified butter, and a layer of clarified butter on top acting as a seal on the surface of the meat. Mrs Beeton actually pointed out that 'if much gravy' was added to the meat it would keep for only a short time whereas 'if a large portion of butter is used, it may be preserved for some time'.

The beef can be stored in the refrigerator for up to a week. Serve potted beef in the same way as a pâté for a first course or as a light meal. It also makes an extremely tasty sandwich filling. Coating the beef with clarified butter and garnishing with herbs gives it an attractive appearance, but this is not strictly necessary.

STEAMING OR BAKING

If boiling is not the most convenient cooking method, the basin of meat can be cooked in a steamer over a saucepan of boiling water (remember to top up the water occasionally). If an ovenproof dish or casserole is used, the meat can be baked at 160°C (325°F/gas 3). It is vital that the dish is tightly covered to seal in all the cooking liquor, so add a layer of foil under a loose-fitting lid.

SCOTCH EGGS

SERVES 4

4 rindless back bacon rashers, finely
   chopped or minced

50 g (2 oz) shredded suet

175 g (6 oz) fresh white breadcrumbs

grated rind of ½ lemon

5 ml (1 tsp) finely chopped parsley

5 ml (1 tsp) finely chopped fresh
   thyme, marjoram or oregano

generous pinch of ground mace

salt

cayenne pepper

2 eggs, beaten

4 hard-boiled eggs

plain flour for coating

oil for deep frying

Mix the bacon with the suet, half the breadcrumbs, the lemon rind, parsley and thyme, marjoram or oregano. Season the mixture with mace, salt and cayenne to taste, then mix well until thoroughly combined. Stir in about half the beaten egg, or slightly less, to make a forcemeat which binds together and can be shaped by hand. Lightly whisk 10 ml (2 tsp) water into the remaining beaten egg.

Divide the forcemeat into quarters. Dust the hard-boiled eggs with a little flour. Flatten a portion of forcemeat into a circle on the palm of one hand. Place an egg on top and gently mould the forcemeat around the egg to enclose it completely. Try to make the coating as even as possible and ensure that it clings to the egg.

Place the remaining breadcrumbs in a large shallow dish. Coat the Scotch eggs in a little flour, then roll them in the beaten egg and coat them with breadcrumbs. Press the breadcrumbs on neatly.

Heat the oil for deep frying to 160°C (325°F) or until it will brown a cube of day-old bread in 2 minutes. Fry the Scotch eggs until they are crisp and golden, turning them in the oil, if necessary, so that they cook evenly. They will need about 10 minutes' cooking.

Drain the Scotch eggs on absorbent kitchen paper and allow them to stand for 5 minutes. They can be served hot or cold. Cut them lengthways in half or quarters; leaving them until completely cold before cutting if they are to be served cold.

ANCHOVY-CRUSTED EGGS

Substitute anchovies for the bacon in the main recipe. Drain a 50 g (2 oz) can of anchovy fillets, then chop them finely.

COOK'S NOTES

Mrs Beeton's variation, using anchovies instead of bacon, makes a tempting starter. The grated rind of a whole lemon can be added for a more pronounced flavour, to balance the strength of the anchovy fillets. A salad garnish of coarsely grated, thinly peeled courgettes with finely chopped spring onion and a little grated red radish would complement either version of the Scotch eggs.

EGG-AND-BREADCRUMB COATING

Mrs Beeton felt that it was 'scarcely necessary' to apply a coating of egg and breadcrumbs. Although, to contemporary taste, the bacon forcemeat is best with the additional coating, the anchovy mixture is good without the layer of egg and breadcrumbs. The coated eggs should be dusted in flour before being fried at the slightly higher temperature of 180°C (350°F), for about half the stated cooking time, until crisp and golden. Serve the eggs with wedges of lemon.

EGGS A LA MAITRE D'HOTEL

SERVES 4

100 g (4 oz) butter

30 ml (2 tbsp) plain flour

300 ml (½ pint) milk

6 hard-boiled eggs (freshly boiled)

15 ml (1 tbsp) finely chopped parsley

10 ml (2 tsp) lemon juice

salt and pepper

Melt half the butter in a small saucepan. Stir in the flour and cook the mixture for a few seconds, then gradually stir in the milk. Bring the sauce to the boil, stirring continuously, then reduce the heat and simmer the sauce gently for 5 minutes, stirring occasionally.

Cut the eggs into quarters and arrange them on a serving dish or on four individual serving plates or shallow dishes. Beat the remaining butter into the sauce, adding it in two or three lumps. When the butter has melted, taste the sauce before stirring in the parsley and lemon juice, with salt and pepper to taste. (Depending on the type and brand, the butter can make the sauce quite salty.) Pour the sauce over the eggs and serve them at once.

COOK'S NOTES

This simple dish of eggs coated with white sauce can also be dressed up for dinner, garnished with fresh herbs and served with fingers of hot toast or croûtes of fried bread to make a classic starter. Shredded smoked salmon, curled into a neat rosette, makes a tempting garnish.

It is also ideal for a mid-week supper, with a couple of chunks of warm crusty bread or some boiled pasta. For a slightly more substantial meal, pipe a border of creamy mashed potato around a gratin dish and brown it under the grill before spooning the eggs coated with sauce into the centre. A tomato salad tastes refreshing with the eggs, particularly if the tomatoes are sun-ripened.

POACHED EGGS WITH SPINACH

SERVES 4

1 kg (2¼ lb) spinach

25 g (i oz) butter

salt and pepper

grated nutmeg

125 ml (4 fl oz) single cream
  (optional)

4 eggs

4 slices of hot buttered toast, crusts
  removed and each cut into four
  triangles

Trim the stalks from the spinach, wash the leaves well, then drain and rinse them. Place the spinach, with the water still clinging to the leaves, in a large saucepan. Cover the pan and cook the spinach for about 3 minutes over high heat, shaking the pan frequently, until it has cooked down considerably and is tender. Drain the spinach in a colander, pressing out the water, then chop it finely.

Melt the butter in the saucepan, add a little seasoning and grated nutmeg, then return the spinach to the pan. If using the cream, heat it gently in a small saucepan, adding a little salt and pepper. Do not allow the cream to simmer or overheat or it will separate. Warm four serving plates or shallow dishes.

Poach the eggs for about 3 minutes, or until they are just set. While the eggs are cooking, divide the spinach between the serving plates, making a slight hollow in the middle of each portion. Drain the eggs and serve one in each hollow. If using the cream, spoon it around and partly over the eggs. Serve immediately, garnished with triangles of hot buttered toast.

COOK'S NOTES

The classic method of poaching an egg is in a frying pan of simmering water with a dash of vinegar added. The vinegar helps to set the egg quickly, thereby keeping it neatly in shape by preventing it from spreading.

1 A fresh egg should be used as the white will be more viscous. It should be chilled. Crack the egg on to a saucer. Swirl the simmering water to create a whirlpool effect.

2 Quickly slide the egg into the middle of the swirl of water. This performance is vital for producing a nicely rounded, plump, poached egg. The egg will cook in about 3 minutes. Have a warmed plate and a sharp pointed knife or kitchen scissors ready. Use a draining spoon to scoop the egg out of the pan and on to the plate.

3 Trim off any straggling bits of white to neaten the egg, mop up any water with absorbent kitchen paper, then simply slide the egg on to the serving dish.

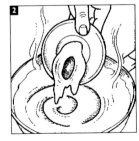
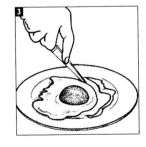

BAKED MUSHROOMS

S E R V E S   4

16 open-cup mushrooms

salt and pepper

about 50 g (2 oz) butter

Set the oven at 200°C (400°F/gas 6). Trim the tops of the stalks off the mushrooms, leaving only a short length in each cap. Use a piece of absorbent kitchen paper and a little salt to wipe the tops of the mushrooms caps, ridding them of any dirt, then stand them, stalks up, in an ovenproof dish.

Season the mushrooms with pepper and place a small knob of butter on top of each cap. Bake the mushrooms for about 20 minutes, until they are well cooked, reduced in size and moist with buttery juices. Towards the end of the cooking time, warm a serving dish for the mushrooms. As soon as they are ready, pile the mushrooms in the dish and pour the cooking juices over the top. Sprinkle lightly with salt and serve at once.

COOK'S NOTES

Select your mushrooms carefully for this recipe – they should be large enough to have lots of flavour. The very small, partially open mushrooms that are pale and delicate are better prepared by other methods. It is equally important to avoid large flat, very mature mushrooms which are best when quickly grilled or pan-fried.

SERVING SUGGESTIONS

Baked mushrooms are delicious on slices of hot buttered toast for breakfast or a satisfying lunch. Toasted muffins or crumpets also make good bases for absorbing the cooking juices. For a starter medium-thick fried croûtes of bread would be more suitable, or the mushrooms can be served in individual dishes, sprinkled with chopped parsley and accompanied by thin slices of wholemeal bread and butter.

Cooked this way, mushrooms are also a mouthwatering accompaniment for grilled bacon, gammon, chops or steaks. Mrs Beeton recommended them for breakfast, luncheon or supper, and stated that they are very good with creamy scrambled eggs.

POTTED MUSHROOMS

SERVES 4

675 g (1½ lb) small closed-cup
  mushrooms

75 g (3 oz) butter

juice of 1 small lemon

salt and pepper

100 g (4 oz) clarified butter*

Place the mushrooms in a colander and rinse them quickly under cold running water, shaking the colander to remove any dirt. Do not soak the mushrooms or prolong the washing process; drain well for 2-3 minutes. Cut the mushrooms into halves or quarters.

Melt the butter in a large saucepan and add the mushrooms. Pour in the lemon juice and add plenty of seasoning. Cook the mushrooms gently for a few minutes, until they begin to give up their liquor, then bring to the boil. Continue cooking at a steady boil (not too fierce, but faster than a simmer) until all the liquor has evaporated and the pieces of mushroom are smaller than when you began.

Begin to stir as the liquid evaporates and continue cooking until the mushrooms are frying in butter. Stir more or less continuously until the mushrooms are pale golden. This stage takes about 45 minutes. Taste the mushrooms for seasoning when most of the liquid has evaporated and they are coated in a thick glaze; at this stage any additional salt will dissolve into the small amount of remaining moisture.

Divide the mushrooms between four small pots or ramekins or place them in one larger dish. Press the mixture down well in each pot, then coat with the clarified butter and allow to cool. Cover and chill overnight or for several days.

Remove the mushrooms from the refrigerator about 30 minutes before serving, otherwise they will be too cool. Serve with hot toast to absorb the butter.

COOK'S NOTES

Imagine having to store mushrooms without a refrigerator and it is easy to understand why Mrs Beeton originally entitled this recipe 'Preserved Mushrooms'. Potting is an excellent way of prolonging the keeping quality of mushrooms. Once she had cooked and preserved the mushrooms in butter, Mrs Beeton would have stored them in a cold larder for several days or more. Before use, they were generally reheated and the excess butter was drained off.

We make wider use of mushrooms today and are more familiar with their flavour, whether they are served hot or cold. These potted mushrooms are extremely good when served with hot toast, but it is important to cut them into quarters, or smaller pieces, so that they are well distributed through the butter. The concentrated mushroom flavour, heightened by frying them in butter after all their liquid has evaporated, is complemented by the lemon. It is important to season the mushrooms well just before all the liquid has evaporated – do this too soon and they could be overseasoned, leave it too late and the salt will not combine with the butter as successfully as it will with the liquid.

SCOTCH RAREBIT

SERVES 4

100 g (4 oz) mature Cheddar cheese, grated

5 ml (1 tsp) prepared English mustard

30 ml (2 tbsp) port

salt and pepper

4 slices of bread

Mix the cheese, mustard and port in a small saucepan. Add seasoning, particularly pepper as the quantity of salt required will depend on the flavour of the cheese. Stir the mixture over low heat until the cheese has melted and all the ingredients are thoroughly combined.

Toast the bread completely on one side and lightly on the second side. Trim off the crusts, if liked, and spread the cheese on the lightly toasted side. Grill the topping until it is golden and bubbling, then serve the Scotch rarebit immediately.

COOK'S NOTES

Mrs Beeton described several versions of toasted cheese, including Welsh rarebit, for which she recommended Cheshire or Gloucester cheese spread with mustard. The cheese was traditionally melted in a 'hot-water cheese dish', which was a dish set over a container of hot water.

As soon as the cheese had browned, the dish was set over the container of hot water and taken to the table. Dry or buttered toast was served with the cheese; occasionally the cheese was spread on toast, then replaced in the dish to keep hot.

MACARONI WITH CHEESE

SERVES 4

225 g (8 oz) macaroni

salt and pepper

100–175 g (4–6 oz) Parmesan cheese, grated

75–100 g (3–4 oz) butter, melted

50 g (2 oz) fresh white breadcrumbs

Cook the macaroni in boiling salted water for about 15 minutes, until tender. Drain the macaroni well, then layer it in a gratin dish, sprinkling each layer with pepper and Parmesan. Trickle a little butter over each layer of macaroni.

Top with the breadcrumbs and remaining butter, then place the dish under the grill and cook until the topping is crisp and golden. Serve at once.

COOK'S NOTES

Originally entitled 'Macaroni, as usually served with the cheese course', this is a plain but rich pasta recipe. It would be slightly too rich to round off a meal for most modern tastes, but it is delicious for lunch or supper, with a crisp salad and plain, warm bread. Serve small portions,

with a finely shredded side salad, for an appetizer.

In the 1861 recipe, the macaroni was boiled in a mixture of milk and water, but it seems rather wasteful by today's methods, to use about 600 ml (1 pint) milk which is discarded.

SCOTCH WOODCOCK

SERVES 4

50 g (2 oz) can anchovy fillets,
    drained
50 g (2 oz) butter, softened
freshly ground black pepper
150 ml (¼ pint) single cream
3 egg yolks
4 slices of hot thick toast

Mash the anchovies with the butter, adding pepper to taste. Heat the cream in a small saucepan but do not let it boil.

Beat the egg yolks, then stir in the cream. When the yolks and cream are well combined, return the mixture to the pan and cook it over gentle heat, stirring constantly, for a few minutes, until slightly thickened. Remove the saucepan from the heat.

Trim the crusts off the toast and spread it with the anchovy butter. Pour the sauce over and serve at once.

50 g (2 oz) can anchovy fillets,
    drained
50 g (2 oz) butter, softened
freshly ground black pepper
2 large eggs
2 egg yolks
150 ml (¼ pint) single cream
4 slices of hot thick toast

SCRAMBLED EGG SCOTCH WOODCOCK

This is a contemporary version. By scrambling eggs with the cream to a soft consistency, the mixture is not as soft as the sauce given in the above recipe.

Mash the anchovies with the butter, adding pepper to taste. Beat the whole eggs with the yolks, then stir in the cream. Pour the mixture into a small saucepan and cook it gently, stirring continuously, until the eggs are just setting and the mixture has thickened to the consistency of creamy, scrambled egg.

Trim the crusts off the toast and spread it with the anchovy butter. Pile the egg mixture on the toast before it thickens further and begins to separate. Serve immediately.

COOK'S NOTES

Mrs Beeton's Scotch Woodcock consisted of a cream sauce poured over toast spread with anchovy paste. Originally, the pounded anchovies were spread on hot buttered toast, but it is easier to make an anchovy butter. Since anchovies are salty, there is no need to season the cream sauce.

For a contemporary interpretation, try the second version of the recipe, where the anchovy toast is topped with creamy scrambled egg. It is useful to rope in an assistant to spread the hot toast with anchovy butter while you scramble the eggs. Spoon the scrambled egg on to the toast as soon as it is ready. The heat retained in a heavy–bottomed saucepan will be sufficient to cause the egg mixture to overcook and separate, so work quickly for perfect results.

POUNDED CHEESE

225 g (8 oz) cheese

40 g (1½ oz) butter

2.5 ml (½ tsp) prepared English
   mustard

Grate the cheese finely. Soften the butter, if necessary, by beating it. Pound the cheese with the back of a mixing spoon, gradually adding the butter to make a smooth paste. Mix in the mustard and pack the cheese into a pot. Smooth the top of the cheese, cover the pot and chill the cheese until required.

The pounded cheese will keep as well as fresh cheese. Any slightly dry cheese or scraps that are beyond their best will keep for 2–3 days once they have been pounded.

SEASONING SUGGESTIONS

The pounded cheese is delicious seasoned with a little ground mace or cayenne pepper in addition to, or instead of, the mustard. Curry powder can also be used to flavour the cheese. Sprinkle in only a little curry powder: for a more pronounced flavour, use curry paste or cook the powder in a little butter over medium heat for 2 minutes, then allow it to cool before mixing it with the pounded cheese. If uncooked curry powder is used in any significant quantity, it gives the cheese a harsh, raw-spice flavour.

COOK'S NOTES

Potted cheese is today's common title for pounded cheese. British hard cheeses, such as Cheddar, Gloucester, Lancashire or Cheshire, would traditionally be used but several international cheeses are equally suitable, for example Edam or Gouda; Stilton or other blue cheeses; or semi-soft cheeses, such as brie or Camembert. The recipe is ideal for using up the slightly dry remains of a traditional wedge of rinded cheese. A mixture of cheeses can also be used, making this an ideal way of recycling scraps from a cheeseboard into a presentable and satisfying savoury. A little port, brandy or sherry can be added to moisten the pounded or potted cheese and add extra flavour.

CHEESE PASTRIES

MAKES ABOUT 24

oil for greasing

225 g (8 oz) puff pastry*

175 g (6 oz) Cheshire, Stilton or
Parmesan cheese, or a mixture of
Parmesan and a mild cheese, grated

1 egg yolk

Grease one or two baking sheets. Set the oven at 220°C (425°F/gas 7). Roll out the pastry into a rectangle measuring about 25 x 15 cm (10 x 6 inches). Sprinkle half the cheese over the middle of the pastry. Fold the bottom third of the pastry over the cheese, then fold the top third down. Give the pastry a quarter turn clockwise, then press the edges together firmly with the rolling pin and roll it out into a rectangle as before. Repeat with the remaining cheese.

Roll out the pastry to a thickness of about 2.5 mm ($\frac{1}{8}$ inch) or slightly thicker. Use cutters to stamp out pastry shapes and place them on the baking sheets. Alternatively, cut the pastry into strips, diamond shapes or triangles. Use a palette knife to transfer the pastry shapes to the baking sheets.

Stir 5 ml (1 tsp) water into the egg yolk, then brush it over the pastry shapes. Bake them for 7–10 minutes, until puffed and golden. Serve freshly baked.

COOK'S NOTES

These taste terrific made with Parmesan cheese. Serve the pastries with drinks or offer them as an accompaniment for plain soups. They can also be used as a garnish for vegetable gratins or boiled vegetables coated with a plain Béchamel or cheese sauce.

ROLLING, FILLING AND FOLDING THE PASTRY

1 Grate the cheese finely and sprinkle it evenly over the middle third of the pastry. Leave a narrow strip down the sides of the pastry free of cheese to prevent it from squeezing out when the pastry if folded and rolled.

2 Fold the bottom third of the pastry over the cheese, fold the top third down and then seal the edges well to keep the cheese in place.

3 To ensure that the cheese stays in place, and blends with the pastry as it is rolled, press ridges into the dough before you actually begin rolling (and thinning) the pastry.

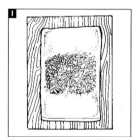
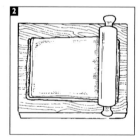
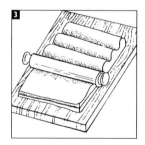

CHEESE RAMEKINS

SERVES 4

75 g (3 oz) butter, melted

50 g (2 oz) fresh white breadcrumbs

60 ml (4 tbsp) milk

4 eggs, separated

salt and pepper

100 g (4 oz) Cheddar cheese, grated

100 g (4 oz) Parmesan cheese, grated

Set the oven at 190°C (375°F/gas 5). Grease four ramekin dishes or individual soufflé dishes with a little of the melted butter. Place the breadcrumbs in a mixing bowl, sprinkle them with the milk and set them aside for 5 minutes.

Beat the egg yolks into the breadcrumb mixture with a little seasoning. Beat in both types of cheese.

Whisk the egg whites until they stand in stiff peaks; do not whisk them for too long or they will become dry. Beat the remaining melted butter into the cheese mixture, then beat in about a quarter of the egg whites. Fold in the remaining egg whites lightly but evenly.

Divide the mixture between the prepared dishes and bake the ramekins for about 30 minutes. The mixture should be risen and golden brown. The ramekins must be served immediately they are cooked. If they are left to stand, the mixture will collapse.

COOK'S NOTES

These are similar to soufflés, but have a slightly firmer texture than creamy, sauce-based soufflés. If you are confident enough to cook a dinner party starter at the last minute, they make an excellent first course; if you are in any doubt, try making the cheese ramekins for a family supper first.

MRS BEETON'S ASIDES ON CHEESE

There were many amusing asides on cheese in the 1861 edition of *Beeton's Book of Household Management,* including the observation that 'a celebrated gourmand remarked that a dinner without cheese is like a woman with one eye'.

As an addition to her recipe for cheese sandwiches (which were toasted in the oven), Mrs Beeton commented correctly that cheese is 'one of the most important products of coagulated milk' and advised that 'in its commonest shape [cheese] is only fit for sedentary people, as an after-dinner stimulant; and in very small quantity. Bread and cheese, as a meal, is only fit for soldiers on march or labourers in the open air, who like it because it "holds the stomach a long time"'.

Stilton cheese was, of course, perfectly acceptable and 'generally preferred to all other cheeses by those whose authority few will dispute. Those made in May or June are usually served at Christmas; or, to be in prime order, should be kept from 10 to 12 months, or even longer.'

FISH &

SEAFOOD

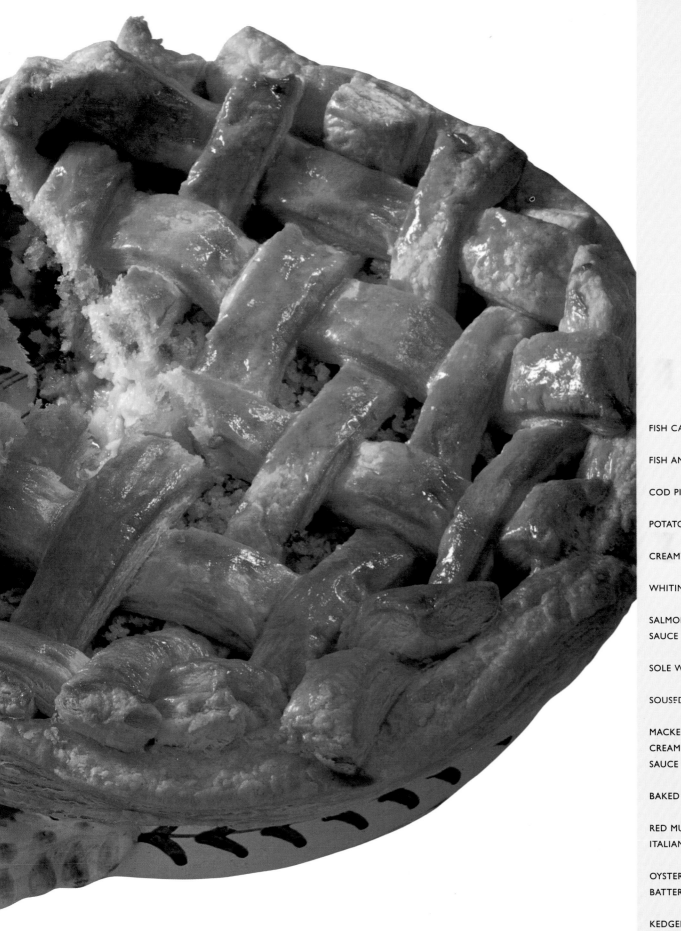

FISH CAKES

MAKES 8

1 small onion, sliced

1 bouquet garni

salt and pepper

450 g (1 lb) white fish, preferably
    cod fillet

450 g (1 lb) potatoes, cut into
    2.5 cm (1 in) chunks

30 ml (2 tbsp) finely chopped parsley

50 g (2 oz) fresh white breadcrumbs

2 eggs

plain flour for coating

100 g (4 oz) dried white breadcrumbs

oil for frying

Place the onion and bouquet garni in a saucepan. Sprinkle in a little salt and pour in 600 ml (1 pint) water. Partially cover the pan and bring the water to the boil. Reduce the heat and simmer the flavoured liquid for 5 minutes. Add the fish and poach it gently, just below simmering point, for 5 minutes, until it is opaque and the flakes separate easily. Remove the pan from the heat, cover it and leave the fish in its cooking liquid until it is cool enough to handle.

Meanwhile, cook the potatoes in boiling salted water for about 10 minutes, until they are tender. Drain and mash them, then press them through a sieve or beat them well until they are smooth.

Remove the fish from the cooking liquid, discard the skin and bones, then use two forks to break up the flesh into fine flakes. Mix the fish and parsley with the potatoes. Add the fresh white breadcrumbs and mix well, adding salt and pepper to taste. Beat in 1 egg.

Lightly beat the remaining egg with 15 ml (1 tbsp) water in a large shallow dish. Pile a little flour on a plate and sprinkle some dried white breadcrumbs on to a third plate or shallow dish.

Divide the fish mixture into quarters, then divide each quarter in half. Take a portion of the mixture and drop it on the flour in one neat spoonful. Using the flour to prevent the mixture from sticking to your hands, press the mixture into a neat round cake. Alternatively, use two palette knives to pat and shape the mixture.

Dip the floured fish cake into the beaten egg, turning it once and spooning the egg over it, then transfer it to the plate of breadcrumbs. Spoon the breadcrumbs over the fish cake, then gently pat them into place all over. Dust off the excess breadcrumbs and transfer the coated fish cake to a plate, ready for cooking. Repeat with the remaining mixture.

Chill the fish cakes for about 15 minutes to set the coating. Heat a little oil in a frying pan and fry the fish cakes for 3–4 minutes, until crisp and golden. Turn them over and cook the second side. Drain the fish cakes on absorbent kitchen paper and serve them freshly cooked.

COOK'S NOTES

FRESH SALMON FISH CAKES

Poach a 450 g (1 lb) portion of thick fresh salmon fillet or enclose it completely in foil and bake it in the oven at 180°C (350°F/gas 4) for 20 minutes. Leave the salmon to cool in its poaching liquid or wrapped in foil. When cool, use the salmon to make the fish cakes. The leftovers from a poached salmon can be used in fish cakes, alone or combined with white fish.

SEASONING FISH CAKES

Chopped parsley, a little thyme and grated lemon rind is a tasty combination for flavouring fish cakes. Alternatively, a little chopped tarragon may be combined with snipped chives.

FISH AND OYSTER BAKE

SERVES 4

450 g (1 lb) cod or haddock fillet,
   cooked

18 oysters

salt and pepper

100 g (4 oz) fresh white breadcrumbs

grated nutmeg

45 ml (3 tbsp) finely chopped parsley

50 g (2 oz) butter, melted

Flake the fish off its skin, discarding any bones. Open the oysters, reserving the liquor from their shells (page 12).

Set the oven at 200°C (400°F/gas 6). Place a third of the fish in an ovenproof dish – a pie dish or gratin dish is ideal. Arrange six oysters on the fish and season the mixture lightly. Sprinkle about a third of the breadcrumbs over the fish and oysters, then add a little nutmeg, seasoning and a third of the parsley.

Repeat the layers twice more. Pour the reserved oyster liquor and half the butter over the fish and oysters before adding the final topping of the remaining breadcrumbs. Trickle the rest of the melted butter over the breadcrumbs. Bake the mixture for 25–30 minutes, until the topping is crisp and golden, the fish is hot and the oysters cooked. Serve at once.

SAUCE TOPPING

Instead of the melted butter; 300 ml (½ pint) Béchamel Sauce★ can be spooned over the final layer of fish and oysters before the breadcrumbs are added, if preferred.

LATTICE BAKE

Set the oven at 220°C (425°F/gas 7). Layer the fish, oysters and breadcrumbs, using only 75 g (3 oz) breadcrumbs and ending with a layer of fish.

Roll out 225 g (8 oz) puff pastry★ and cut a narrow strip to line the rim of the dish. Dampen the rim and press the strip of pastry in place. Cut the remaining pastry into 1 cm (½ inch) wide strips and arrange them in a lattice over the top of the bake. Dampen the edges of the strips and press them on the pastry rim when the lattice is complete, then trim off the ends of the pastry. Brush the lattice with a little beaten egg and cook the bake for 20–25 minutes, until the pastry topping has puffed up well and is golden.

COOK'S NOTES

Oysters were an economical ingredient in Mrs Beeton's day, so she made lavish use of them in dishes of this type, but for today's cook the recipe also works well without them. Add the oysters for a special-occasion dish or a first course, when you may prefer to cook the mixture in individual ovenproof shell dishes or individual oval gratin dishes.

The moist layers of breadcrumbs and fish are full of flavour and have a wonderfully crisp topping, making this an extremely good supper dish. The basic recipe is likely to become a family favourite. It is excellent with cod, but also an ideal way of using canned salmon or tuna. The variations, although interesting, do not have the appealing simplicity of the basic method for everyday cooking.

COD PIE

SERVES 4

short crust pastry* made with

175 g (6 oz) plain flour

450 g (1 lb) cod fillet, skinned and cut

into chunks

2.5 ml (½ tsp) grated nutmeg

1.25 ml (¼ tsp) ground mace

salt and pepper

10 oysters

25 g (1 oz) butter

30 ml (2 tbsp) plain flour

300 ml (½ pint) fish stock*

grated rind of 1 lemon

150 ml (¼ pint) single cream

milk or beaten egg to glaze

Set the oven at 180°C (350°F/gas 4). Roll out the short crust pastry to the same shape as a 900 ml (1½ pint) pie dish, but about 4 cm (1½ inches) larger all around. Cut a strip from around the edge of the pastry, dampen the rim of the dish and press the pastry strip on to it.

Place the cod chunks in the dish and sprinkle them with the nutmeg, mace and seasoning. Open the oysters, reserving the liquor from their shells. Melt the butter in a small saucepan. Stir in the flour and cook the mixture gently for 1 minute. Stir in the stock and the reserved liquor from the oysters, then cook, stirring, until the sauce comes to the boil. Remove from the heat and stir in the lemon rind, cream and oysters, with seasoning to taste. Pour the oyster mixture into the dish and mix it lightly with the seasoned cod chunks. Dampen the pastry rim and cover the pie with the lid.

Trim off the excess pastry, knock up the edge and pinch it into decorative flutes or scallops. Roll out the pastry trimmings and cut out leaves or other decorative shapes to place on top of the pie. Brush the pastry with a little milk or beaten egg and bake the pie for 45 minutes or until golden brown.

COOK'S NOTES

In Mrs Beeton's day, oysters were an economical ingredient, widely used in sauces, stuffings and fish mixtures for pies or bakes. As an inexpensive alternative in the above recipe, and in the potato-topped fish pie opposite, add chopped hard-boiled eggs or lightly sautéed, sliced mushrooms to the sauce. Chopped parsley, chives and tarragon can be added to the sauce, either singly or as a mixture.

SHELLFISH FOR PIES

Scallops These are delicious in a special fish pie, made with a light puff pastry topping instead of the homely short crust pastry. Separate the bright corals and slice the white nuggets of flesh. Add both to the sauce as in the main recipe. To make this filling even more special, use dry white wine instead of the fish stock.

Prawns Peeled cooked prawns can be added to the sauce instead of the oysters.

POTATO-TOPPED FISH PIE

SERVES 4

250 ml (8 fl oz) milk

450 g (1 lb) cod fillet

12 oysters (optional)

900 g (2 lb) potatoes, boiled until
    tender

50 g (2 oz) butter

salt and pepper

Set the oven at 200°C (400°F/gas 6). Pour 175 ml (6 fl oz) of the milk into a frying pan or large saucepan and heat it gently to just below simmering point. Add the fish fillet and poach it gently for 2 minutes, or until it is half- to three-quarters cooked and the flakes can be separated. Remove from the heat and cool slightly.

Open the oysters, if using, and set them aside in the reserved liquor from their shells. Drain and mash the potatoes with half the butter, the remaining milk and salt and pepper to taste. Drain the fish, reserving the cooking liquid, and flake it, discarding the skin and any bones.

Place the fish in a deep ovenproof dish and top it with the oysters and their liquor, if using. Season the fish well with salt and pepper before pouring in the reserved cooking liquid. Melt the remaining butter and pour it over the fish mixture. Spread the mashed potatoes evenly over the top and score them with a fork. Bake the pie for about 30 minutes, or until golden brown on top.

COOK'S NOTES

Unlike modern recipes for fish pies, in which the fish is coated with a Béchamel or cheese sauce, in this case the fish is simply moistened with the milk in which it was poached. The result is a pie which is lighter than usual and it makes a pleasing change. As the liquid in this pie is thinner than the now-popular sauce, it will bubble over more easily during cooking. So be sure to use a dish which is deep enough to prevent the milk from boiling out from under the potato topping.

Oysters are not an essential ingredient in the pie – Mrs Beeton used them for the economical ingredient they were in her day – but good-quality, thick cod will give by far the best results as both the flavour and texture of the fish contribute to the quality of the cooked pie. It is also important to season the fish well or the result will be rather bland.

PERFECT POTATO TOPPINGS

Topping any type of moist base with mashed potato can be difficult as the sauce or liquid tends to rise around the edge or between the portions of potato as they are added. The trick is to start by placing modest spoonfuls of potato all around the edge – this helps to prevent the liquid rising just inside the rim of the dish. Then cover the middle with potato before filling in with any remaining potato. Do not be tempted to smooth the top until the pie is completely covered. Use a fork to press the potato down lightly, working very gently at first, and fill any tiny gaps around the edge of the dish.

CREAMY CURRIED COD

SERVES   4

675 g (1½ lb) thick cod fillet

45 ml (3 tbsp) plain flour

15 ml (1 tbsp) good-quality curry
    powder

salt and pepper

pinch of cayenne pepper (optional)

50 g (2 oz) butter

1 large onion, thinly sliced

300 ml (½ pint) fish stock★

150 ml (¼ pint) single cream

Skin the cod fillet and cut it into chunks, discarding any bones. Mix the flour and curry powder with a good sprinkling of salt and pepper in a bowl. Add the cayenne, if using, then turn the chunks of cod in the mixture.

Melt the butter in a large frying pan. Add the pieces of cod, reserving any leftover seasoned flour. Cook the cod in the butter until browned, then turn the pieces and brown the other side. Use a slotted spoon to remove them from the pan.

Add the onion to the butter remaining in the pan and cook it, stirring occasionally, until it is soft. Stir in the reserved seasoned flour, then pour in the stock and bring the sauce to the boil, stirring continuously. Reduce the heat and replace the cod, then simmer the curry gently for 10 minutes.

Finally, stir in the cream and heat the curry briefly without allowing it to boil. Serve freshly cooked, with boiled basmati rice.

COOK'S NOTES

This basic recipe is quick and easy to prepare. It tastes extremely good, provided it is made with one of the good-quality curry powders available at all larger supermarkets. Thick cod fillet gives the best results as thinner pieces are already well cooked by the time they have been quickly browned in the first stage of cooking, so tend to disintegrate by the time they have been simmered in the sauce. Yogurt can be used instead of cream.

LEMON HERB RICE ACCOMPANIMENT
For a complementary, lively flavour contrast, combine the grated rind of 1 lemon with 30 ml (2 tbsp) chopped fresh coriander leaves, 15 ml (1 tbsp) chopped parsley, 30 ml (2 tbsp) chopped peeled cucumber and 1 finely chopped garlic clove. Add a bay leaf when boiling the basmati rice and toss the cooked rice with the lemon mixture. The fresh flavours of the lemon, herbs and cucumber, combined with the clean taste of basmati rice, balance the creamy fish curry.

WHITING AU GRATIN

SERVES 4

40 g (1½ oz) butter

175 g (6 oz) mushrooms, roughly
    chopped

30 ml (2 tbsp) chopped parsley

salt and pepper

grated nutmeg

4 whiting fillets

150 ml (¼ pint) dry sherry or Madeira

50 g (2 oz) fresh white breadcrumbs

1 lemon, cut into wedges

Set the oven at 190°C (375°F/gas 5). Grease an ovenproof dish or gratin dish with a little of the butter, then melt the remaining butter in a small saucepan. Mix the mushrooms and parsley, adding salt and pepper and a little nutmeg to taste.

Spoon half the mushroom mixture into the dish, then lay the whiting fillets on top. Sprinkle with the remaining mushroom mixture, then gently pour the sherry or Madeira over the fish and topping. Sprinkle the breadcrumbs over the top and trickle the melted butter evenly over them.

Bake the gratin for about 20 minutes, or until the topping is browned and the fish cooked through. Garnish with lemon wedges and serve at once.

COOK'S NOTES

Whiting is a member of the cod family. Smaller than cod, it yields thinner fillets which have a firm, slightly dry texture and delicate flavour. Small fish are sold whole, in which form they can be baked, while larger fish are filleted.

This well-flavoured gratin is equally good when made with other types of white fish, including haddock, cod or monkfish, or oily fish, such as mackerel. The original recipe called for whole fish (cleaned ready for baking), but fillets are more successful.

The sherry or Madeira must be dry, as a sweet fortified wine would not taste good with the fish. Dry white wine can be used instead.

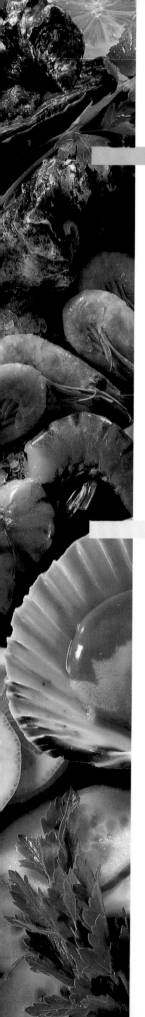

SALMON *with* CAPER SAUCE

SERVES 4

4 x 175–225 g (6–8 oz) portions
  salmon fillet

75 g (3 oz) butter

2 parsley sprigs, finely chopped

1 shallot, finely chopped

salt and pepper

grated nutmeg

12.5 ml (2½ tsp) plain flour

250 ml (8 fl oz) fish stock★ or water

30 ml (2 tbsp) drained capers, roughly
  chopped

10 ml (2 tsp) vinegar from capers

2.5 ml (½ tsp) anchovy essence
  (optional)

Set the oven at 200°C (400°F/gas 6). Lay the salmon in an ovenproof dish and dot with a third of the butter. Sprinkle the parsley, shallot, salt, pepper and nutmeg over the fish and cover the dish. Bake the salmon for 20–30 minutes, or until it is cooked and the flesh flakes easily.

Cut the remaining butter into dice and place these in a saucepan. Sprinkle the flour over the butter. Pour in the stock or water. Whisk the mixture over medium heat, reducing the heat as the water gets hotter, until the butter has melted and combined with the other ingredients. Bring to a full boil, then remove the pan from the heat. Stir the capers, vinegar and anchovy essence (if liked) into the sauce.

Transfer the salmon to serving plates, then stir the cooking juices from the dish into the caper sauce. Pour the sauce over the salmon and serve immediately. New potatoes or creamy mashed potatoes and broccoli, carrots and French beans are excellent accompaniments.

COOK'S NOTES

The combination of ingredients is unusual, as is the method used to make the sauce but the results are highly successful. At first, it seems as though the sauce cannot possibly work, but as the butter melts the ingredients blend together beautifully. It is important to bring the sauce to a full boil and to whisk it all the time.

Do taste the sauce before adding the anchovy essence, particularly if fish stock is used, as it completely alters the nature of the mixture and you may prefer to leave it out. A proportion of dry white wine can be used instead of all water or stock – about half would be appropriate.

Tomato sauce is given as an alternative to caper sauce to dress the baked salmon fillets. The following quantities are based on one of Mrs Beeton's original sauces – the result bears little resemblance to the type of rich tomato sauce we might make today, but it is good with the salmon.

TOMATO SAUCE

Cut 900 g (2 lb) ripe tomatoes into quarters and place them in a saucepan with 4 chopped shallots, 2 cloves and a blade of mace. Add 300 ml (½ pint) white stock★. Season to taste. Bring to the boil, then reduce the heat and cover the pan. Simmer the sauce gently for 1 hour. Rub the sauce through a fine sieve. Alternatively, purée it in a blender or food processor, then sieve it to remove the seeds. Return the sauce to a large saucepan, bring it to the boil and boil hard for 5 minutes to reduce it and concentrate the flavours slightly. Taste the sauce for seasoning and add 5 ml (1 tsp) sugar, if you like. Serve instead of the caper sauce in the main recipe.

SOLE WITH MUSHROOMS

SERVES 4

salt and pepper

8 sole fillets

25 g (1 oz) butter

25 g (1 oz) plain flour

300 ml (½ pint) fish stock*

150 ml (¼ pint) milk

175 g (6 oz) small button mushrooms

300 ml (½ pint) single cream

a little lemon juice

parsley sprigs and lemon slices to
    garnish

Season the sole fillets. Starting at the head end, roll up the fillets and secure them with wooden cocktail sticks. Place them in a flameproof casserole or saucepan. Cream the butter and flour to a paste and set this beurre manié aside. Warm a serving dish for the sole, have a piece of foil ready to cover the dish and warm the grill compartment or oven to keep the sole hot while the sauce is prepared.

Season the fish, then pour the stock and milk over the rolls. Heat the liquid until it just simmers, then cover the pan and reduce the heat to poach the sole gently for 5–7 minutes, or until the rolls are just cooked.

Use a slotted spoon to drain the fish rolls and transfer them to the warm dish. Cover the fish and keep it hot. Bring the cooking liquid to the boil and boil it for 2 minutes to reduce it slightly. Reduce the heat and whisk knobs of the beurre manié into the simmering liquid to make a thick sauce – the sauce will be too thick at this stage, but juices from the mushrooms will thin it. Stir in the mushrooms and simmer the sauce for 2 minutes, stirring occasionally.

Add the cream to the sauce and heat it gently without boiling. Taste the sauce for seasoning and add a little lemon juice to taste. Pour the sauce over the sole and garnish the dish with parsley and lemon.

COOK'S NOTES

Originally, this was a recipe for whole soles, poached in a mixture of milk and water (which was then discarded) and served with a mushroom sauce. Either Dover or lemon sole can be used; fillets are easier to cook and serve than the whole fish in the original recipe.

Dover sole is often cooked whole as its fillets are quite small. The fishmonger will remove the tough skin, leaving the fish ready for grilling or baking. These alternative methods can be used instead of poaching, if preferred, and the sauce prepared while the fish is cooking. Brush the fish

with melted butter and season it lightly before grilling or baking.

Plaice fillets can be used instead of sole for equally good results. The plain, creamy dish benefits from a contrasting accompaniment, such as slightly crunchy carrots and broccoli. Firm little new potatoes complement the dish; alternatively, the fish can be served in a gratin dish edged with a piped border of mashed potatoes. Brown the piped potatoes under a hot grill before arranging the fish in the gratin dish.

SOUSED HERRINGS

SERVES 6

6 herrings, gutted, heads removed and
  boned

2 bay leaves

6 cloves

6 allspice berries

1 blade of mace

salt

cayenne pepper

about 600 ml (1 pint) vinegar

Set the oven at 160°C (325°F/gas 3). Lay three herrings in an ovenproof dish, placing them skin sides down. Arrange the bay leaves, cloves, allspice and mace on the fish. Sprinkle with salt to taste and add a pinch of cayenne. Place the remaining herrings on top, laying them skin side up.

Pour in enough vinegar to just cover the herrings. Cover the dish and bake the herrings for 1 hour, until they are just cooked. Leave them to cool in their cooking liquid, then chill them for several hours or overnight.

Drain the herrings and pat them dry on absorbent kitchen paper. Serve them cold, with bread and butter and a salad of thinly sliced cucumber.

COOK'S NOTES

The herrings can be stored in an airtight container, submerged in the vinegar in which they were cooked, for 4–5 days. Ordinary malt vinegar can be used, but, for a finer flavour, use wine vinegar. The exact quantity required will depend upon the shape and size of the dish. In addition to the flavourings used above, sliced onion is a popular ingredient. Mackerel can also be soused by this method.

BONING HERRINGS

You do not have to be skilled or brave to bone small round fish, like herrings and mackerel, as it is a simple, comparatively clean, task. It works particularly well for mackerel, but removing all the fine bones from herrings is fiddly and time consuming.

1 The fish should be gutted and the head should be removed. Lay it skin side up on a board and rub it firmly along the length of the backbone, from the tail towards the head. Repeat this, rubbing outwards from the bone towards both sides of the fillet. The aim is to press the bones away from the flesh of the fish.

2 Turn the fish over and snip the backbone at the tail end. Then carefully lift it off the fish, removing if from the tail towards the head. As the main bone is removed, the small bones will come away with it.

3 Pick out any remaining bones. A pair of tweezers (bought and kept solely for kitchen use) is useful for removing the fine bones from herrings.

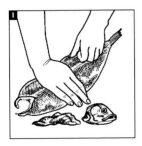
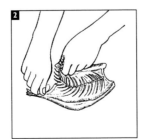
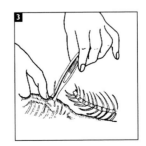

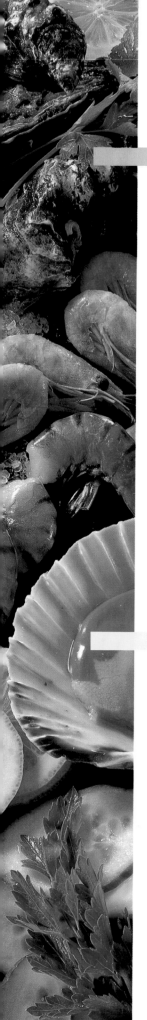

MACKEREL *with* CREAMED GOOSEBERRY SAUCE

SERVES   4

1 onion, thinly sliced

1 bay leaf

4 large fennel sprigs

salt and pepper

4 small mackerel, cleaned

fennel sprigs to garnish

GOOSEBERRY SAUCE

450 g (1 lb) gooseberries

50 g (2 oz) butter

15 ml (1 tbsp) plain flour

50 g (2 oz) sugar

45 ml (3 tbsp) single cream

a little grated nutmeg

Place the onion, bay leaf and fennel in a fairly deep frying pan or saucepan large enough to hold the mackerel. A roasting tin can be used, with foil for a cover instead of a lid. Pour in water to a depth of about 2.5 cm (1 inch) and stir in a generous seasoning of salt and pepper. Heat the water gently until it just boils, then cover the pan and remove it from the heat. Leave the water and flavourings to infuse for 15 minutes.

Meanwhile, make the sauce: place the gooseberries in a pan and add 150 ml (¼ pint) water. Heat gently until the water is boiling, then cover the pan and reduce the heat. Cook the gooseberries for about 20 minutes or until they are soft, stirring occasionally. Rub the cooked fruit through a fine sieve.

Melt the butter in a saucepan and stir in the flour. Gradually add the gooseberry purée, stirring continuously. Stir in the sugar and bring the sauce to the boil. Simmer the sauce, stirring occasionally, for 3–4 minutes.

Arrange the mackerel in the cooled water in the pan or roasting tin and cook over medium heat until just boiling. Then reduce the heat, cover and poach the fish for 5 minutes. Turn the mackerel, replace the cover and continue to cook gently for a further 5–7 minutes, or until the flesh is firm and opaque. Lift out the mackerel, draining them thoroughly and place them on a heated serving dish. Remove the skin from the fish.

Add the cream and a little nutmeg to the sauce and heat it gently, if necessary, but do not let it boil. Garnish the mackerel with fennel sprigs and serve the sauce separately.

COOK'S NOTES

Both the cooking method for the mackerel and the unusual milk-based gooseberry sauce are surprisingly successful in the above recipe: the sauce perfectly complements the poached fish and the result is delicious. However, the sauce does not go well with grilled mackerel, one of the various ways Mrs Beeton generally recommended for cooking the fish. She also suggested frying fillets in a coating of egg and breadcrumbs. The following accompaniments are better suited to grilled or fried fish.

SAUCES FOR MACKEREL
As well as the gooseberry sauce described above, which is based on stewed fruit with a small quantity of creamy Béchamel sauce, Mrs Beeton suggested serving plain melted butter, maître d'hôtel sauce, caper, fennel or

anchovy sauce with mackerel. Both Mrs Beeton's fennel and caper sauces are richer but still complementary.

Fennel Sauce Cut 100 g (4 oz) unsalted butter into small pieces and place them in a saucepan with 30 ml (2 tbsp) plain flour. Whisk in 300 ml (½ pint) water and heat the sauce gently, whisking continuously, until the butter has melted. Bring the sauce to a full boil, whisking until it is smooth. Add 30 ml (2 tbsp) finely chopped fennel and simmer the sauce gently for 1–2 minutes.

Caper Sauce Finely chop 45 ml (3 tbsp) drained capers. Follow the recipe for Fennel Sauce, but add capers instead of fennel. Stir in 15 ml (1 tbsp) liquid from the capers. Add 15 ml (1 tbsp) anchovy essence if you like. Bring the sauce to simmering point and then serve it at once.

BAKED MACKEREL

SERVES 4

4 medium mackerel

50 g (2 oz) butter

1 small onion, very finely chopped

1 rindless bacon rasher, finely diced
   or chopped

100 g (4 oz) fresh white breadcrumbs

15 ml (1 tbsp) chopped parsley

15 ml (1 tbsp) chopped fresh dill,
   fennel or tarragon

25 g (1 oz) suet

a little grated nutmeg

salt and pepper

1 small egg, beaten

Clean the mackerel, removing the heads and tails. Bone them following the instructions for boning herrings on page 59. Set the oven at 200°C (400°F/gas 6).

Melt half the butter in a small saucepan. Add the onion and cook for 5 minutes. Stir in the bacon, cook for 1-2 minutes, then allow to cool slightly. Put the breadcrumbs in a bowl and stir in the herbs and suet. Add the onion and bacon, with the butter from the pan, a little nutmeg and seasoning to taste. Mix in the egg to bind this stuffing or forcemeat.

Divide the stuffing into four. Press one portion together into a neat sausage shape and place it on one mackerel fillet. Fold the mackerel over the stuffing and secure the edges of the fillet with a wooden cocktail stick. Repeat with the remaining stuffing and mackerel.

Place the stuffed mackerel in an ovenproof dish and season lightly, then dot with the remaining butter. Cover and cook for 35-40 minutes, until the mackerel and stuffing are cooked through. Serve piping hot, with the cooking juices poured over.

COOK'S NOTES

Originally, the mackerel were stuffed with heads and tails on, but they are easy to bone and far more pleasant to eat when this has been done. Mrs Beeton suggested that the fish could be cooked in a little wine – about 60 ml (4 tbsp) dry white wine can be poured into the dish.

Mackerel are deep sea fish which migrate between the Mediterranean and Atlantic waters as far north as Iceland. They have a reputation for being voracious eaters and attacking large objects during the spring after near hibernation in deep waters over winter.

The mackerel has a striking appearance, with bold dark stripes on vivid green-blue skin. It tastes delicious. The fish visit British shores from spring through summer; small fish caught early in the season have fine flesh with a superior flavour.

The oily flesh deteriorates rapidly in quality, so it is important to look for mackerel with bright eyes and avoid any dull-skinned, stale specimens. Historically, because of the rapidity with which this fish decays, fishermen were allowed to sell mackerel on a Sunday.

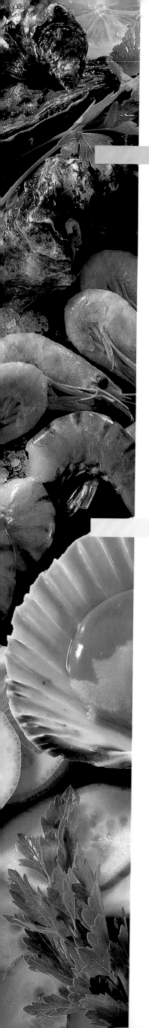

RED MULLET

with ITALIAN SAUCE

S E R V E S   4

2 shallots, finely chopped

100 g (4 oz) closed cup or button
    mushrooms, finely chopped

50 g (2 oz) lean cooked ham,
    chopped

300 ml (½ pint) white stock*

4 red mullet, gutted

about 15 g (½ oz) butter, melted,
    for greasing

salt and pepper

150 ml (¼ pint) Béchamel sauce*

2.5 ml (½ tsp) sugar

a few drops of garlic vinegar

a little lemon juice

Place the shallots, mushrooms, ham and stock in a saucepan. Bring to the boil, reduce the heat, cover the pan and simmer the mixture for 25 minutes.

Meanwhile, set the oven at 190°C (375°F/gas 5) and cut four double-thick pieces of greaseproof paper, each large enough to enclose a mullet completely. Brush the middle of one piece of paper with a little of the melted butter and place a red mullet on top. Brush the fish with a little more butter, season it and then fold the paper around it. Fold and pinch the edges of the paper together to enclose the fish completely. Repeat with the remaining fish. Place them on a baking sheet or in a roasting tin. Bake the fish for 30 minutes.

Purée the cooked mushroom mixture in a food processor or blender, or press it through a fine sieve. Stir in the Béchamel sauce and sugar, with salt and pepper to taste. Add a little garlic vinegar and lemon juice to taste. Reheat the sauce.

Transfer the mullet to warmed serving plates and spoon some of the sauce on to each plate beside the fish. Serve the remaining sauce separately.

COOK'S NOTES

Mrs Beeton commented that red mullet should never be served plain boiled. Cooking suggestions from the first edition of her work include baking in oiled paper or broiling in oiled paper, broiling being a term used for cooking quickly over direct heat on a hot plate or griddle.

SAUCES FOR RED MULLET

In addition to the Italian sauce, Mrs Beeton suggested anchovy sauce, melted butter or a sauce made with sherry and the cooking juices from the baked fish.

Sherry Sauce Bake the mullet in buttered foil, adding a knob of butter and a sprinkling of salt and pepper to the packet. Drain the cooking liquor from the fish into a small saucepan and add 250 ml (8 fl oz) dry sherry. Cream

15 g (½ oz) plain flour with 25 g (1 oz) butter. Heat the sauce until boiling, then reduce the heat and whisk lumps of the butter and flour paste into the simmering sauce. Bring to the boil, then reduce the heat and simmer for 2 minutes. Stir in 2.5 ml (½ tsp) anchovy essence (if liked) and a pinch of cayenne. Taste for seasoning and add a little salt, if necessary. Serve with the baked mullet.

Anchovy Sauce Cut 100 g (4 oz) unsalted butter into small pieces and place these in a saucepan with 30 ml (2 tbsp) plain flour. Whisk in 300 ml (½ pint) water. Heat, whisking continuously, until the butter has completely melted and the sauce is smooth. Bring to a full boil. Add 15 ml (1 tbsp) anchovy essence (or to taste), check the seasoning and serve.

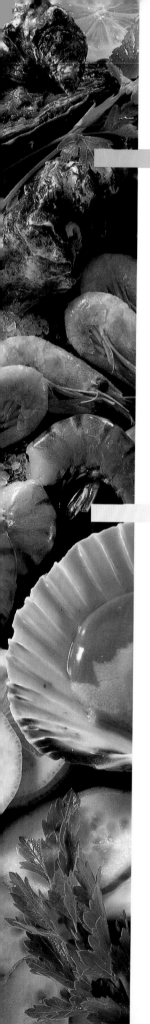

OYSTERS FRIED IN BATTER

SERVES 4

20 oysters

100 g (4 oz) plain flour plus extra for
    coating

salt and pepper

grated nutmeg

1 egg

100 ml (3½ fl oz) milk

oil for deep frying

lemon wedges to serve

Shell the oysters, reserving the liquor from the shells. Remove their dark, slightly frilly edges. Pour the liquor into a small saucepan and add the oysters. Heat them gently until the liquor just begins to simmer and the oysters are opaque and barely firm. Remove them from the heat at once, drain them and dry them on absorbent kitchen paper. Dust the oysters lightly with flour.

Sift the flour into a bowl and add seasoning, with a little grated nutmeg. Make a well in the middle of the flour and break in the egg. Pour in a little of the milk, then gradually beat the egg and milk together, incorporating the flour and adding the remaining milk in stages to make a smooth, fairly thick batter. Beat the batter thoroughly until it is smooth and light.

Heat the oil for deep frying to 190°C (375°F). Dip the oysters individually into the batter to coat them; deep fry them briefly until the batter is crisp and light brown. Use a slotted spoon to remove the oysters from the pan and drain them thoroughly on absorbent kitchen paper. Serve immediately with lemon wedges, so that a little lemon juice can be squeezed over the oysters before they are eaten.

COOK'S NOTES

This is a good way of making the most of a few oysters as the batter makes them more substantial and preserves their succulent texture without masking their flavour. The speedy cooking method is perfect for firming the oysters to perfection and enhancing their flavour to the full. The quantities given are sufficient for a light meal or starter.

NATIVE OYSTERS

Britain is famous for flat oysters, known as native oysters, which are renowned for their sweet taste compared to the Pacific oysters, introduced to Europe and America from Japan, or other types found in Mediterranean waters.

The taste and texture of the oysters depend on the waters in which they are reared. Colchester, in particular, has a reputation for the high quality of its oysters; also on the east coast, Whitstable is known for its oyster beds. In the south-west, Cornwall is another region where oysters thrive. Freshly harvested Irish oysters are traditionally slipped down as an accompaniment to creamy topped Guinness stout.

British oysters are in season during months with an 'r' in their names, that is from September through to April.

KEDGEREE

225 g (8 oz) long-grain rice

salt and pepper

450 g (1 lb) smoked haddock

4 eggs

25 g (1 oz) butter

10 ml (2 tsp) made English mustard

Place the rice in a saucepan. Add 600 ml (1 pint) water and a little salt. Bring the water to the boil, then reduce the heat and stir the rice once. Cover the pan closely and cook the rice gently for 15–20 minutes, until the water has been absorbed and the grains are tender. Leave the rice to stand in the covered pan, off the heat.

Meanwhile, place the smoked haddock in a frying pan or saucepan and add just enough water to cover the fish. Heat the water to simmering point, then poach the fish gently for about 5 minutes, until it is firm and the flakes separate easily. Drain the fish and flake the flesh off the skin, discarding any bones along with the skin.

Cook the eggs in boiling water for 8 minutes, then drain them and rinse them under cold running water. Shell the eggs and cut them into quarters. Melt the butter in a large saucepan. Stir in the mustard, then add the fish and rice. Lightly toss the ingredients together. Lastly add the eggs; fold them gently into the rice mixture. Serve the kedgeree at once.

COOK'S NOTES

Modern recipes for kedgeree tend to be spicy, flavoured with turmeric and curry spices or good-quality curry powder, so sampling Mrs Beeton's simple kedgeree was a new experience and – indeed – a delicious one! Combined with rice and fish, the English mustard gives the dish a distinct, yet mild, and refreshingly uncomplicated flavour.

Mrs Beeton intended her recipe for leftover cooked fish – any cold fish could be used, white or smoked. Cooked salmon is especially good or lightly cooked cod can be excellent. This was a traditional breakfast dish,

served alongside the range of cold meats and grills offered on a country house breakfast buffet.

To ensure that it is evenly distributed, it is important to stir the mustard into the melted butter before adding the fish and rice. The dish can be enriched by using double the quantity of butter. Of course, if you want to make a spicy kedgeree, you can add a little turmeric or good-quality curry powder to the butter, but it really is worth trying this recipe as it stands as a deliciously individual, light alternative to the heavily seasoned foods we so often eat today.

POULTRY &
GAME

ROAST STUFFED CHICKEN

50 g (2 oz) gammon or rindless
    bacon, finely chopped

50 g (2 oz) shredded suet

grated rind of ½ lemon

5 ml (1 tsp) finely chopped parsley

5 ml (1 tsp) finely chopped mixed
    fresh herbs

salt and pepper

cayenne pepper

pinch of ground mace

175 g (6 oz) fresh white breadcrumbs

2 eggs, lightly beaten

1 x 1.5–1.8 kg (3½–4 lb) oven–ready
    chicken

50 g (2 oz) plain flour plus a little
    extra for dusting

25 g (1 oz) butter

900 ml (1½ pints) vegetable cooking
    water

Set the oven at 180°C (350°F/gas 4). Mix the gammon or bacon, suet, lemon rind and herbs, then add salt, cayenne and mace to taste. Stir in the breadcrumbs and add enough beaten egg to bind the ingredients into a moist forcemeat.

Use a small, pointed knife to loosen the skin over the breast of the chicken: cut the membrane under the skin at the vent end (between the legs) of the chicken to form a gap under the skin. Carefully insert the point of the knife into the gap and ease the skin away from the meat without cutting through the skin. When there is sufficient space, use a teaspoon or dessertspoon to continue loosening the skin up over the breast. The other, more traditional, method for doing this is to insert your fingers under the skin.

Use a small spoon to push the forcemeat between the skin and the breast of the chicken. As the forcemeat is packed in, it can be eased over and around the top of the bird by gently pushing from outside the skin. Insert enough forcemeat to cover the breast evenly and make the bird look extremely plump.

Truss the chicken neatly and dust it with a little plain flour. Place the bird in a roasting tin and sprinkle it generously with salt and pepper. Dot the butter on the top of the chicken and roast it for 30 minutes. Cover the top of the breast with foil and continue cooking for a further 1–1½ hours. Baste the chicken occasionally during cooking, replacing the foil each time, but taking it off the breast for the final 15–20 minutes.

Transfer the chicken to a warmed serving platter, cover it with foil and keep it hot. If there is a lot of fat in the tin, pour off the excess but retain a shallow layer (sufficient to absorb the flour). Stir in the flour over medium heat. Cook the mixture, stirring, for 2–3 minutes, to brown the paste slightly. If the meat juices in the roasting tin are already well browned, this will not be necessary. Gradually pour in the vegetable cooking water and bring the gravy to the boil, stirring continuously to incorporate roasting residue from the tin. Simmer the gravy for 3–5 minutes, then taste it and season if necessary. Serve the piping hot gravy with the roast chicken and forcemeat.

COOK'S NOTES

The comparatively small proportion of gammon or bacon makes a delicious forcemeat. The original recipe used double the quantity of suet but the smaller amount is more in keeping with today's taste. It is worth stuffing the top of the breast as this not only boosts the flavour of the bird, but also protects the delicate meat and keeps it succulent during roasting.

CHECKING COOKING PROGRESS
When the chicken is cooked, the meat will be white and firm, not pink and soft. It is important to check the thick area of meat around the thigh area by making a discreet slit with a small pointed knife. Any sign of blood in the juices – or uncooked meat – indicates that the chicken is not cooked through. Check both sides of the bird to be sure.

CHICKEN CUTLETS

SERVES 4

4 skinned, boneless chicken breasts

salt and white pepper

cayenne pepper

ground mace

40 g (1½ oz) plain flour plus extra for
    dusting

I egg, beaten

50 g (2 oz) dried white breadcrumbs

50 g (2 oz) butter, preferably
    clarified★

2 carrots, finely diced

I onion, finely chopped

600 ml (1 pint) chicken stock★

I strip of lemon peel

30 ml (2 tbsp) mushroom ketchup

Lay each chicken breast in turn between two sheets of greaseproof paper and beat out with a rolling pin. The chicken should be thin and even in thickness all over. Season the chicken breasts with salt and white pepper, a pinch of cayenne and a generous pinch of mace. Dust them with a little flour, then dip them in beaten egg and coat them in breadcrumbs.

Melt about three-quarters of the butter in a saucepan. Add the carrots and onion. Cook, stirring occasionally, for 15 minutes. Stir in the measured flour then gradually stir in the stock and bring the sauce to the boil, stirring continuously. Stir in the lemon peel and mushroom ketchup. Reduce the heat, cover the pan and simmer the sauce for 30 minutes.

Meanwhile, heat the remaining butter with the oil in a frying pan and fry the chicken over moderate heat, allowing about 10 minutes on each side, until the coating is crisp and golden and the chicken is cooked through. Drain the chicken on absorbent kitchen paper and serve on warmed plates.

Taste the sauce for seasoning before removing the lemon peel and spooning it around or behind the chicken portions. Serve the remaining sauce separately.

COOK'S NOTES

To avoid overbrowning the coating before the chicken is cooked, it is important to follow the first instruction in the method. The thick portion towards the middle of a chicken breast is the area of meat to concentrate on when thinning; it should be about 5 mm (¼ inch) thick.

Mrs Beeton fried her chicken cutlets in butter. This does give the breadcrumb coating a splendid flavour; however oil can be used or a small knob of butter combined with oil. Clarified butter is always best for frying as it neither overbrowns nor burns. Another useful alternative is to bake the chicken in a shallow baking tin which has been greased with melted butter or oil. Dot a little butter on each portion and cook for about 25 minutes at 200°C (400°F/gas 6).

GARNISHING SUGGESTION

Garnishing the cutlets with cooked vegetables is better than using salad ingredients which would cool the sauce and make it less pleasant to eat. Slice a leek thinly and separate the slices into rings. Cut a carrot in half lengthways and slice it thinly. Sweat the leek and carrot together in a little butter in a small covered saucepan for about 10 minutes, until both vegetables are just tender. Arrange a small pile of the vegetables as a garnish for each chicken portion and add a small sprig of parsley.

ACCOMPANIMENTS

Creamy mashed potatoes or waxy boiled new potatoes taste delicious with the crunchy chicken. The sauce is quite plain and tastes good with all vegetables – try lightly cooked shredded cabbage, spring greens or kale. In winter, serve Brussels sprouts or mashed swede with carrots.

CHICKEN PIE

50 g (2 oz) gammon or rindless
  bacon, finely chopped

50 g (2 oz) shredded suet

grated rind of ½ lemon

5 ml (1 tsp) finely chopped parsley

5 ml (1 tsp) finely chopped mixed
  herbs

salt and pepper

cayenne pepper

ground mace

175 g (6 oz) fresh white breadcrumbs

2 eggs, lightly beaten

3 skinless boneless chicken breasts

6 slices of lean cooked ham

3 hard-boiled eggs (optional, see
  Cook's Notes)

grated nutmeg

175 g (6 oz) puff pastry★

Set the oven at 220°C (425°F/gas 7). Mix the gammon or bacon, suet, lemon rind and herbs, then add salt, cayenne and mace to taste. Stir in the breadcrumbs and add three-quarters of the beaten egg to bind the forcemeat.

Slice the chicken breasts in half at a slant. Layer the chicken, ham, forcemeat and hard-boiled eggs (if using) in a 1.5 litre (2¾ pint) pie dish. Season each layer with mace, nutmeg, salt and pepper. Pour in 300 ml (½ pint) water.

Roll out the pastry on a lightly floured surface to the same shape as the dish but about 2.5 cm (1 inch) larger all round. Cut off a 1 cm (½ inch) strip from around the edge of the pastry, dampen the rim of the dish and press the pastry strip on to it. Dampen the strip and lay the lid on top. Trim off the excess pastry, knock up and flute the edge, then use any trimmings to decorate the crust with pastry leaves. Brush the pastry with the reserved beaten egg and make a small hole in the centre of the pie.

Bake the pie for 15 minutes to set the pastry, then reduce the oven temperature to 180°C (350°F/gas 4) and bake it for a further 30 minutes. Cover the pastry loosely with foil and continue to bake the pie for 45 minutes. Serve the pie hot or cold.

CHICKEN PIE WITH SAUSAGEMEAT

Sausagemeat can be used instead of the forcemeat.

COOK'S NOTES

This pie is fabulous – it is so well flavoured, and it looks so attractive when cut and served cold, that it is bound to become a family favourite. When it was tested, the hot pie tasted slightly odd with hard-boiled eggs in the filling, especially when the pie was served with gravy, but the eggs were an excellent addition when the pie was served cold. So if you plan to serve the pie hot, omit the egg. If you do not have a large pie dish, use a gratin dish or a wide casserole that is not too deep. If the dish does not have a rim, pinch the pastry around the top edge.

Originally, the pie was made with a jointed chicken, including the bones. The remnants of the carcass were boiled to make a stock and this was poured into the cooked pie before serving. However, the pie is quite full, so it is easier to make a gravy to serve separately: melt 50 g (2 oz) butter in a saucepan and cook 1 finely chopped onion with 1 finely diced carrot, 1 diced celery stick and 1 bay leaf until softened and lightly browned. Stir in 50 g (2 oz) plain flour and cook this paste over medium heat until lightly browned. Gradually stir in 900 ml (1½ pints) good chicken stock★ and bring the gravy to the boil. Reduce the heat, cover the pan and simmer the gravy for 15 minutes. Remove the bay leaf. Taste and adjust the seasoning before serving the gravy.

CURRIED CHICKEN

SERVES 4

50 g (2 oz) butter

8 chicken thighs or 4 chicken quarters

3 onions, sliced

1 cooking apple, peeled, cored and
    chopped

salt and pepper

15 ml (1 tbsp) good-quality curry
    powder

15 ml (1 tbsp) plain flour

450 ml (¾ pint) chicken stock*

15 ml (1 tbsp) lemon juice

60 ml (4 tbsp) single cream

Melt the butter in a flameproof casserole or large, heavy-bottomed saucepan. Brown the chicken portions all over, then use a slotted spoon to remove them from the pan.

Fry the onions and apple in the fat remaining in the pan until they are lightly browned. Season the mixture, then stir in the curry powder and flour. Gradually pour in the stock and bring the sauce to the boil, stirring continuously. Replace the chicken and regulate the heat so that the sauce simmers steadily. Cover the pan and cook the curry for 45 minutes, or until the chicken portions are cooked through.

Stir the lemon juice and cream into the sauce and taste it for seasoning. Do not allow the sauce to boil once the cream has been added. Serve the curry with plain boiled rice, preferably basmati rice.

CURRY OF COOKED CHICKEN

The curry can be made from leftover cooked chicken, but the flavour is far better if fresh poultry is used.

COOK'S NOTES

Mrs Beeton's curry may be totally different from the vast variety of authentic Indian dishes we enjoy today, but this does not mean it should be ignored. Try it – you may be well pleased with the light, plain but spicy flavour. It is good with basmati rice.

There are some good-quality commercial spice mixes, including many varieties of curry powder and garam masala. Although the latter is a mild, roasted spice mixture intended as much as a garnish as for flavouring a sauce, it can be used instead of curry powder if a mild-flavoured sauce is required. Alternatively, try this mixture from the original book, attributed by Mrs Beeton to Dr Kitchener. Fenugreek seeds are incredibly hard – they resemble tiny pebbles and are virtually impossible to grind unless they are first softened by soaking.

INDIAN CURRY POWDER

Mix 50 g (2 oz) coriander seeds, 25 g (1 oz) cinnamon sticks, 15 g (½ oz) dark mustard seeds and 7 g (¼ oz) allspice berries in a heavy-bottomed saucepan or frying pan. Roast the spices over low heat, shaking the pan occasionally, until they are aromatic. Do not allow them to brown or they will taste bitter. Set the spice mixture aside to cool.

Grind the roasted spices. Mix in 15 g (½ oz) ground ginger, 25 g (1 oz) ground fenugreek and 7 g (¼ oz) cayenne pepper. The latter is extremely hot and can be omitted if preferred as it does overpower the spice mix. Store the powder in an airtight jar in a cool, dark cupboard. Alternatively, the spice mix can be frozen in an airtight container

CHICKEN AND RICE CROQUETTES

225 g (8 oz) risotto rice

450 ml (¾ pint) chicken stock★

salt and pepper

25 g (1 oz) butter

175 g (6 oz) cooked chicken, minced or finely chopped

1 hard-boiled egg, mashed (optional)

cayenne pepper

1.25 ml (¼ tsp) ground mace

grated rind of ½ lemon

a little lemon juice

30 ml (2 tbsp) double or single cream

2 eggs

a little flour

75 g (3 oz) dried white breadcrumbs

oil for deep frying

8-10 parsley sprigs, washed and dried

Place the rice in a saucepan with the stock. Add a little salt and bring the stock to the boil. Stir the rice once, then cover the pan and reduce the heat to the lowest setting. Leave the rice to cook gently for 15 minutes. Turn the heat off but do not remove the lid from the pan; leave the rice to stand for a further 15 minutes. Add the butter to the cooked rice and mix it in with a fork. Tip the rice into a bowl and allow it to cool.

Meanwhile, mix the chicken and egg (if using). Add a little seasoning, a pinch of cayenne, the mace and lemon rind. Moisten the mixture with the lemon juice and cream so that it binds together. Taste the chicken mixture for seasoning, then chill it.

To shape the croquettes, wet your hands under cold water. Take a spoonful of the rice – a portion about the size of a small tomato – and flatten it on the palm of one hand. Place a small portion of the chicken mixture in the middle, then shape the rice around it. Set the croquette aside on a platter and rinse your hands before shaping the next one. When all the mixture has been shaped, chill the croquettes for at least 30 minutes.

Beat the eggs with 30 ml (2 tbsp) water. Dust the croquettes in flour, then dip them in the egg mixture and coat them in breadcrumbs. Chill the croquettes for at least 30 minutes to set the coating.

Heat the oil for deep frying to 190°C (375°F) and fry the croquettes until they are crisp and golden. Drain the croquettes on absorbent kitchen paper and keep them hot while cooking successive batches. Finally, deep fry the parsley sprigs in the hot oil for a few seconds, until they are bright green, then drain them well. Serve the croquettes hot, garnished with the deep-fried parsley.

COOK'S NOTES

These Italian-style croquettes make an excellent starter or main course. For a starter, allow two or three croquettes each and garnish them with a small portion of salad made by dressing finely shredded vegetables with soured cream or mayonnaise.

For a main course, try serving the croquettes with a robust leafy salad – with peppery rocket, watercress, crisp Iceberg lettuce or full-flavoured Little Gem hearts, lots of chopped spring onion and plenty of coarsely shredded basil (when in season). Add an oil-based dressing and offer warm crusty bread to balance the richness of the meal.

TOMATO DRESSING

This is a good dressing for leafy salads. Peel, seed and chop 4 ripe tomatoes (preferably plum tomatoes). Sprinkle the tomatoes with 2.5 ml (½ tsp) caster sugar, salt, pepper and 5 ml (1 tsp) mustard powder. Add a finely chopped garlic clove, if you like, and 30 ml (2 tbsp) balsamic vinegar. Use a hand whisk to gradually incorporate 90 ml (6 tbsp) virgin olive oil, whisking quite hard. Do not worry about breaking up the tomatoes further – the idea is to partially mash them, making some pulpy and leaving some pieces of chopped tomato.

SAUTEED CHICKEN WITH PEAS

SERVES 3–4

about 225 g (8 oz) skinned, boneless
cooked chicken (the leftovers from
a roast bird are ideal)

salt and pepper

pinch of ground mace

15 ml (1 tbsp) plain flour

50 g (2 oz) butter

300 ml (½ pint) chicken stock

225 g (8 oz) frozen peas

Cut the chicken into bite-sized pieces and season these well with salt, pepper and a good pinch of mace. Sprinkle over the flour and coat the chicken evenly in it.

Melt the butter in a large frying pan. Add the chicken, reserving any dregs of flour, and quickly sauté the pieces until they are lightly browned. Sprinkle in the reserved flour, then stir in the stock and bring the mixture to the boil, stirring all the time.

Add the frozen peas and bring the sauce back to the boil. Reduce the heat, cover the pan and simmer the mixture gently for 10 minutes, until the peas are cooked. Taste the mixture for seasoning before serving the sauté.

SAUTEED CHICKEN WITH MUSHROOMS

About 225 g (8 oz) sliced mushrooms can be added instead of peas: sauté them with the chicken and their flavour will be more intense.

COOK'S NOTES

This is a traditional way of transforming the leftovers from a Sunday roast into a tasty meal for Monday. It goes well with mashed potatoes or can be spooned into split baked potatoes. Plain cooked rice or pasta are also suitable accompaniments.

Chicken is now an everyday food, but in Mrs Beeton's day it would have been a luxury choice, which is why every last bit was used to full advantage. A sandwich would not have been Mrs Beeton's way of using up the remains of a roast fowl.

Peas, being seasonal, were also very much a speciality. During the late 18th and early 19th centuries, June 4th was a significant date for gardeners on grand country-house estates as that was the day when they were urged to bring in the first peas of the season to mark the birthday of George III. Since the King liked to sample the first peas of the season on his birthday, fashionable society people were keen to follow suit.

Until the turn of this century, freshly cooked peas were sold by street vendors. The hot peas were dipped into seasoned melted butter flavoured with vinegar and sucked out of their pods. Freezing has, of course, revolutionized our attitude to peas, which have become so inexpensive and commonplace that they are today the most humble of vegetables. Even so, there is nothing quite like the taste of freshly picked raw peas – the perk for the person doing the podding – nor their superb flavour when freshly boiled and tossed with a little butter and pepper.

ROAST DUCK WITH SAGE AND ONION STUFFING

SERVES 4

1 x 1.8 kg (4 lb) oven-ready duck
  with giblets

5 onions

1 carrot, sliced

1 celery stick, sliced

1 bay leaf

2 parsley sprigs

10 large fresh sage leaves

50 g (2 oz) butter, cut into small
  pieces

100 g (4 oz) fresh white breadcrumbs

salt and pepper

1 egg yolk

45 ml (3 tbsp) plain flour

Place the giblets from the duck in a saucepan. Thickly slice 1 onion and add the slices to the pan with the carrot, celery, bay leaf and parsley. Add water to cover and bring it to the boil. Reduce the heat, cover the pan and simmer the stock gently for 1 hour. Strain the duck stock and boil it further, if necessary, until it is reduced to 600 ml (1 pint).

Cook the remaining onions whole in simmering water for 2 minutes. Add the sage leaves just before draining the onions, to blanch them for a few seconds. Chop the drained onions and sage finely, then mix the butter into them until it has melted; stir in the breadcrumbs. Add seasoning to taste and bind the stuffing with the egg yolk.

Set the oven at 190°C (375°F/gas 5). Spoon the stuffing into the duck and truss it. Put the duck on a wire rack in a roasting tin and prick the skin all over with a fork or skewer to release the fat. Sprinkle the duck generously with salt, then roast it for 1¾ hours, basting it occasionally with the pan juices and pouring away the excess fat if necessary. Test by piercing the thickest part of the thigh with the point of a sharp knife. The juices should run clear.

Transfer the duck to a heated platter, remove the trussing string and keep hot. Pour off most of the fat from the roasting tin, sprinkle in the flour and cook, stirring, for 2 minutes. Gradually stir in the stock and bring the gravy to the boil, then lower the heat and simmer, stirring, for 3–4 minutes. Add salt and pepper to taste and serve the gravy with the duck.

COOK'S NOTES

If the duck is sold without giblets, the cooking water from boiling vegetables can be used to make the gravy.

ACCOMPANIMENTS FOR ROAST DUCK

Although fresh peas are the classic vegetable accompaniment, frozen petit pois dressed with butter and tossed with a little chopped tarragon or mint can be served instead. Slightly crisp carrots, sugar snap peas or French beans are all suitable vegetables, with new potatoes or boiled potatoes topped with a little chopped parsley.

Sharp apple sauce★ is another traditional accompaniment or a tangy jelly, such as crab apple, redcurrant or rowanberry, can be served. Sweet-sour flavours complement the richness of duck. This is perfectly illustrated by the use of bitter Seville orange in Bigarade Sauce, a traditional accompaniment for roast duck.

QUICK BIGARADE SAUCE

Pare the rind thinly from 1 Seville orange and cut it into fine strips. Simmer the strips in water for 5 minutes, or until tender, then drain them and set them aside. Boil the strained giblet stock until it is reduce to 300 ml (½ pint), then add 300 ml (½ pint) red wine to make up the volume. Follow the instructions for making the gravy, using only 30 ml (2 tbsp) plain flour. Add the juice of the orange and the rind when the gravy boils, then simmer for 5 minutes. Finally, add 15–30 ml (1–2 tbsp) redcurrant jelly, to taste, and stir until it has melted. The sauce can be further sharpened with more Seville orange juice or lemon juice.

DUCK RAGOUT

SERVES 4

1 x 1.8 kg (4 lb) oven-ready duck
    with giblets

salt and pepper

1 bay leaf

1 small carrot, sliced

1 celery stick, sliced

3 onions, sliced

4 large fresh sage leaves or small
    sprigs

2 fresh lemon thyme sprigs or a strip
    of pared lemon rind and thyme
    sprigs

40 g (1½ oz) butter

25 g (1 oz) plain flour

Set the oven at 220°C (425°F/gas 7). Place the duck breast down on a rack in a roasting tin, prick the skin all over and rub it with plenty of salt and pepper. Roast the duck for 15 minutes, then turn it over and roast it for a further 15 minutes.

Meanwhile, place the giblets, bay leaf, carrot, celery and 1 onion in a saucepan with water to cover. Bring to the boil, skim off any scum and reduce the heat. Cover the pan and cook the giblets for 45 minutes.

When the duck is browned, remove it from the oven. Lower the temperature to 180°C (350°F/gas 4). The duck can be placed whole in a large ovenproof casserole, but it is more practical to cut it into four portions. To joint the duck, place it breast down on a large board and split it in half. Use a meat mallet or rolling pin to tap the knife through the bones. Cut both halves into two portions, splitting the breast meat so that most of it rests with the wing joint. Use scissors or a pointed knife to trim away any small bones and the ends of the breast bone. Put the whole or jointed duck into the casserole.

Pour a little of the roasting fat into a frying pan and fry the remaining onions until they are evenly browned, stirring occasionally. Add the onions to the casserole with the herbs. Strain the giblet stock straight over the duck. Add plenty of salt and pepper and return the ragout to the oven. There should be plenty of stock, so the casserole should not need to be covered. Cook for 1 hour, turning the joints halfway through cooking, and basting if necessary. The duck should be very tender and the cooking liquid should be richly flavoured.

Transfer the whole duck or joints to a serving dish or plates. Pour the stock into a saucepan, if necessary, or put a flameproof casserole on the hob. Discard the herbs – there should be about 600 ml (1 pint) cooking liquid. If there is more than this, reduce it by boiling; if less add a little more water. If adding water, swirl it around the casserole to incorporate all the cooking sediment. Cream the butter and flour to a paste.

Heat the cooking liquid until just simmering, then whisk in knobs of the butter mixture. Continue to whisk until the sauce boils, then reduce the heat and simmer the sauce for 2–3 minutes. Taste the sauce for seasoning, then pour it over the duck and serve at once.

COOK'S NOTES

This is ideal for today's birds that are bred to be less fatty. The duck can be served whole but it is often more practical to joint it for ease of serving, particularly when presenting the ragout at a dinner party. Minted peas and turnips are suitable vegetable accompaniments, along with boiled or roast potatoes.

VARIATION

Duck with Orange and Red Wine Pare the rind and squeeze the juice from 1 orange. Add both to the duck in the casserole, with the herbs and onions. Pour over 300 ml (½ pint) red wine and 300 ml (½ pint) of the giblet stock. Cover and continue as in the main recipe.

ROAST GOOSE

1 goose with giblets

5 onions

1 carrot, sliced

1 celery stick, sliced

1 bay leaf

2 parsley sprigs

10 large fresh sage leaves

75 g (3 oz) butter, cut into small
   pieces

100 g (4 oz) fresh white breadcrumbs

salt and pepper

1 egg yolk

½ lemon

5 ml (1 tsp) prepared English mustard

250 ml (8 fl oz) port

cayenne pepper

30 ml (2 tbsp) plain flour

Place the giblets from the goose in a saucepan. Thickly slice 1 onion and add the slices to the pan with the carrot, celery, bay leaf and parsley. Add water to cover the ingredients generously and bring it to the boil. Reduce the heat, cover the pan and simmer the stock gently for 1 hour. Strain the stock and boil it further, if necessary, until it is reduced to 600 ml (1 pint).

Cook the remaining onions whole in simmering water for 2 minutes. Add the sage leaves just before draining the onions, to blanch them for a few seconds. Chop the drained onions and sage finely, then mix two-thirds of the butter into them until it has melted. Stir in the breadcrumbs. Add seasoning to taste and bind the stuffing with the egg yolk.

Set the oven at 230°C (450°F/gas 8). Weigh the goose and calculate the cooking time at 20 minutes per 450 g (1 lb). Remove the excess fat usually found around the vent. Rinse the inside of the bird, then rub the skin with lemon and season the bird with salt and pepper.

Stuff the body of the bird with the sage and onion stuffing and truss the legs and wings neatly.

Put the goose on a rack in a roasting tin, place it in the oven and immediately lower the temperature to 180°C (350°F/gas 4). Roast for the calculated time. Drain fat away from the roasting tin occasionally. About 20 minutes before the end of the cooking time, mix the mustard with the port, a pinch of cayenne and a little salt. Drain off the excess fat from the roasting tin, then slowly trickle the port mixture over the goose. Continue to roast the bird until it is cooked.

Transfer the goose to a serving platter, cover it with tented foil and keep it hot. Stir the giblet stock into the pan juices and bring to the boil. Reduce the heat and simmer the gravy for 2–3 minutes, scraping the sediment off the roasting tin. Cream the remaining butter with the flour to a smooth paste, then whisk knobs of this into the simmering gravy, continuing to whisk until the gravy thickens. Simmer the gravy for a further 2 minutes, stirring occasionally, then taste it for seasoning. Serve the gravy with the roast goose.

Although a goose is a large bird, it yields a small proportion of meat. While the carcass is large and well covered with fat, the fillets of meat from the breast are comparatively small. Modern breeding methods are producing leaner birds, but they still yield a significant quantity of fat. Stand the goose on a rack. It is essential to use a fairly deep roasting tin as the goose will yield a great deal of fat; drain this away at least twice during cooking.

Goose fat was put to many uses in the Victorian household, where nothing was wasted. Apart from being an excellent medium for cooking, in particular for roasting potatoes, goose fat was an ingredient for furniture polish when beeswax was not available. It was also used to protect against illness by being rubbed into the chest of anyone, and children in particular, who showed the first signs of developing a cold or cough.

ROAST GUINEAFOWL

SERVES 2–3

1 oven-ready guineafowl

salt and pepper

25 g (1 oz) butter

2–3 rindless streaky bacon rashers

a little flour

bread sauce* to serve

Set the oven at 180°C (350°F/gas 4). Place the guineafowl in a roasting tin. Sprinkle the bird with seasoning, then dot it with butter, spreading some over the thighs as well as on the breast. Lay the bacon rashers over the breast.

Roast the guineafowl for 1–1½ hours or until cooked through, basting frequently. About 20 minutes before the end of the cooking time, remove the bacon, baste the bird and dredge the breast with flour. Serve with bread sauce.

COOK'S NOTES

Guineafowl is a domesticated bird originating from Africa, where it is found wild and in great abundance. A wandering bird which tends to run around rather than fly, the guineafowl is about the size of a small chicken but with slightly longer legs.

The delicate-flavoured flesh is not as gamey as that of pheasant but slightly more distinctive than chicken. It can be quite dry, so it should be barded or covered during cooking. Guineafowl can also be braised or casseroled,

whole or jointed. Traditionally, it was valued as an alternative to pheasant when the latter was out of season.

Dredging poultry and game birds with flour before and during roasting is rather an old-fashioned technique that is usually overlooked today. In fact, it gives the skin a particularly crisp texture, which is a bonus for those who regard the roasted skin on a chicken or guineafowl as a special treat. The pan juices can be used to make a delicous gravy.

PIGEON PIE

SERVES 6

1 onion, sliced

50 g (2 oz) butter

450 g (1 lb) rump steak, cubed

salt and pepper

ground mace

2 oven-ready pigeons (see Cook's
    Notes)

1 thin gammon steak

250 ml (8 fl oz) beef stock* or
    chicken stock*

175 g (6 oz) puff pastry*

beaten egg to glaze

Set the oven at 220°C (425°F/gas 7). Cook the onion in half the butter for about 5 minutes, until it is slightly softened, but not browned.

Place the steak in a pie dish and sprinkle the onion on top. Season the meat well and sprinkle it with a generous pinch of mace. Cut the remaining butter in half and place a piece in the body cavity of each pigeon. Place the pigeons on the steak, nestling them in neatly. Sprinkle with seasoning and a little mace. Trim the rind from the gammon, then cut the gammon steak in half and lay one piece over each bird. Pour in the stock.

Roll out the pastry to the same shape as the pie dish, but 4 cm (1½ inches) larger all around. Cut a 2.5 cm (1 inch) strip from around the edge. Dampen the rim of the dish and press the pastry strip on to it, then dampen the pastry. Lay the pastry lid in place, trim off the excess pastry and knock up the edges. Flute the rim of the pie and use the pastry trimmings to make a garnish of leaves.

Cut a small hole in the middle of the pie and glaze it with beaten egg. Bake the pie for 15 minutes, then reduce the temperature to 160°C (325°F/gas 3) and cook the pie for a further 2 hours. Cover the top of the pie loosely with foil after 1 hour to prevent the pastry from overbrowning. Serve the pie piping hot.

COOK'S NOTES

Plentiful and inexpensive, pigeons are often considered to be the poor relations of the game world. They tend to be quite tough, so are best casseroled or cooked by another moist, slow method to complement the rich flavour of their dark breast meat.

They are most presentable when the small breast fillets are removed and braised or stewed in a rich stock made from the rest of the carcass. Red wine, mushrooms, diced bacon and a seasoning of juniper berries are all complementary ingredients. The tart flavours of crab apple or rowanberry jelly, or orange rind and juice contrast well with pigeon. The meat is also good finely diced or minced and used in a pâté or terrine.

VICTORIAN-STYLE PIE GARNISH

The original finishing touches for the pie included making a hole on the top into which was inserted the reserved feet from the pigeons, claws outermost, as an indication of the contents. This type of gruesome garnish is rarely appreciated by today's diners!

BONELESS PIGEON PIE

Pigeon pie has a superb flavour, but making it with whole birds does present difficulties when it comes to cutting and serving. It is far better to use the breast fillets from three pigeons, boiling the remainder of the birds to make a delicious stock for the pie. If you use breasts, dice the gammon and sprinkle it evenly over the top of the filling. Omit the second portion of butter.

STEWED VENISON

SERVES 6–8

225 g (8 oz) pork fat or fatty belly of
   pork, thinly sliced

salt and pepper

2.5 ml (½ tsp) ground allspice

300 ml (½ pint) port

1.6 kg (3½ lb) haunch or shoulder of
   venison joint

50 g (2 oz) butter

I large onion, finely chopped

I carrot, diced

I celery stick, diced

I bay leaf

900 ml (1½ pints) hot beef stock*,
   chicken stock* or game stock*

2.5 ml (½ tsp) black peppercorns

2.5 ml (½ tsp) allspice berries

25 g (1 oz) plain flour

redcurrant jelly to serve

Lay the pork fat or belly slices in a large shallow dish and season them well. Sprinkle the ground allspice over, then pour in the port. Turn the slices in the port and seasoning to coat both sides, then cover the dish and chill the fat or pork for 2–3 hours.

Set the oven at 160°C (325°F/gas 4). Trim any fat and membrane off the venison. Drain the marinated slices or fat or pork, reserving the marinade, and wrap them around the joint, tying them on. Place the joint in a large casserole.

Melt half the butter in a small saucepan and fry the onion, carrot and celery until lightly browned. Add the bay leaf and stir in some of the stock – enough to allow the cooking residue to be scraped off the pan and incorporated. Bring the mixture to the boil, stirring, then add it to the casserole with the remaining stock and reserved marinade. Tie the whole peppercorns and allspice berries in a small piece of muslin and add them to the casserole.

Cover the casserole tightly and cook the venison for 3–3½ hours. Baste the meat occasionally, if necessary, and turn the joint halfway through cooking. Cream the flour with the remaining butter. Stir knobs of this beurre manié into the cooking juices about 30 minutes before the end of the cooking time. Stir until all the paste has melted, then replace the casserole in the oven.

When the venison is tender, lift it out of the casserole, remove the barding fat and carve the meat into thick slices. Discard the bay leaf and the spices in the muslin bag, then ladle the cooking juices over the venison. Serve with redcurrant jelly.

COOK'S NOTES

Some of Mrs Beeton's recipes for braised meats and long-cooked meat pies excluded onions; this was a typical example. Most Victorian cooks would have had a ready supply of good stock simmering on the stove and Mrs Beeton was occasionally cautious in her use of flavouring ingredients. Onion, carrot, celery and a bay leaf have been added to the ingredients to update this fine recipe.

ACCOMPANIMENT IDEAS

Plain flavours best complement a rich casserole – creamy mashed potatoes or plain boiled potatoes dressed with a little melted butter and finely chopped parsley are perfect

for mopping up all the sauce. Today's cook also has the choice of pasta or gnocchi as excellent alternatives to potatoes. Large, chunky pasta shapes go well with rich venison stew, while potato gnocchi – available chilled or frozen from delicatessens or shops offering a broad range of fresh pasta – are delicious and satisfying.

Braised celery or fennel, carrots, Brussels sprouts and braised red cabbage make ideal vegetable accompaniments. Braised vegetables are best cooked with the simplest of seasonings and only a small amount of liquid. A sauce-coated vegetable dish, such as a gratin with Béchamel sauce, would not be a good choice.

JUGGED HARE

SERVES 6

1 hare, jointed with liver and blood
    reserved

60 ml (4 tbsp) plain flour

salt and pepper

75 g (3 oz) butter

900 ml (1½ pints) beef stock★

1 lemon

1 onion

6 cloves

1 bouquet garni

1.25 ml (¼ tsp) ground allspice

300 ml (½ pint) port

redcurrant jelly to serve

FORCEMEAT

50 g (2 oz) gammon or rindless
    bacon, finely chopped

50 g (2 oz) shredded suet

grated rind of ½ lemon

5 ml (1 tsp) finely chopped parsley

5 ml (1 tsp) finely chopped fresh
    mixed herbs

cayenne pepper

pinch of ground mace

175 g (6 oz) fresh white breadcrumbs

1 egg, lightly beaten

Set the oven at 180°C (350°F/gas 4). Dust the portions of hare with the flour and season them well. Melt 50 g (2 oz) of the butter in a frying pan and brown the hare joints all over, reserving any flour left over from coating them. Transfer the joints to a casserole. Stir the reserved flour into the fat remaining in the pan, then gradually stir in about half the stock and bring it to the boil, stirring. Stir in salt and pepper to taste, then turn off the heat under the pan.

Cut the lemon into quarters and add these to the hare. Stud the onion with the cloves and add it to the casserole with the bouquet garni and allspice. Add the thickened stock from the pan and stir in the remaining stock. Cover the casserole tightly and place it in the oven. Cook the hare for 3 hours.

For the forcemeat, mix the gammon or bacon, suet, lemon rind and herbs, adding salt, cayenne and mace to taste. Stir in the breadcrumbs and add the beaten egg to bind the mixture. Mould small balls of this forcemeat and fry them in the remaining butter until lightly browned.

Remove the bouquet garni and lemon quarters from the casserole. Reduce the oven temperature to 150°C (300°F/gas 2). Finely chop the liver, place it in a bowl and add a little of the cooking liquid from the casserole. Mash the liver into the hot liquid. Add the port and the hare's blood, then stir this mixture into the casserole. Top with the forcemeat balls and cover the casserole, then return it to the oven and cook for a further 10–15 minutes.

Serve the hare garnished with the forcemeat balls, with the cooking juices ladled over the joints. Offer redcurrant jelly as an accompaniment.

COOK'S NOTES

Traditionally, the point of jugged hare was to thicken the casserole with the reserved blood. The butcher will reserve the blood and liver for you if the hare is ordered in advance. To prevent the blood from coagulating, 5 ml (1 tsp) vinegar must be added to it and it must be stored in a covered container in the refrigerator.

In her original recipe, Mrs Beeton did not add the blood, which was legitimate because the title was given to recipes that were not enriched in that way, but were cooked in a deep pot or 'jug'. If you do add blood to the sauce, do not boil it or cook it at too high a temperature after the blood has been added as this will curdle the mixture.

HASHED HARE

remains of roast hare

1 blade of mace

3 allspice berries

1 onion, sliced

1 bouquet garni

salt and pepper

40 g (1½ oz) butter

40 g (1½ oz) plain flour

45 ml (3 tbsp) port

30 ml (2 tbsp) mushroom ketchup

2 thin slices of white bread, crusts
   removed

handful of parsley, finely chopped

redcurrant jelly to serve

Cut all the meat off the hare carcass, slicing any larger portions and cutting any irregular chunks into bite-sized pieces. Cut any stuffing into small portions.

Break up the carcass and place it in a large saucepan. Add the mace, allspice berries, onion, bouquet garni and a generous sprinkling of salt and pepper. Pour in water to cover the bones and bring it to the boil. Reduce the heat, cover the pan and simmer the stock for 1 hour. Strain the stock, then return it to the rinsed-out pan and boil it until it has reduced to about 450 ml (¾ pint).

Meanwhile, cream the butter and flour to a smooth paste. Whisk lumps of this beurre manié into the gently simmering stock and continue to whisk until the sauce thickens. Add the port and mushroom ketchup, then taste the sauce for seasoning.

Add the hare meat and any stuffing to the sauce and simmer it gently for about 5 minutes, or until the meat is hot. While the hare is reheating, toast the bread and cut it into small triangles. Transfer the hashed hare to a serving dish and sprinkle it generously with chopped parsley. Garnish with the toasted bread triangles and serve at once with the redcurrant jelly.

COOK'S NOTES

The number of servings which this recipes yields depends, of course, on the amount of meat left on the hare carcass. If the amount is small, the dish can be bulked out to serve four by frying 100 g (4 oz) chopped rindless bacon with 1 chopped onion and adding 100 g (4 oz) thinly sliced mushrooms. Add the reduced stock to the fried ingredients, then thicken the sauce as in the main recipe.

HARE

Hare is in season throughout the year but it must not be sold from March to July. It is at its best from October to January. Traditionally, hare is particularly popular in country areas, especially in Yorkshire, where jugged hare was considered to be a local speciality and a festive Christmas dish.

Two types of hare are fairly common in Britain, the English (or brown) hare and the Scottish (or blue) hare. Brown hare is considered to have the best flavour.

HASHED DISHES

Hash, derived from the French hacher, is the name given to foods that have been cut up. It is also synonymous in culinary terms with reheated foods and leftovers, especially meat, which may be minced or finely chopped, combined with sauce and mixed with ingredients to extend it, typically mashed potatoes.

Hash can be served with rice, pasta, creamed or baked potatoes. A border of piped mashed potatoes can be browned under the grill, then filled with hash.

RABBIT A LA MINUTE

SERVES 4

3 dried mushrooms

600 ml (1 pint) hot chicken stock

675 g (1½ lb) boneless rabbit portions

salt and pepper

30 ml (2 tbsp) plain flour

2.5 ml (½ tsp) ground mace

25 g (1 oz) butter

30 ml (2 tbsp) chopped parsley

60 ml (4 tbsp) dry sherry

Soak the mushrooms in about a quarter of the hot stock for 30 minutes. Drain and slice them, discarding any tough stems and reserving the soaking liquid. Strain the liquid through a muslin-lined sieve or a coffee filter paper to remove any grit.

Cut the rabbit portions into small, fairly thin pieces. Season them well and dust them with flour and the mace. Melt the butter in a large deep frying pan and brown the rabbit portions all over, turning them frequently until they are well cooked. Sprinkle any leftover flour and mace over the rabbit.

Add the mushrooms and their soaking liquid, the parsley, remaining stock and sherry. Bring the liquid to the boil, then lower the heat slightly and cover the pan. Cook at a rapid simmer for 20 minutes or until the rabbit is tender. Taste for seasoning and serve.

COOK'S NOTES

With this recipe, Mrs Beeton was exhibiting her knowledge of Eastern European cookery. The dish has a delicious flavour, thanks to the rich dried mushroom and sherry sauce. Although the recipe works well as it stands, the flavour and texture are even better if it is simmered for a further 20 minutes.

Several different types of dried mushroom are sold in delicatessens and specialist stores, particularly Italian and Polish food shops. Dried ceps (the Italian porcini), are readily available. Most large supermarkets sell sliced dried mushrooms. These only need a short soaking time and are sufficiently clean for the stock to be used without straining.

If dried mushrooms are not available, substitute 100 g (4 oz) fresh wild mushrooms; failing this, use sliced chestnut mushrooms and sauté them separately in a little oil or butter before adding them to the rabbit. Continue cooking the mushrooms until all the liquid they yield has evaporated – this concentrates their flavour slightly.

SERVING SUGGESTIONS
Creamy mashed potatoes or plain boiled potatoes are ideal accompaniments. Potato gnocchi may not be very British, but they are good with this type of sauce. Braised red cabbage is a 'must' with this dish.

RAGOUT OF RABBIT

SERVES 4

675 g (1½ lb) boneless rabbit portions

salt and pepper

45 ml (3 tbsp) plain flour

50 g (2 oz) butter

2 large or 3 medium onions, sliced

4 rindless streaky bacon rashers,
    diced

450 ml (¾ pint) chicken stock*

2 thick slices of lemon

1 bay leaf

150 ml (¼ pint) port

Coat the rabbit portions with the salt, pepper and flour. Melt the butter in a heavy-bottomed saucepan or flameproof casserole and brown the rabbit portions all over. Use a slotted spoon to remove the portions from the pan.

Cook the onions in the fat remaining in the pan, stirring them occasionally, until they are well browned. Add the bacon and cook for 2 minutes. Stir in any flour left over from coating the rabbit, then pour in the stock and bring the sauce to the boil, stirring all the time.

Replace the rabbit portions, add the lemon slices and bay leaf and cover the pan. Simmer the ragout gently for about 45 minutes, or until the rabbit portions are cooked. Stir in the port and bring the ragout to the boil, then simmer for 3–5 minutes. Taste the sauce for seasoning before serving the rabbit.

COOK'S NOTES

'Excellent' and 'yum' were just two of the comments scribbled on the recipe when this was tested; it is a jolly good rabbit stew. If the budget does not stretch to port, substitute red wine and add the pared rind from half a lemon rather than the two slices, which contribute tangy juice.

DUMPLINGS

Dumplings are an excellent accompaniment for rabbit ragout. Follow a standard recipe for suet pastry* and roll it into small dumplings, about the size of eggs. Cook the dumplings in simmering salted water for 15–20 minutes. Use a slotted spoon to remove the dumplings and serve them as soon as they are cooked.

SUSSEX HARD DUMPLINGS

These are extremely plain, flour-and-water dumplings. Season 225 g (8 oz) self-raising flour well and mix in 150 ml (¼ pint) water or milk. Roll small egg-sized balls of the dough. Cook them in simmering stock or water for 15–20 minutes. Use a slotted spoon to remove the dumplings and serve them as soon as they are cooked.

MEAT DISHES

ROAST RIBS OF BEEF *with* YORKSHIRE PUDDING

SERVES 6–8

2.5 kg (5½ lb) forerib of beef

50 g (2 oz) plain flour plus extra for
    dusting

50–75 g (2–3 oz) beef dripping

salt and pepper

900 ml (1½ pints) vegetable cooking
    water

YORKSHIRE PUDDING

100 g (4 oz) plain flour

1 egg, beaten

150 ml (¼ pint) milk

Set the oven at 230°C (450°F/gas 8). Dust the meat with flour but do not salt it. Place the meat in a roasting tin and dot the dripping over and around it. Roast the joint for 10 minutes. Lower the oven temperature to 180°C (350°F/gas 4). Baste the meat thoroughly, then continue to roast for a further 1¾ hours for rare meat to 2¼ hours for well-done meat. Baste the joint frequently during cooking.

Meanwhile, make the Yorkshire pudding batter. Sift the flour into a bowl and add a pinch of salt. Make a well in the centre of the flour and add the egg. Beat a little of the milk into the egg, then gradually beat in the rest of the milk, working in the surrounding flour. Beat vigorously until the mixture is smooth and bubbly, then stir in 150 ml (¼ pint) water.

About 30 minutes before the end of the cooking time, pour a little of the dripping into a small roasting tin or six 7.5 cm (3 inch) Yorkshire pudding tins. Place the tin or tins in the oven for a short while, until the fat is very hot, then carefully pour in the batter. Bake a large pudding for 30–40 minutes (depending on the size of the tin – the larger the tin, the thinner the layer of batter and the shorter the cooking time) or 15–20 minutes for individual puddings.

When the beef is cooked, salt it lightly. Transfer it to a warmed serving plate. Cover it with tented foil and set it aside to rest while you make gravy. Pour off the excess fat from the roasting tin, leaving a shallow layer to absorb the flour. Stir in the flour, scraping the base of the tin to incorporate the sediment. Gradually stir in the vegetable cooking water and bring the gravy to the boil, stirring all the time. Reduce the heat and simmer the gravy for about 5 minutes. Taste and season, then serve the gravy with the roast beef and Yorkshire pudding.

COOK'S NOTES

The traditional method of cooking Yorkshire pudding is in a large tin below the joint, so that some of the cooking juices from the meat fall into the pudding to give it an excellent flavour. This was, of course, extremely practical when joints were suspended on hooks or skewered on rotisseries for roasting.

To achieve the same result in a modern oven, the joint would have to be placed directly on the wire shelf, unless it is cooked on a spit. To minimize spitting, roast the meat in the tin until you are ready to put the pudding in the oven, then remove the meat from the tin, allowing excess cooking juices to drip off, and place it on the shelf above the pudding batter.

Individual puddings may look neat, but a large pudding tastes better, having a good proportion of lightly crisped centre to crusty edge. Cut into portions for serving.

ACCOMPANIMENTS FOR ROAST BEEF
Mrs Beeton garnished the joint of beef with 'tufts of scraped horseradish' and sent a dish of horseradish sauce to the table. Since fresh horseradish is not the easiest ingredient to prepare, it seems a waste to use it as a mere garnish; however, good, hot horseradish sauce is a must for a classic roast rib of beef. English mustard is another popular accompaniment, while those who prefer a milder condiment plump for creamed horseradish.

COLLARED BEEF

SERVES 8-10

2.5 kg (5½ lb) thin end of flank of
   beef, boned

40 g (1½ oz) sugar

175 g (6 oz) coarse salt

large handful of parsley, finely
   chopped, stalks reserved

2 large fresh sage sprigs, finely
   chopped

2 large fresh marjoram sprigs, finely
   chopped

2 large fresh thyme sprigs, finely
   chopped

2.5 ml (½ tsp) ground allspice

salt and pepper

2 carrots, sliced

2 celery sticks, sliced

2 large onions, sliced

Select beef which is not too fatty. Remove any gristle, then lay the beef in a large dish or plastic container. Rub the sugar and salt all over the meat, making sure the top is well covered with these seasonings. Cover the dish or container and chill the meat for 3 days. Turn the meat every day, spooning the pickling juices that will have formed in the container over it with any undissolved sugar and salt.

Mix the chopped herbs with the allspice and plenty of seasoning. Drain the meat and lay it on a board. Spread the herb mixture evenly over the beef, then roll it up tightly into a neat round joint. Tie the joint securely. Wrap it in a piece of muslin and tie this around the meat in several places.

Place the carrots, celery and onions in a large saucepan with the reserved parsley stalks. Place the beef on top; pour in enough water to cover the joint. Bring the water to simmering point, skimming off the scum which rises to the surface. Reduce the heat so that the water is barely simmers; and cover the pan tightly. Cook the beef gently for 4½ hours, until it is completely tender. If the liquid is simmering gently, there is no need to top it up during cooking. Check, however, that the meat is not cooking too rapidly and add a little extra boiling water, if necessary, to keep the joint covered.

Allow the meat to cool in its cooking liquid for 2 hours, then remove it and place it in a deep dish without unwrapping it. Top the meat with a plate and weight it down. Leave the joint to cool, then chill it overnight, still weighted. To serve, unwrap the joint and slice it thinly.

COOK'S NOTES

Although this recipe requires forward planning to allow for pickling and pressing, it is otherwise quite simple and the result is absolutely splendid. The superbly flavoured cold beef is delicious with salads, new or baked potatoes or as a filling for sandwiches.

Originally, saltpetre was added to the sugar and salt, and the beef was pickled for a week to ten days. Saltpetre (potassium nitrate) was widely used by butchers and at home for pickling meat. Today, nitrate and nitrite are both commercial preservatives, but saltpetre is not available from local butchers or chemist shops for home use.

It is essential to turn the beef and ensure it is well covered or basted with the salt and sugar mixture or the brine which develops.

ALTERNATIVE JOINTS OF BEEF

Flank is a comparatively fatty joint which requires long, slow cooking. Once widely used, it is today quite difficult to obtain as the bulk of it is minced. Brisket of beef is a good alternative. Today's joints are less fatty than many traditional cuts, both due to the rearing of the animals and because the meat is trimmed by the butcher. Joints which are sold boned and rolled should be untrussed for coating with the pickle mixture. Silverside is an excellent choice for salting and boiling.

RUMP STEAK *with* OYSTER SAUCE

16 oysters

50 g (2 oz) butter

15 ml (1 tbsp) plain flour

200 ml (7 fl oz) milk

salt and pepper

900 g (2 lb) rump steak

Open the oysters, reserving the liquor from their shells, and place them in a small saucepan. Add the reserved liquor and cook the oysters for 2–3 minutes, until they are just opaque, without allowing the liquor to reach simmering point. Remove the pan from the heat. Cut away the dark frilly edges from the oysters, then replace the oysters in the liquor.

Melt the butter in a saucepan and stir in the flour. Cook this thin paste for 1 minute, stirring, then gradually stir in the milk and bring the sauce to the boil. Reduce the heat and simmer the sauce for 3 minutes, stirring occasionally, then add seasoning to taste. Leave the sauce over very low heat, stirring it occasionally, while grilling the steak.

Heat the grill to the hottest setting and have four plates warming, ready to serve the steaks immediately they are cooked. Cut the steak into four portions and grill them for about 2½–6 minutes on each side, depending on how thick the steak is and how well done you like it. Rump steak that is about 2 cm (¾ inch) thick will be rare after 2½ minutes or well done after 6 minutes on each side.

A couple of minutes before the rump steaks are ready, add the oysters and their cooking liquor to the sauce and heat them through without allowing the sauce to simmer. Check the seasoning and serve the oyster sauce spooned partly over and around the steaks.

COOK'S NOTES

This is an interesting recipe and a change from the steak and oyster combination famous as a filling for pies or puddings. Here the oysters in sauce are little more than a fine-flavoured condiment to complement and moisten the steak. The small quantity of sauce enhances, rather than drowns, the flavour of the simple grilled meat.

Take care to avoid overheating and toughening the oysters as their soft, almost creamy texture is important for the success of the sauce. By way of contrast, a crisp green side salad and crisply fried or firm, waxy new potatoes are excellent accompaniments.

One old wives' tale claims that eating oysters on St James' day, July 25th, will ensure that there will be no shortage of money for the rest of the year; however, this is difficult to achieve as native oysters are not in season until there is an 'r' in the month.

Oysters can be frozen and are then ideal for adding to sauces or for using in pies. Freeze the raw oysters in the liquor from their shells, packing about half a dozen in a small container or polythene bag. They can certainly be kept for up to 1–2 months and it is best to thaw them partially before cooking.

BEEF COLLOPS

675 g (1½ lb) rump steak, beaten and

    cut into thin slices, about 7.5 cm

    (3 inches) long

50 g (2 oz) plain flour

salt and pepper

50 g (2 oz) butter

1 small onion, finely chopped

600 ml (1 pint) good beef stock★

1 bouquet garni

15 ml (1 tbsp) Harvey's or

    Worcestershire sauce or

    mushroom ketchup

Toss the meat slices in the flour, adding plenty of salt and pepper. Melt the butter in a large frying pan, flameproof casserole or heavy-bottomed saucepan. Add the steak and fry the pieces until browned on all sides. Use a slotted spoon to remove the meat from the pan.

Add the onion to the fat remaining in the pan and fry it until it has softened and is beginning to brown. Stir in any flour left over after dusting the meat and cook it for about 5 minutes, stirring all the time, until the flour begins to brown.

Gradually add the stock, stirring continuously, then add the bouquet garni, sauce or mushroom ketchup, with salt and pepper to taste. Bring to the boil, stirring constantly, then lower the heat and replace the meat. Simmer the meat gently for 10 minutes and serve.

MINCED COLLOPS

Minced steak can be used instead of the meat strips. Fry the onion first until lightly browned, then add the meat and brown it. Sprinkle in the flour and stir in the stock, then add the remaining ingredients and cook in the main recipe. Cover the pan and simmer the minced steak for 20 minutes. Sippets★ of toasted bread make a good garnish for the collops.

COOK'S NOTES

This is a plain but tasty dish of beef steak with onions. Creamy mashed potatoes, buttery shredded cabbage and simply cooked carrots are good accompaniments.

Collop Monday, also known as Shrove Monday, Poets' Day and Peasen Monday, was the name traditionally given to the day before Shrove Tuesday at the beginning of Lent. Originally, collops (thick slices) of bacon were cooked with eggs to finish these rich foods before the Lenten fast. Other meats eaten up before the fast included pork, which was eaten with pease pudding. In Lancashire it was customary on Collop Monday for the mill owners to distribute pennies to the children and many schools closed after morning lessons so that the youngsters could congregate at the local mills.

The image of courteous children waiting patiently for treats is not necessarily accurate: in Yorkshire youngsters demanded sweets from local confectioners with the cry of 'Pray, Dame, a collop or we will give you a wallop'.

Poets' Day probably comes from the Eton custom of writing verses to be read on the Monday before Lent. These verses were meant as farewells to the good eating which was not to be allowed again until Easter.

ROASTED ROLLED STEAK

SERVES 4

50 g (2 oz) gammon or rindless
    bacon, finely chopped

50 g (2 oz) shredded suet

grated rind of ½ lemon

5 ml (1 tsp) finely chopped parsley

5 ml (1 tsp) finely chopped mixed
    herbs

salt and pepper

cayenne pepper

pinch of ground mace

175 g (6 oz) fresh white breadcrumbs

1 egg, lightly beaten

900 g (2 lb) thick-cut rump steak, in
    one or two pieces

50 g (2 oz) clarified butter★

25 g (1 oz) plain flour

750 ml (1¼ pints) vegetable cooking
    water

Set the oven at 200°C (400°F/gas 6). Mix the gammon or bacon, suet, lemon rind and herbs, adding salt, cayenne and mace to taste. Stir in the breadcrumbs and add the beaten egg to bind the ingredients into a forcemeat.

Lay the steak between two sheets of greaseproof paper and beat it with a rolling pin or steak mallet to thin it slightly so that it is the same thickness all over. Season the steak well and spread the forcemeat over half of it, if it is in one piece, or over one portion if it is in two pieces. Roll up the steak to enclose the forcemeat; wrap the unfilled piece around the filled steak if there are two portions. Tie the steak firmly to keep it in shape and place it in a roasting tin.

Dot the clarified butter over the steak and roast it for 10 minutes. Reduce the heat to 180°C (350°F/gas 4) and continue roasting the steak for 1¼ hours. Baste the roll frequently during cooking.

Transfer the cooked steak to a serving plate, cover it and keep it warm. Stir the flour into the pan juices and cook the paste, stirring it often, until the flour browns lightly. Stir in the vegetable cooking water and bring the gravy to the boil, stirring continuously. Boil the gravy for about 3 minutes, until it has reduced and all the cooking residue from the pan has been incorporated. Taste and season the gravy before serving it with the rolled stuffed steak.

COOK'S NOTES

BEEF OLIVES

These are now the more familiar version of rolled steak. Mrs Beeton's method for making beef olives was simple and successful. Beat out small slices of lean beef steak (braising steak works well) until thin. Brush the steaks with beaten egg, then sprinkle them with seasoning and finely chopped mixed herbs (parsley, thyme and marjoram or your favourite combination). Roll up the steaks and secure them with skewers or wooden cocktail sticks.

Place the rolls in a casserole and pour in 600 ml (1 pint) beef stock★. Lay 2 or 3 rashers of bacon over the top and cover the casserole. Cook the beef olives gently for 2 hours, either by simmering them on the hob or cooking them in the oven at 160°C (325°F/gas 3). Thicken the cooking juices by stirring in a few pieces of beurre manié (made by creaming equal quantities of softened butter and plain flour together). Pour the sauce over the beef olives.

STEWED BEEF

SERVES 6

25 g (1 oz) butter

900 g (2 lb) stewing beef or braising
    steak, cut into 2.5–5 cm (1–2 inch)
    chunks

3 onions, thinly sliced

3 carrots, thinly sliced

2 turnips, diced

salt and pepper

15 ml (1 tbsp) mushroom ketchup,
    liquid from pickled walnuts or
    Harvey's or Worcestershire sauce

30 ml (2 tbsp) plain flour

Melt the butter in a flameproof casserole or heavy-bottomed saucepan and fry the beef or steak until the chunks are browned on both sides. Use a slotted spoon to remove the meat, then fry the vegetables in the fat remaining in the pan. Stir the vegetables until the onions are slightly softened.

Replace the meat and add plenty of seasoning. Pour in 600 ml (1 pint) water, or enough to just cover the ingredients, then bring the stew slowly to simmering point. Cover the pan tightly and simmer the stew very gently for 2½–3 hours, or until the meat is tender.

Add the ketchup, walnut liquid or sauce and additional seasoning if necessary. Blend the flour to a smooth paste with a little cold water, then stir in a few spoonfuls of the hot liquid from the stew. Stir the flour mixture into the stew and bring it to the boil, stirring to thicken the cooking liquid smoothly. Reduce the heat and simmer for 1–2 minutes before serving.

NOTE

The stew will be less rich if it is cooked the day before it is required, then cooled and chilled. This allows any fat to be lifted off the surface, so that the stew merely needs to be heated before being served.

COOK'S NOTES

YEAST DUMPLINGS

These were made using a basic bread dough*, mixed with milk instead of water, and served with meat gravy or as a sweet dish, with melted butter and sugar.

To make yeast dumplings, take small portions of dough, about 50 g (2 oz), and roll them into neat balls, then place these on a floured baking sheet. Cover the dumplings loosely with greased polythene or foil and leave them in a warm place until they have doubled in size.

The dumplings must be served as soon as they are cooked or they will become heavy. Bring a large saucepan of water to the boil and gently add the dumplings, using a slotted spoon. Cover the pan and simmer them for 20 minutes. Turn the dumplings halfway through cooking, but take care not to knock the air out of the mixture or the dumplings will be leaden. Remove them with a slotted spoon and serve at once, breaking the dumplings open with two forks.

TOAD-IN-THE-HOLE

SERVES 4–6

15 g (½ oz) butter

175 g (6 oz) plain flour

salt and pepper

4 eggs

600 ml (1 pint) milk

675 g (1½ lb) lean rump steak, cut into 4 cm (1½ in) cubes

1 lamb's kidney, trimmed and finely diced

1 small onion, finely chopped

Set the oven at 190°C (375°F/gas 5). Using the butter, grease an ovenproof dish – a large gratin dish or lasagne dish is ideal; alternatively, a roasting tin can be used.

Season the flour with salt and pepper and make a well in the middle. Add the eggs and pour in a little milk. Gently beat the egg mixture, gradually pouring in the remaining milk and working in the flour to make a smooth batter. Beat the batter thoroughly until it is smooth and light.

Season the steak cubes well, then place them in the greased dish. Distribute the kidney and onion between the steak cubes. Pour the batter over the meat and bake the toad-in-the-hole for about 1–1¼ hours, until the batter is risen, browned and crisp, and the meat cooked. Serve at once.

VARIATIONS

The remains of cold roast beef or lamb can be substituted for steak; rare roast beef is particularly suitable. The sliced meat should be seasoned well before being placed in the dish. Mushrooms can be used instead of the kidney.

COOK'S NOTES

We know toad-in-the-hole as a savoury pudding of sausages cooked in batter, but Mrs Beeton included no fewer than three versions of this recipe in her original book. The first, entitled Baked Beef-steak Pudding, used slightly less batter; the second (on which the above recipe is based) included a small quantity of minced onion or shallot as an optional extra; and the third used sliced cold cooked mutton instead of steak.

The recipe given here is delicious – it tastes rather like roast beef and Yorkshire pudding rolled into one, with a hint of that wonderful savoury kidney flavour for good measure. Tender steak is essential – braising or stewing cuts are too tough – and the kidney must be cut into very small pieces as its texture does not go well with the baked batter (but the flavour is superb). Trim off the rim of fat around rump steak and use it to flavour a rich onion gravy to serve with the toad-in-the-hole. Offer generous portions of everyday vegetables as accompaniments, for example Brussels sprouts, cabbage, carrots, mashed swedes or parsnips. Since the batter is quite filling, only those with the most ravenous appetites will want potatoes.

ONION GRAVY

Melt 40 g (1½ oz) beef dripping, beef suet, lard or butter in a small to medium saucepan. Add the fat trimmed from the rump steak in one piece and brown it all over. If suet is used, the small amount of flour coating will brown in the bottom of the pan and this will help to give the gravy a good colour. Stir in 3 thinly sliced onions, then leave them to cook for about 20 minutes, or longer, until they are browned in places. Turn the onions occasionally.

Stir in 40 g (1½ oz) plain flour and cook, stirring frequently, until the paste begins to brown slightly. Gradually stir in 750 ml (1¼ pints) beef stock⋆. If beef stock is not available, chicken stock⋆ or vegetable stock⋆ can be used. Bring the gravy to the boil, stirring, then reduce the heat and simmer, uncovered, for 30 minutes, stirring occasionally.

Remove the piece of steak fat from the gravy, then add salt and pepper to taste. Serve the piping hot gravy poured over portions of the toad-in-the-hole.

BRAISED STUFFED
SHOULDER OF LAMB

SERVES 6

50 g (2 oz) gammon or rindless
  bacon, finely chopped

50 g (2 oz) shredded suet

grated rind of ½ lemon

5 ml (1 tsp) finely chopped parsley

5 ml (1 tsp) finely chopped fresh
  mixed herbs

salt and pepper

cayenne pepper

pinch of ground mace

175 g (6 oz) fresh white breadcrumbs

1 egg, lightly beaten

1 shoulder of lamb, boned

2 onions, sliced

½ head of celery, sliced

1 bouquet garni

1.1 litres (2 pints) lamb stock or
  chicken stock*

2 streaky bacon rashers

Set the oven at 180°C (350°F/gas 4). Mix the gammon or bacon, suet, lemon rind and herbs, then add salt, cayenne and mace to taste. Stir in the breadcrumbs and add enough of the beaten egg to bind the ingredients into a forcemeat.

Fill the boned shoulder of lamb with the forcemeat and sew up the joint with a trussing needle and string or heavy buttonhole thread (used double). Place the onions, celery and bouquet garni in a large casserole and put the shoulder of lamb on top. Pour in the stock, leaving the top of the meat exposed. Season the lamb well. Lay the streaky bacon over the lamb. Cover the casserole and place it in the oven.

Cook the lamb for 30 minutes, then remove the lid. Cook for 1 hour more, then lift off the bacon and continue to cook the lamb for a further 30–40 minutes. Transfer the lamb to a serving dish and spoon the celery and onions around it.

COOK'S NOTES

Peas and Stewed Cucumbers with Onions (page 116) were among the original accompaniments suggested for the stuffed shoulder of lamb. New potatoes would complete the menu.

MUSHROOM STUFFING

A well-flavoured mushroom stuffing is delicious with lamb. Chop 225 g (8 oz) open-cup mushrooms fairly finely and fry them in 50 g (2 oz) butter in a large saucepan. Continue to cook until the liquid which runs from the mushrooms evaporates completely. Stir the mushrooms towards the end of cooking to prevent them from sticking to the pan.

Mix 100 g (4 oz) fresh white breadcrumbs, 60 ml (4 tbsp) chopped parsley, 15 ml (1 tbsp) chopped fresh tarragon, thyme or savory and a little grated nutmeg with the mushrooms. Add salt and pepper to taste. Bind the stuffing with 30 ml (2 tbsp) dry sherry and a little beaten egg, if necessary. The stuffing should be quite dry for braised lamb but moist if the joint is to be roasted.

ROLLED LOIN OF LAMB

SERVES 6

1 x 1.4–1.6 kg (3–3½ lb) boned and
   rolled double loin of lamb, bones
   reserved, trimmed

salt and pepper

1.25 ml (¼ tsp) ground allspice

2.5 ml (½ tsp) ground mace

2.5 ml (½ tsp) grated nutmeg

6 cloves

600 ml (1 pint) lamb stock, chicken
   stock* or vegetable stock*

125 ml (4 fl oz) port

30 ml (2 tbsp) mushroom ketchup

30 ml (2 tbsp) plain flour

25 g (1 oz) butter

100 g (4 oz) button mushrooms

STUFFING

50 g (2 oz) shredded suet

50 g (2 oz) cooked ham, chopped

15 ml (1 tbsp) finely chopped parsley

5 ml (1 tsp) chopped fresh thyme

grated rind of ½ lemon

175 g (6 oz) fresh white breadcrumbs

2.5 ml (½ tsp) ground mace

pinch of cayenne pepper

1 egg, beaten

60 ml (4 tbsp) milk

Open out the lamb and season the inside lightly. Mix the allspice, mace and nutmeg, then rub these spices all over the meat. Cover the lamb and marinate it for 24 hours in the refrigerator.

Set the oven at 180°C (350°F/gas 4). Make the stuffing. Mix the suet, ham, parsley, thyme, lemon rind, breadcrumbs and mace. Add salt and pepper to taste. Sprinkle the cayenne over the mixture, stir in the egg and add enough milk to bind it lightly.

Spread the stuffing evenly over the lamb, roll it up and tie it neatly. Pierce the lamb and stick the cloves into the joint. Put the lamb bones in the bottom of a roasting tin and pour over just enough stock to cover them. Place the lamb on top and cook it for about 2½ hours, adding extra stock or water during cooking so that the level of the liquid remains just below the top of the bones and joint. Baste the joint occasionally with the cooking juices.

When the lamb is cooked, transfer it to a heated serving platter. Tent foil over the lamb and leave it to rest while you make the sauce. Remove the bones and skim off most of the fat from the liquid in the roasting tin. Stir in the port and mushroom ketchup, then bring the mixture to simmering point. Beat the flour and butter to a smooth paste. Whisking all the time, gradually add small lumps of the butter and flour mixture to the sauce. Continue whisking until the sauce boils and thickens. Slice the mushrooms and stir them into the sauce. Reduce the heat and simmer for 3 minutes. Add salt and pepper, if necessary, before serving the sauce with the lamb. Offer redcurrant jelly and/or mint sauce as additional accompaniments.

COOK'S NOTES

The original recipe called for a joint of mutton, double the size of the loin of lamb suggested here. The mutton was part baked, then stewed. Mutton is seldom available today, but is worth seeking out. Some mail-order organic meat suppliers offer it and it is also available from a number of city butchers, particularly those that offer halal meat. However, the comparatively smaller joint of lamb also gives excellent results and is perhaps more appropriate for our households. Cooking it over the braising bones gives an excellent result, with succulent meat and a rich sauce.

IRISH STEW

SERVES 6

900 g (2 lb) potatoes, thickly sliced

1.4 kg (3 lb) neck of lamb, trimmed of
excess fat

2 large onions, thickly sliced

salt and pepper

Set the oven at 190°C (375°F/gas 5). Arrange a layer of potatoes in the bottom of a large casserole. Add a layer of meat and onions, seasoning each layer very well. Continue to layer the ingredients, ending with a thick layer of vegetables.

Pour in 600 ml (1 pint) hot water and cover the casserole tightly. Bake the stew for 2½ hours. Try to avoid removing the lid. It is, however, a good idea to check the casserole halfway through cooking and to top up the liquid if necessary. Serve the stew piping hot.

USING BREAST OF LAMB

An economical stew can be prepared by simmering two breasts of lamb in 900 ml (1½ pints) lightly salted water for 1 hour. Drain the lamb and reserve the stock. Cut the lamb into small pieces, discarding the bones and excess fat. Layer the lamb with the potatoes and onions. Skim the fat off the stock and add the stock to the casserole instead of water.

COOK'S NOTES

Apparently Irish stew was originally made with young goat (kid). The important difference between this and other meat and vegetable stews is that potatoes and onions are the only vegetables.

There is no need to add stock when making an Irish stew; with plenty of seasoning, the slow-cooked lamb provides ample flavour. The potatoes should be thickly sliced, or small ones halved, so that they retain their shape. A deep pot is essential and it must be tightly covered throughout cooking, using an underlying layer of foil if the lid does not fit closely. For a brown crust, remove the lid at the end of the stated cooking time and increase the oven temperature to 200°C (400°F/gas 6). Return the stew to the oven for about 20 minutes more.

The result will be a hearty hotpot, with plenty of potatoes and meat to satisfy eager winter appetites. Serve lightly cooked carrots and lightly boiled cabbage, dressed with plenty of butter and pepper, as accompaniments.

CASSEROLE OF BREAST OF LAMB

SERVES 4

1 large breast of lamb, boned and
   trimmed of excess fat

2–3 rindless bacon rashers, diced

25 g (1 oz) plain flour

salt and pepper

2 onions, sliced

1 bouquet garni

225 g (8 oz) shelled fresh or frozen
   peas

Cut the lamb into pieces about 5 cm (2 inches) square and place these in a flameproof casserole or heavy-bottomed saucepan. Add the bacon. Heat the pan gently until the fat runs from the lamb and bacon, then increase the heat and fry the meats until the pieces of lamb are browned on both sides.

Pour off any excess fat from the pan and sprinkle the flour over the lamb. Season the meat generously and stir in enough water to just cover the lamb. Add the onions and the bouquet garni, then bring the water to the boil, stirring continuously. Reduce the heat and cover the pan, then simmer the lamb gently for 1½ hours, until it is completely tender.

Cook the peas in boiling salted water until tender, allowing 20 minutes for fresh vegetables or 5 minutes for frozen peas. Skim any fat from the surface of the lamb, discard the bouquet garni and taste the sauce for seasoning. Stir in the peas and serve the lamb immediately.

COOK'S NOTES

Breast of lamb is a somewhat underrated cut. With a little attention it can make a delicious roast for two or the base of an aromatic curry, particularly with the addition of spices with citrus-like flavours, such as ginger, lemon grass and cardamom.

ROASTING BREAST OF LAMB
Use one of the many high-quality sausagemeats as a stuffing, such as pork and leek, and add the grated rind of ½ lemon, with a good sprinkling of chopped fresh parsley.

Spread the sausagemeat over the seasoned, trimmed, boned breast of lamb, and roll it up neatly, then tie it securely with string to keep it in shape. Weigh the stuffed lamb before placing it in a small roasting tin.

Sprinkle a little chopped rosemary or savory over the lamb and roast it at 180°C (350°F/gas 4), allowing 30 minutes per 450 g (1 lb), plus an additional 30 minutes. Baste the lamb occasionally during cooking. Discard the excess fat from the pan, then use the juices to make gravy to serve with the meat.

BOILED LEG OF LAMB
with CAPER SAUCE

SERVES 6–8

2 onions, sliced

2 carrots, sliced

1 turnip, sliced

5 ml (1 tsp) salt

1 bouquet garni

10 black peppercorns

2 kg (4½ lb) leg of lamb, trimmed

CAPER SAUCE

225 g (8 oz) butter

25 g (1 oz) plain flour

475 ml (16 fl oz) milk

60 ml (4 tbsp) chopped capers

30 ml (2 tbsp) pickling vinegar from
    the jar of capers

Place the onions, carrots, turnip, salt, bouquet garni and peppercorns in a large saucepan or stockpot. Pour in enough water to half-fill the pan and bring it to the boil. Have a kettle of boiling water ready to top up the cooking liquid, if necessary, when the lamb is added. Lower the lamb into the boiling water, adding more water to cover the meat, if necessary. Bring the water back to the boil and reduce the heat immediately so that the liquid simmers very gently.

Skim the surface of the water, cover the pan with a tight-fitting lid and cook the lamb gently for 2½–3 hours or until it is tender.

For the caper sauce, cut the butter into small knobs and place these in a saucepan with the flour. Gradually pour in the milk, whisking continuously. Heat the sauce gently and continue stirring or lightly whisking it until the butter melts and the sauce boils. Immediately remove the pan from the heat and add the capers and vinegar, with seasoning to taste.

Drain and carve the lamb, then serve it on a platter, coated with the caper sauce. Carrots, mashed turnips and lightly cooked fresh spinach would be suitable vegetable accompaniments.

COOK'S NOTES

The idea of boiled lamb may not have much appeal for modern cooks, but this recipe gives the most wonderful result. It is surprising to discover that boiled lamb has a sweet, distinctive, yet delicate, flavour which tastes delicious with a piquant, peppery caper sauce. The leg of lamb will provide neat slices for six portions, but there is enough meat to serve eight. Do not skimp on the sauce – to serve eight, make an additional half quantity.

PRESENTING BOILED LAMB

To make a superbly flavoured meal that looks as good as it tastes, present the boiled lamb carefully. Carve the joint into slices and overlap these neatly on a warmed large platter. Arrange bright new-season carrots and sugar snap peas or other vegetables on the platter. Pour some of the sauce over the meat, then serve the remaining sauce in a sauceboat or jug.

FLAVOURING AND USING THE STOCK

Make a good sized bouquet garni to add to the pan, with a couple of bay leaves, a length of celery stick with leaves, several sprigs of parsley and thyme, and a generous sprig of rosemary.

The stock from cooking the meat can be reserved for making soup or for flavouring lamb casseroles and stews. Cool, strain and chill the cooking liquid, lift off and discard the layer of fat on the surface, then freeze the stock.

BECHAMEL SAUCE

Instead of making the rich butter sauce, 600 ml (1 pint) Béchamel sauce★ can be used as the base. Add the capers and beat in an additional 25 g (1 oz) butter just before serving.

BOILED BACON WITH BROAD BEANS

1.8 kg (4 lb) bacon joint

2 bay leaves

1 blade of mace

2 onions, sliced

1 carrot, sliced

1 celery stick, sliced

1.4 kg (3 lb) broad beans, shelled

salt

25–50 g (1–2 oz) butter

large handful of parsley, chopped

freshly ground black pepper

Tie the bacon into a neat shape, if necessary. Place the joint in a large saucepan and pour in cold water to cover it. Bring the water slowly to the boil, skimming off any scum as it surfaces, then drain the joint. Replace the bacon in the pan and add the bay leaves, mace, onions, carrot and celery. Pour in cold water to cover.

Bring the water to the boil, again removing any scum, then immediately reduce the heat so that the water simmers. Cover the pan and cook the bacon for 1¾ hours. Do not allow the water to boil rapidly at any stage.

Towards the end of the cooking time for the bacon, bring a saucepan of salted water to the boil and cook the broad beans. Small young beans require 5 minutes' cooking; older beans should be boiled for 10–15 minutes. If the beans are very large and old, the skins should be removed or they will remain tough even when the beans themselves are tender.

Remove the rind from the bacon as soon as it is cooked: cut off any binding, then make a shallow slit into the rind. Working from the slit around the joint, carefully cut off the rind, leaving an even layer of fat on the meat. The rind will come away easily while the joint is hot; when cold it will be much more difficult to remove it to leave a smooth coating of fat.

Drain the cooked beans and toss them with the butter, parsley and a good sprinkling of freshly ground black pepper. Stand the joint of bacon on a serving dish and surround it with the beans.

COOK'S NOTES

In Mrs Beeton's day, curing methods meant that a joint had to be soaked for several hours before cooking and ham was traditionally blanched or par-boiled before baking. If you soak meat cured by modern methods, however, you will deprive it entirely of flavour, so soaking is seldom necessary. Always check with the butcher if you are in any doubt about the saltiness of the meat.

COOKING TIMES

As a general rule, allow 20 minutes per 450 g (1 lb) plus an additional 20 minutes. Bacon should be boiled. When tender, the rind can be removed and the joint browned in the oven. Hams can be par-boiled, then baked or baked from raw. To finish a cooked joint in the oven, set the temperature at 200°C (400°F/gas 6). Remove the rind from the joint and cook it for about 20–30 minutes. The fat may be glazed with honey or coated with soft brown sugar before baking.

To bake a ham from raw or after it has been par-boiled, set the oven at 180°C (350°F/gas 4) and cover the joint with foil. About 30 minutes before the end of the cooking time, remove the foil and cut off the rind.

The fat may be scored with diamond cuts and studded with whole cloves before the joint is glazed and baked.

STUFFED LEG OF PORK
with APPLE SAUCE

SERVES 6

4 large onions

175 g (6 oz) fresh white breadcrumbs

45 ml (3 tbsp) chopped fresh sage or

15 ml (1 tbsp) dried sage

salt and pepper

40 g (1½ oz) butter, melted

1 egg

1.5 kg (3¼ lb) boned joint from leg of

pork, scored

30 ml (2 tbsp) oil

40 g (1½ oz) plain flour

900 ml (1½ pints) vegetable cooking

water

APPLE SAUCE

3 large cooking apples

25 g (1 oz) butter

50–75 g (2–3 oz) sugar

Place the onions in a saucepan, cover them with water and bring it to the boil. Cook the onions for 5 minutes, then drain them. As soon as they are cool enough to handle, chop the onions and mix them with the breadcrumbs. Add the sage, plenty of seasoning, the butter and the egg to bind the stuffing.

Set the oven at 180°C (350°F/gas 4). Make sure the pork rind is well scored. Fill the cavity left by the bone with some of the stuffing, then tie the joint into a neat shape. Place the remaining stuffing in a buttered, ovenproof dish and set it aside.

Place the joint in a roasting tin and rub plenty of salt into the rind. Trickle the oil over. Roast the pork for about 2 hours, basting it occasionally, until it is cooked through. Place the dish of stuffing in the oven halfway through cooking and trickle a little of the fat from the roasting tin over the top of the stuffing.

Make the sauce when you first put the joint in the oven so that it has time to cool down before being served. Peel, core and slice the apples, placing them in a bowl of cold water to prevent them from turning brown. Drain the apples and cook them with a sprinkling of water (just enough to prevent them from burning) until they are soft and pulpy. Beat them well until smooth, then stir in the butter and sugar to taste. Transfer the sauce to a serving dish.

Lift the roast pork on to a serving platter, cover it and keep it warm. Pour off the excess fat from the roasting tin, then stir in the flour and cook it over medium heat until it is has browned slightly. Gradually stir in the vegetable cooking water and bring the gravy to the boil, stirring continuously. Lower the heat and simmer the gravy for 2–3 minutes, stirring occasionally to incorporate the cooking residue off the roasting tin. Strain the gravy, if necessary, before serving it with the pork, stuffing and apple sauce.

COOK'S NOTES

Mrs Beeton waxed lyrical on the subject of pork, stating that 'there is no domestic animal so profitable or so useful to man as the much-maligned pig, or any that yields him a more varied or more luxurious repast'.

When buying pork for roasting, make sure that the butcher scores the pork rind well. If you are buying it in a supermarket, check that the joint is well scored. If necessary, use a sharp knife to score the rind at home. Singe the rind by running a lighted match over it to burn off any hairs. Light the match and allow the smoke to burn away for a second or two before singeing the pork.

SERVING PORK CRACKLING
The crackling can be sliced off the pork before it is carved and cut into small portions which can be served alongside the neatly sliced stuffed meat. Stuffed pork is usually served thickly sliced. If the rind has been so well scored that the crackling can be easily cut, then carve it neatly with the meat. Areas of rind which have not become bubbly and crisp should be removed and discarded before the meat is carved.

SAUSAGEMEAT CAKES

MAKES 8

450 g (1 lb) boneless belly of pork,
  skinned

350 g (12 oz) rindless bacon (offcuts
  will do very nicely)

15 g (½ oz) salt

freshly ground black pepper

1.25 ml (¼ tsp) grated nutmeg

15 ml (1 tbsp) chopped parsley

50 g (2 oz) fresh breadcrumbs

flour for shaping

dripping or oil for frying

Finely chop the pork and bacon: a food processor is ideal for this, otherwise use a large, very sharp knife or cleaver. Add the salt, plenty of pepper, nutmeg, parsley and breadcrumbs. Pound the mixture until the ingredients bind together.

Wet your hands and shape the mixture into eight neat round cakes. Knead each cake so that the mixture binds firmly, then dust them with flour.

Heat just enough dripping or oil in a frying pan to prevent the cakes from sticking. Cook them fairly slowly so that they are thoroughly cooked through by the time they are well browned on both sides. This should take about 30 minutes. Serve the cakes freshly cooked.

COOK'S NOTES

The original recipe for these sausagemeat cakes did not have any breadcrumbs but they do help to give the mixture a workable consistency which could only otherwise be achieved by pounding the mixture for some time in a large mortar. Mrs Beeton would have used pork and bacon with a far higher proportion of fat, which would have given the mixture a softer consistency and enable it to bind together more easily than lean meat. In fact, Mrs Beeton commented on the simplicity and ease with which this version of sausagemeat could be formed into small cakes or patties.

Well-flavoured organic pork with a slightly more traditional proportion of fat is available from some independent butchers or from one of the reputable mail-order meat suppliers who specialise in traditionally reared and prepared meats and meat products.

OXFORD SAUSAGES

MAKES 36

450 g (1 lb) boneless belly of pork,
   minced

450 g (1 lb) minced veal

225 g (8 oz) shredded suet

450 g (1 lb) fresh white breadcrumbs

5 ml (1 tsp) freshly ground black
   pepper

5 ml (1 tsp) salt

grated rind of ½ lemon

2.5 ml (½ tsp) grated nutmeg

6 fresh sage leaves, chopped

2.5 ml (½ tsp) chopped fresh savory

2.5 ml (½ tsp) dried marjoram

sausage skins (optional) for filling

Mix all the ingredients until they are thoroughly combined. Fill sausage skins, following the instructions below, or shape the mixture into small cakes. To prevent the mixture from sticking while you are shaping the cakes, run your hands under cold running water occasionally. Cakes should be floured before being fried.

When cooking home-made sausages, do not prick the skins. Fry or grill them, using moderate heat so that the skins do not burst. Alternatively, set the oven at 200°C (400°F/gas 6) and lightly grease a roasting tin with oil. Place the sausages in the tin and bake them for about 30 minutes, turning once, until they are browned and crisp. Drain the sausages on absorbent kitchen paper before serving them.

COOK'S NOTES

Mrs Beeton's recipe for Oxford sausagemeat is typical of that used to make good-quality British sausages, with well-seasoned, coarsely minced meat flavoured with herbs. Slim, fine-textured pork chipolatas are traditionally delicately flavoured while the meaty, chunky breakfast sausages that originated in Aberdeen have a more robust flavour.

FILLING SAUSAGE SKINS
Don't let the idea of handling sausage skins deter you from making this wonderful recipe. Once you are accustomed to the soft texture of natural skins you will find them no more off-putting than raw poultry or seafood.

Cut the sausage skin into manageable lengths – each no longer than 0.9 m (1 yd) – and soak these in cold water for at least 30 minutes, preferably overnight. Drain, rinse and drain again, repeating this process until all the salt has been removed. Put the skins in a bowl; cover with fresh water.

Fit a large piping bag with a large 2.5 cm (1 inch) nozzle. Put some of the sausagemeat into the bag and press it down to fill the nozzle. Carefully open the end of one of the sausage skins. With the filled bag resting on the work surface, carefully push the sausage skin as far up the nozzle and the outside of the piping bag as possible. When most of the skin is on the nozzle, start squeezing out the mixture.

When a little of the skin has been filled, tie a neat knot in the end. Continue to fill the sausage skin, keeping up a low steady pressure on the piping bag, at the same time allowing the skin to flow off the end of the nozzle, so that the skin fills evenly without bursting. Tie a knot in the end of the skin.

The length of sausage may either be twisted at regular lengths to make conventional sausages, or looped round, pinwheel fashion, to make a single large sausage.

DORMERS

MAKES 6

225 g (8 oz) cold roast lamb

75 g (3 oz) cooked long-grain rice

50 g (2 oz) fresh white breadcrumbs

salt and pepper

30 ml (2 tbsp) chopped fresh mint

about 60 ml (4 tbsp) gravy, stock
  or milk

1 egg, beaten

50 g (2 oz) dried white breadcrumbs

oil for shallow frying

Finely chop the lamb, using a food processor if possible. Add the rice and fresh breadcrumbs with plenty of salt and pepper, then stir in the mint, with just enough gravy, stock or milk to bind the mixture.

Shape the mixture into six sausages or patties. Beat the egg with 15 ml (1 tbsp) water. Coat the dormers in egg and then in the dried breadcrumbs. Chill the dormers for about 1 hour to allow the mixture and coating to become firm.

Heat the oil in a large shallow frying pan. Fry the dormers for 10-15 minutes, until golden brown on both sides. Drain on absorbent kitchen paper and serve the dormers piping hot.

COOK'S NOTES

Many old favourite recipes for leftovers from a roast joint, like rissoles and these cakes of cooked meat and rice, involved messy preparation using a mincer or strenuous chopping and pounding. Today's food processors make light work of these tasks.

The original recipe for dormers (which were shaped into sausages) included suet, an ingredient which was often added to enrich fairly dry or plain mixtures. Finely chopped or grated onion and 5 ml (1 tsp) ground mace can be added to the dormers; and chopped fresh thyme can be used instead of the mint.

SPRING CELEBRATIONS: ROAST LAMB AND OAK APPLE DAY   .

Traditionally, lamb is enjoyed during spring, and Mrs Beeton particularly recommended lamb from animals reared on the South Downs: 'Among epicures, the most delicious sorts of lamb are those of the South-Down breed, known by their black feet; and of these, those which have been exclusively suckled on the milk of the parent ewe, are considered the finest'.

While spring lamb provided a festive meal for city dwellers, country activities were focused on May Day long before bank holidays were invented. May 29th was known as Oak Apple Day. The oak trees were beaten and shaken so that oak apples fell to the ground. Garlands of oak and hawthorn were hung on buildings and oak apples were gilded to decorate the displays which were also adorned with flowers and ribbons. Oak apple day is still celebrated in some villages, particularly in the West Country.

RISSOLES

225–350 g (8–12 oz) cooked meat or
    poultry, minced or finely chopped

225 g (8 oz) fresh white breadcrumbs

grated rind of ½ lemon

30 ml (2 tbsp) chopped parsley

5 ml (1 tsp) chopped fresh sage

5 ml (1 tsp) chopped fresh thyme,
    marjoram or savory

salt and pepper

25 g (1 oz) butter

1 onion, finely chopped

1 egg, beaten

60 ml (4 tbsp) milk

plain flour for shaping

oil or dripping for frying

fried parsley to garnish (optional)

Mix the meat with the breadcrumbs, lemon, herbs and seasoning to taste. Melt the butter in a small pan and cook the onion until softened but not browned, then add it to the rissole mixture. Mix in the beaten egg, adding a little extra milk to bind the ingredients to a fairly soft, but not sticky, mixture.

Shape the mixture into eight round balls, cones or cakes on a lightly floured surface. Heat a little oil or dripping and fry the rissoles until they are well browned on both sides. Garnish with fried parsley and serve the rissoles piping hot.

Instead of adding a garnish of fried parsley, the rissoles could be served with thoroughly reheated leftover gravy or fresh gravy made with dripping from a roast joint or bird and stock boiled from bones or a carcass.

COOK'S NOTES

Onions did not feature in the original recipe but they are now so widely appreciated as a basic flavouring that without them the rissoles would seem bland. Mashed potatoes have superseded breadcrumbs as the popular base, making a lighter mixture and stretching a small amount of meat even further.

RISSOLES WITH POTATOES

Substitute 450 g (1 lb) mashed potatoes for the breadcrumbs. There is no need to add egg and milk to the mixture. Chill the shaped rissoles for at least 30 minutes, until firm, then coat them in egg and about 75 g (3 oz) dry white breadcrumbs. Fry the rissoles until golden.

CALF'S LIVER AND BACON

SERVES 4

450 g (1 lb) calf's liver

plain flour for dusting and thickening
the sauce

salt and pepper

50 g (2 oz) butter

8 rindless bacon rashers

30 ml (2 tbsp) lemon juice

150 ml (¼ pint) water

lemon slices to garnish

FORCEMEAT BALLS

50 g (2 oz) gammon or rindless
bacon, finely chopped

50 g (2 oz) shredded suet

grated rind of ½ lemon

5 ml (1 tsp) finely chopped parsley

5 ml (1 tsp) finely chopped fresh
mixed herbs

cayenne pepper

pinch of ground mace

175 g (6 oz) fresh white breadcrumbs

1 egg, lightly beaten

Remove any skin and tubes from the liver, then cut it into thin slices and dust these with flour, seasoning them well.

Mix all the ingredients for the forcemeat and shape the mixture into eight balls. Melt half the butter in a large frying pan; cook the forcemeat balls over medium heat, rolling them in the pan to brown them evenly and cook them through. Use a slotted spoon to transfer the balls to a bowl lined with absorbent kitchen paper and keep them warm. Set a serving platter to warm.

Fry the bacon in the fat remaining in the pan, then drain it well and transfer it to the serving platter. Melt the remaining butter in the pan and fry the liver, browning the slices quickly on both sides. Do not use fierce heat nor overcook the liver or it will become tough – about 4 minutes is long enough. Arrange the liver with the bacon on the serving platter.

Sprinkle 5 ml (1 tsp) flour into the fat remaining in the pan and stir it in. Pour in the lemon juice and water. Bring the pan juices to the boil, stirring, and boil them rapidly for 1 minute to deglaze the pan. Taste the sauce for seasoning before serving it to one side of the liver and bacon.

Arrange the forcemeat balls on the platter with the liver and bacon. Garnish the dish with lemon slices and serve it at once.

COOK'S NOTES

Lamb's liver can be cooked in the same way as the calf's liver but the heat should be slightly lower and it should be cooked for a few minutes longer. Whereas it is traditional to serve calf's liver slightly pink in the middle, lamb's liver should be cooked through. Again, it should not be fried too fiercely nor for so long that it becomes tough.

LIVER AND BACON HOTPOT

SERVES 4

5 large potatoes

salt and pepper

225 g (8 oz) lamb's or pig's liver, trimmed

225 g (8 oz) rindless bacon rashers

large bunch of parsley

2 large fresh sage leaves

2 onions, finely chopped

large knob of butter

Set the oven at 180°C (350°F/gas 4). Cook the potatoes in boiling salted water for 10 minutes, then drain and slice them.

Meanwhile, slice the liver into small pieces and cut the bacon rashers in half. Finely chop the parsley and sage. Layer the potatoes, liver, bacon, herbs and onions in a deep ovenproof dish, seasoning the layers well and ending with an even layer of sliced potatoes.

Sprinkle 60 ml (4 tbsp) water over the hotpot, then dot the top with butter. Cover the dish and bake the hotpot for 1 hour.

Remove the lid and add a little extra butter if the tops of the potatoes look rather dry, then return the hotpot to the oven and cook for a further 30 minutes, until the potatoes are browned on top.

COOK'S NOTES

Even if you have never particularly liked liver, do try this tempting hotpot. The small pieces of liver are well balanced by the other ingredients and the result is delicious.

In Mrs Beeton's day, this dish — and others like it — would have been allowed to cook gently in the simmering oven of the coal-fired kitchen range for several hours, then transferred to the main oven to finish cooking if necessary. It was also a popular dish for placing in the bottom of the oven on baking days as it would not easily spoil or overcook as the oven temperature was adjusted to accommodate different cakes and pastries. At the end of the baking session, the hotpot would simply be left to simmer in the residual heat of the oven until required for supper.

ALTERNATIVE INGREDIENTS
Layered hotpots based on potatoes and onions make welcome supper dishes on cold winter days. In the simplest form, layered potatoes and onions, well seasoned, moistened with a little milk and topped with cheese make a tasty dish. Shredded cabbage and peeled and thinly sliced apple are delicious additions, especially when bacon is included in the layers.

SPEEDY SOLUTIONS
With the right choice of cooking container, layered vegetable and bacon dishes can be ready in half the time they would traditionally take if they are partially cooked in the microwave before being transferred to the oven to finish cooking at a slightly higher temperature. This method doesn't work well for liver however, which would toughen and cook unevenly.

VEGETABLES

ARTICHOKE FRITTERS

SERVES   4

4 cooked globe artichoke bottoms

100 g (4 oz) plain flour, plus extra for
    dusting

salt and pepper

1 egg yolk

150 ml (¼ pint) milk

oil for deep frying

8 parsley sprigs

1 lemon, cut into wedges

75 g (3 oz) hot melted butter to
    serve (optional)

Cut each artichoke bottom into quarters and coat the pieces with flour and a little salt and pepper.

Sift the measured flour into a bowl and add a little seasoning. Make a well in the middle, then add the egg yolk and a little of the milk. Stir the yolk and milk together, then gradually beat in the remaining milk, working in the flour to make a fairly thick coating batter. Beat the batter hard until it is smooth and light.

Heat the oil for deep frying to 190°C (375°F). Dip the artichoke pieces in the batter to coat them completely, then drop them into the hot oil and fry them until the batter is crisp and golden.

Drain the artichoke fritters on absorbent kitchen paper and arrange them on serving plates. Fry the parsley sprigs for a few seconds, drain them on absorbent kitchen paper and arrange them beside the fritters with the lemon wedges. If serving the butter, pour it into four dishes or saucers and offer it with the fritters.

COOK'S NOTES

COOKING GLOBE ARTICHOKES

Thoroughly wash the artichokes, swishing them about in a bowl of cold water before rinsing them well. Trim off each stalk to about 2.5 cm (1 inch) below the head and slice off the top of the bud. Sprinkle the cut artichokes with a little lemon juice to prevent them from discolouring. Remove any loose and wide-set lower leaves, then trim the points off the remaining leaves with scissors.

Cook the artichokes in boiling salted water for about 30 minutes – small vegetables will be ready sooner but large ones can take up to 45 minutes. To test, try pulling off one of the lower leaves; it should come off easily if the artichoke is cooked. Drain the artichokes well.

REMOVING THE CHOKE

Separate the leaves and pull out the ones from the centre to reveal the cone of soft leaves covering the choke. Pull this group of leaves out and it should bring with it the hairy choke which it covers. The choke is a cushion of fine hairs covering the bottom of the vegetable. Use a teaspoon to gently scoop out every remaining hair. If the choke did not come away cleanly with the leaves, it should be possible to scrape it out in one or two neat portions.

ARTICHOKE BOTTOMS

After the choke has been removed you will see the small cupped bottom, which is the prize portion of the vegetable, sometimes referred to as the 'fond'. The remaining stalk should be trimmed so that the artichoke sits neatly on a plate. The larger leaves each have a small edible nugget at the base, and this is usually dipped in melted butter or sauce, then eaten before the rest of the leaf is discarded. If the bottoms alone are required, all the leaves can be removed and thrown away.

Canned artichoke bottoms are a useful storecupboard ingredient for dinner party first courses – they can be topped with pâté, or served with smoked salmon rolls or a complementary salad.

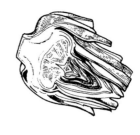
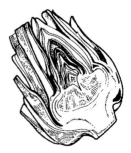

JERUSALEM ARTICHOKES WITH BRUSSELS SPROUTS

SERVES 4

675 g (1½ lb) Jerusalem artichokes

juice of ½ lemon

salt

450 g (1 lb) Brussels sprouts, trimmed

300 ml (½ pint) hot Béchamel sauce*

Wash and thinly peel the artichokes. As soon as they are prepared, place them in cold water acidulated with lemon juice to prevent them from discolouring. Cook the artichokes in steadily simmering water for 10–15 minutes until tender.

Meanwhile, cook the Brussels sprouts in boiling salted water for 5–7 minutes, until tender but not soft. Drain both types of vegetable separately.

Turn the artichokes into the middle of a serving dish. Coat them with Béchamel sauce, then arrange the sprouts around them and serve immediately.

COOK'S NOTES

Jerusalem artichokes and Brussels sprouts are combined most successfully in this dish, with their contrasting flavours married by the Béchamel sauce. Serve the artichokes and sprouts as a side dish for grilled meats or poultry. Alternatively, before arranging the sprouts around the artichokes, add a topping of grated cheese mixed with a handful of fresh white breadcrumbs. Brown this topping under a hot grill. Add the sprouts and serve as supper dish or vegetarian treat..

Jerusalem artichokes have a reputation for being horribly fiddly to clean but modern cultivars are less knobbly and therefore trap less soil, so they are not too difficult to scrub or peel.

The tubers discolour quickly once peeled, so it is important to drop them straight into cold water, preferably with a good squeeze of lemon juice added or, failing that, with a shake of salt swirled in.

COOKING REMINDERS

Jerusalem artichokes can be cooked in their skins. Select tubers which have fairly thin, unblemished skin and scrub them thoroughly. When cooking the tubers, do not boil the water too rapidly or they will break up. Par-boiling followed by baking is a good method as the artichokes are less likely to break up or 'fall'. They can be coated in sauce or buttered and sprinkled with breadcrumbs and/or cheese before baking.

Microwave cooking is also a good method for small quantities of tubers. Drain them but leave them quite wet and place them in a roasting bag or covered dish with a knob of butter. Follow times suggested by the microwave manufacturer for new potatoes and rearrange the vegetables halfway through cooking.

WAYS TO USE JERUSALEM ARTICHOKES

- Serve plain boiled and buttered.
- Make into a delicate soup (page 19).
- Coat with Béchamel or cheese sauce.
- Boil, mash and sieve, then enrich the purée with a little cream or soft cheese.
- Par-boil, slice and sauté in butter, then serve sprinkled with snipped chives.

ASPARAGUS PUDDING

SERVES   4

225 g (8 oz) asparagus

45 ml (3 tbsp) plain flour

salt and pepper

4 eggs

50 g (2 oz) cooked ham, minced or
   finely chopped

50 g (2 oz) hot melted butter, plus
   extra for greasing the dish

300 ml (½ pint) milk

Grease a 900 ml (1½ pint) soufflé dish or similar container suitable for steaming the pudding. Prepare a large saucepan of boiling water topped with a steamer. Cut a piece of double-thick greaseproof paper and another of foil, each large enough to cover the pudding.

Trim the asparagus, boil the spears until just tender, then drain and slice them. Mix the flour with seasoning, then add the eggs, ham, half the melted butter and a little of the milk. Gradually beat the ingredients together until smooth, then beat in the remaining milk to make a smooth batter.

Stir the asparagus into the batter, then turn it into the dish. Cover the dish with the paper and foil, tying the cover securely around the rim to prevent steam from entering. Steam the pudding for 1½ hours, or until set. The time may vary according to the shape of the container.

Turn out the pudding on to a warmed serving dish and pour the remaining melted butter around it. Serve the pudding at once.

COOK'S NOTES

Mrs Beeton suggested that this asparagus pudding should be served as a side dish with the second course; in fact, it makes a very good light lunch or supper. Individual puddings (cooked in small basins or individual soufflé dishes) make an appetizing starter. Crisply grilled bacon rolls and thin brown bread and butter would complement the pudding.

STEWED RED CABBAGE

SERVES 6

15 g (½ oz) butter

50 g (2 oz) lean gammon, finely diced

I small red cabbage, shredded

300 ml (½ pint) chicken stock* or
   vegetable stock*

50 ml (2 fl oz) vinegar

salt and pepper

15 ml (I tbsp) sugar

Melt the butter in a flameproof casserole or heavy-bottomed saucepan and fry the gammon until lightly cooked. Stir in the cabbage, stock, vinegar and seasoning. Bring the mixture to the boil, then cover the pan closely and cook the cabbage very gently for 1 hour.

Remove the lid from the pan and stir in the sugar. Increase the heat to high and cook the cabbage for 3–5 minutes, stirring often, until some of the excess liquid has evaporated, leaving the cabbage juicy.

COOK'S NOTES

Malt vinegar was most probably the usual type used in Mrs Beeton's day. While malt vinegar is quite acceptable in this recipe for red cabbage, a rich wine vinegar (such as dark balsamic vinegar) will give a deeper flavour. Cider vinegar gives a milder flavour.

This is another recipe to which you may like to add an onion. Cut it in half and slice it thinly before cooking it with the gammon.

SERVING WITH SAUSAGES

Mrs Beeton suggested sending fried sausages to table with the cabbage, laying them around the cabbage as a garnish. Today, most large supermarkets offer an interesting selection of continental sausages, many of which are delicious with braised red cabbage. Try, for example, crisp grilled *bratwurst*, garlic-laden Toulouse-style sausages or meaty *wiejska*, a large Polish boiling sausage which can be sliced and simmered with the cabbage or simmered separately, then grilled and sliced.

Smoked pork sausage, with or without garlic, is an economical choice. Ready cooked, it only needs to be reheated in boiling water or under the grill before being sliced and tossed with the cabbage. Smoked pork sausage can also be heated in the microwave.

STEWED CUCUMBERS
WITH ONIONS

SERVES 4

2 cucumbers

25 g (1 oz) butter

1 large onion, thinly sliced

150 ml (¼ pint) chicken stock* or

    vegetable stock*

salt

cayenne pepper

grated nutmeg

1 egg yolk

Peel the cucumbers and halve them lengthways. Scoop out the seeds from the middle of the cucumbers and cut them into 5 mm (¼ inch) thick slices.

Melt the butter in a saucepan and fry the onion for 5 minutes. Add the cucumbers and cook them, stirring, for 2 minutes, then pour in the stock and add salt, a pinch of cayenne and a little nutmeg. Bring to the boil, reduce the heat and cover the pan. Simmer the cucumbers steadily for 15 minutes.

Beat the egg yolk with a little of the cooking juice from the pan. Taste the cucumbers for seasoning, then turn the heat off or down to the lowest setting. Stir the beaten egg into the cucumber and cook the vegetables for a few seconds, but do not allow the sauce to boil or it will curdle. Serve at once.

COOK'S NOTES

Mrs Beeton frequently suggested serving stewed cucumbers with lamb or mutton chops, rump steak or other meats. They go well with grilled meats, including gammon, pork and lamb or with fish dishes.

To thicken the sauce slightly, mix 5 ml (1 tsp) cornflour to a smooth paste with a little cold water. Stir in one or two spoonfuls of the cooking liquid from the cucumber, then pour the cornflour mixture into the pan, stirring continuously. Bring the sauce to the boil, then remove the pan from the heat and add the egg yolk as in the main recipe. A little single cream can be added with the eggs to enrich the sauce.

DRESSED CUCUMBER

SERVES 4

1 cucumber, peeled

salt and pepper

45 ml (3 tbsp) salad oil

60 ml (4 tbsp) vinegar

Slice the cucumber very thinly and place it in a dish. Season the cucumber and sprinkle the oil and vinegar over the slices. Turn the slices in the dressing, then serve the salad immediately.

This is a favourite accompaniment for boiled salmon and an excellent addition to all sorts of salads. The cucumber can also be used as a garnish, for example with lobster salad.

COOK'S NOTES

The classic cucumber salad is often overlooked today, when the choice of salad ingredients is so wide. However, it makes a refreshing accompaniment for many classic dishes and its distinctive flavour is delicious with a variety of plain cooked foods, such as salmon (hot or cold), grilled poultry and rich meats like grilled lamb or pork. Peel the cucumber for a good salad and take care to slice it thinly and evenly. Add the seasoning and dressing just before serving the salad.

Snipped chives and chopped dill, fennel, tarragon or parsley can be sprinkled over the salad.

FRIED CUCUMBER
This was another of Mrs Beeton's simple dishes. Peeled and evenly sliced cucumber was mopped dry, then dusted with flour and fried in hot oil or butter. The slices were turned and stirred as they were cooked briskly until browned. Fried cucumber was traditionally served with rump steak.

BEETROOT WITH
ROAST ONIONS

450 g (1 lb) pickling onions or button
onions
salt and pepper
50 g (2 oz) butter
675 g (1½ lb) small beetroot

Set the oven at 200°C (400°F/gas 6). Peel the onions, cook them in boiling salted water for 5 minutes, then drain them and place them in a small roasting tin or dish. Season the onions well and dot them with half the butter, then roast them for about 45 minutes, stirring occasionally, until evenly browned.

Meanwhile, cook the beetroot in boiling water for about 1 hour, or until tender. Drain away the water and pour cold water over the beetroot in the saucepan. Slip the peel off the beetroot under the cold water, then place the peeled vegetables in a serving dish. Melt the remaining butter and pour it over the beetroot. Surround with the roasted onions, pouring their buttery juices over the beetroot. Serve the vegetables immediately.

COOK'S NOTES

This is a delicious, unusual vegetable dish. It is the ideal accompaniment for grilled sausages, gammon or pork chops, or for boiled or baked ham. In a strange way, the onions act as a type of seasoning for the beetroot. It is important to season the onions well with salt and pepper so that they bring out the flavour of the beetroot.

It is not worth buying out-of-season beetroot. The beets may look small but they can be extremely tough and some remain hard even after they have been boiled for 2 hours or more. By this time they are, of course, completely devoid of flavour. When fresh raw beetroot is not available, try the long-life, vacuum-packed beetroot which is not preserved with vinegar or acetic acid.

GLAZING THE ONIONS ON THE HOB
Roasting onions to serve with beetroot is a good idea when the oven is already in use but it is otherwise a rather extravagant use of the cooker. As an alternative, blanch the onions for 2 minutes, then drain them and melt the butter in a saucepan. Add the onions and cook them in the butter, stirring often and keeping the pan half covered, for about 30 minutes, until they are evenly glazed and lightly browned.

BRAISED CELERY

SERVES 4

1 head of celery, trimmed

150 ml (¼ pint) white stock* or

chicken stock*

salt and pepper

25 g (1 oz) butter

15 ml (1 tbsp) plain flour

pinch of ground mace

grated nutmeg

30 ml (2 tbsp) double cream

Cut the celery into 10 cm (4 inch) lengths and place in a saucepan. Add the stock and seasoning. Heat the stock until it simmers, then cover the pan tightly and braise the celery for about 30 minutes, or until it is tender.

Cream the butter with the flour to a smooth paste. Use a slotted spoon to transfer the celery to a warmed serving dish. Whisk lumps of the butter and flour paste into the simmering stock and continue whisking until the sauce boils and thickens. Add the mace and just a little nutmeg, then stir in the cream and heat the sauce gently without allowing it to boil. Taste the sauce for seasoning before pouring it over the celery.

COOK'S NOTES

Mrs Beeton found celery to be an 'exceedingly useful vegetable for flavouring soups, sauces, etc.' and as an ingredient for a winter salad. She recommended that celery be kept, root downwards, in a twin-handled celery glass half filled with water.

FLAVOURING BRAISED CELERY

This is a very plain recipe. Braised celery is often flavoured by sautéing a finely chopped small onion and diced small carrot in a little butter before adding the celery and stock. A bay leaf and sprig of thyme can be added with the liquid. Some cooks prefer not to thicken the sauce, but a little thickening makes the sauce coat the celery and it tends to bring the flavours together well.

CELERY CURLS

1   Cut 10 cm (4 inch) lengths of celery from the tops of the stalks. Shred the lengths into narrow strips, leaving them attached by about 2.5 cm (1 inch).

2   Place the strips in iced water and leave them to stand for about an hour or until they have curled. Use the curls as a garnish for savoury dishes, salads or on a cheeseboard.

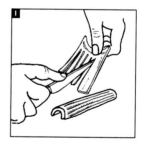
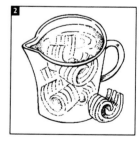

HARICOT BEANS WITH ONIONS

175 g (6 oz) haricot beans, soaked
   overnight in cold water to cover

40 g (1½ oz) butter

4 onions, finely chopped

salt and pepper

15 ml (1 tbsp) plain flour

150 ml (¼ pint) full-flavoured stock or
   good, thin gravy (see Cook's
   Notes)

Drain the beans. Boil them in plenty of fresh water for 10 minutes, then lower the heat, cover the pan and simmer the beans for about 40 minutes or until they are tender.

Melt the butter in a saucepan and cook the onions for 15–20 minutes, stirring them often, until they are thoroughly softened and browned in places. Season to taste, then stir in the flour and gradually pour in the stock or gravy. Bring the mixture to the boil, stirring, then reduce the heat, cover the pan and simmer the onion sauce for 2–3 minutes.

Drain the cooked beans and stir them into the sauce. Taste the mixture, adjust the seasoning if necessary and serve piping hot.

COOK'S NOTES

This was one recipe that was put to the bottom of the testing pile because it sounded rather dull – but what a surprise when it was cooked! Made with good stock or gravy (pork gravy, when tested) the result was extremely tasty and a bowlful of the beans made a satisfying supper, with some crusty bread to mop the small quantity of juices.

Mrs Beeton used 'good brown gravy' in this recipe, with a thickening of flour. The choice of stock depends on personal taste – both chicken and vegetable stock are suitable. Gravy left over from roast chicken or pork is excellent; however, if the gravy is well thickened, the flour should be reduced or omitted. For a vegetarian dish, use vegetable stock, but do check that it is well flavoure; if necessary, boil it down to concentrate the flavour before adding it to the dish.

BOILING DRIED BEANS
Soaking dried beans for several hours or overnight greatly reduces the cooking time. Do not add salt to the cooking water as this would prevent the beans from becoming tender, even with prolonged cooking. For the same reason, avoid using salted stock. Season dried beans only after they have been thoroughly cooked.

ALTERNATIVE BEANS
Soya beans are an excellent source of high-quality vegetarian protein, while chick peas or flageolet beans are also ideal for this type of dish, the latter going particularly well with grilled or roast lamb.

SERVING SUGGESTIONS
The beans make a moist, satisfying side dish for grilled meats, such as sausages, kebabs, chops and steaks. They are also good with roast lamb.

Serve the beans as a filling for baked potatoes or with pasta, topping them with crumbled, crisp grilled bacon and crumbled Stilton cheese.

CREAMED MUSHROOMS

75 g (3 oz) butter

10 ml (2 tsp) plain flour

450 g (1 lb) button mushrooms,
    trimmed of excess stalk, halved
    if large

dash of lemon juice

salt and pepper

150 ml (¼ pint) single cream

1.25 ml (¼ tsp) grated nutmeg

Cream about a third, or slightly less, of the butter with the flour to make a smooth paste. Set it aside. Melt the remaining butter in a saucepan and add the mushrooms, lemon juice and seasoning to taste. Turn the mushrooms in the butter, then cover the pan closely and cook them gently for 20 minutes.

Gradually stir pieces of the butter and flour paste into the mushrooms, allowing each portion to melt into the cooking liquid before adding the next. Bring the liquid to the boil, stirring until it thickens.

Stir in the cream and nutmeg. Heat the sauce gently, without allowing it to boil. Serve the mushrooms as soon as the sauce is hot.

COOK'S NOTES

This is a simple, classic method for cooking mushrooms, encouraging them to create their own rich sauce from the butter and the liquor they yield during the gentle, comparatively long, cooking.

SERVING SUGGESTIONS
For a first course or supper dish, spoon the creamed mushrooms over rounds of hot buttered toast or crisp fried bread croûtes and sprinkle them with snipped chives,

chopped parsley or crumbled grilled bacon. The mushrooms are extremely versatile as a side dish, complementing grilled fish, poultry or meat. They make a tempting filling for baked potatoes and a tasty topping for rice or pasta, when a sprinkling of freshly grated Parmesan cheese may be added.

The creamed mushrooms are also suitable for filling pastry cases, such as tartlets or vols-au-vent, and savoury pancakes. They make a very special filling for omelettes.

BAKED SPANISH ONIONS

SERVES **4**

4 Spanish onions or large mild onions

salt and pepper

butter to serve

Pull the roots off the onions and trim off the tops, with any loose outer layers of peel, to leave the onions covered with a neat and even layer of peel. Rinse them well, then cook them in boiling salted water for 30 minutes.

Set the oven at 190°C (375°F/gas 5). Drain the onions and mop them dry with absorbent kitchen paper. Place the onions on a baking sheet or in a shallow dish and bake them for about 1 hour, or until they are tender. Serve the onions in their skins, in the same way as baked potatoes. They should be cut open and sprinkled with salt and pepper to taste, then topped with knobs of cold butter. The buttery onion flesh is scooped out of the skin with a fork or spoon.

COOK'S NOTES

Before the dawning of the microwave era and fast food, baked potatoes were a wonderful winter suppertime treat, especially when they were cooked in the dying embers of a bonfire on November 5th or in the ashes under an open fire. Now, of course, baked potatoes have become standard fare and serve as practical bases for tasty and nutritious toppings and sauces of an international flavour. For a taste of nostalgia, try these baked onions as an alternative to plain old-fashioned baked potatoes.

Generous knobs of butter are an essential accompaniment, salt is a questionable seasoning but a little freshly ground black pepper goes very well. Fairly thinly sliced bread and butter tastes rather good with the baked onions.

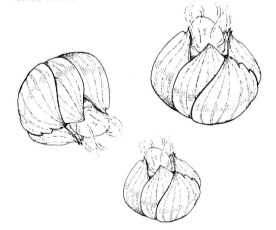

STEWED SPANISH ONIONS

SERVES 4

4 Spanish onions or large mild onions
salt and pepper
25 g (1 oz) butter
600 ml (1 pint) chicken stock* or
vegetable stock*

Peel the onions, taking care when trimming off the ends to avoid removing so much that the outer layers of onion are loosened. Place the onions in a pan or casserole in which they fit fairly snugly side by side. Add seasoning and the butter, then pour in the stock.

Bring the stock to the boil, reduce the heat immediately so that it simmers very gently and cover the pan tightly. Cook the onions gently for about 2 hours or until they are completely tender.

Transfer the onions to a warmed serving dish and boil the stock hard until it is reduced to a small quantity of rich liquor. Pour this over the onions and serve them at once.

COOK'S NOTES

Onions were not as popular in Mrs Beeton's recipes as they are in today's savoury dishes, where they feature as an essential flavouring ingredient. However, she commented that, 'Spanish onions, which are imported to this country during the winter months are, when properly roasted, perfectly sweet, and equal to many preserves'.

SERVING SUGGESTIONS
Stewed Spanish onions were presented as a favourite accompaniment to roast shoulder of mutton. Whole large onions are surprisingly filling, so give them due space on the menu rather than treating them as an interesting aside to other vegetables.

These taste good with positive flavours, like those of duck, venison, gammon (grilled or boiled) and lamb, and with foods that have a bit of bite to their texture, such as nutty grains like wild or brown rice and barley.

PEASE PUDDING

350 g (12 oz) yellow split peas,
soaked overnight in cold water

1 small onion, chopped

salt and pepper

25 g (1 oz) butter

1 large egg

Drain the peas and put them in a saucepan. Pour in cold water to cover, then add the onion. Bring the liquid to the boil, skim off any scum that forms on the surface, then reduce the heat and partially cover the pan. Cook the peas gently for about 1 hour or until tender but not mushy.

Drain the peas thoroughly. Press them through a sieve or purée them in a blender or food processor. Beat in the butter and egg.

Pile the mixture on to a floured dampened pudding cloth. Gather up the corners of the cloth and tie them together or bind them together with string. Suspend the pudding from a wooden spoon placed over a saucepan of boiling salted water. Top up the water if necessary so that the pudding is fully submerged. Simmer the pudding gently for 1 hour.

To serve the pudding, lift the spoon and drain the pudding well. Place the pudding on a plate or shallow dish. Untie the cloth and gently peel it away from the sides of the pudding – take care or the pudding may crumble. Use a large fish slice to transfer the pudding to a serving dish, or cut it into wedges and place these straight on to individual plates. Serve the pudding promptly.

COOK'S NOTES

Pease pudding was traditionally served with boiled leg of pork or boiled beef; it is also good with boiled ham or bacon, or with grilled gammon or bacon. It also goes well with crisp grilled sausages and onion gravy or with faggots and gravy.

Pease pudding tastes rather like dry, flavoursome mashed potato and is especially good when seasoned with freshly ground black pepper. Chopped herbs can be added, if you like: parsley, chives and thyme go well. You may well be tempted to serve the creamy, puréed peas as they are, instead of adding the egg and boiling the pudding. They are delicious instead of mashed potatoes.

STEAMING OR BAKING

Instead of using a pudding cloth, the mixture can be steamed in a greased basin or baked in a greased ovenproof dish. Cover the dish with foil and bake it for about 45 minutes at 180°C (350°F/gas 4).

POTATO RISSOLES

MAKES ABOUT 10

50 g (2 oz) butter

1 large onion, finely chopped

salt and pepper

450 g (1 lb) potatoes, boiled and
    mashed

10 ml (2 tsp) chopped parsley

a little plain flour for dusting

2 eggs, beaten

75 g (3 oz) dried white breadcrumbs

lard or oil for shallow frying

Melt the butter and cook the onion, stirring often, until soft but not browned. Season the mashed potato generously, then stir in the parsley and onion, with all the butter from the pan. Allow the mixture to cool completely.

Shape the cold potato mixture into small balls on a lightly floured surface. Coat them in beaten egg and breadcrumbs. Chill the rissoles for at least 15 minutes to set the coating and firm the mixture before cooking.

Melt the lard or heat the oil and fry the rissoles, turning them in the fat, for 6–9 minutes, until golden brown all over. Drain on absorbent kitchen paper and serve the rissoles freshly cooked.

VARIATION

A little finely chopped or minced cooked ham or tongue can be added to the rissoles if you like.

COOK'S NOTES

These simple rissoles are very tasty. In the original recipe, the onion was optional and you may still like to omit it if you are preparing the rissoles as a dinner party potato dish, for example as an accompaniment to a sophisticated main dish which is carefully flavoured and seasoned. Add the butter to the mashed potato, using slightly less than the quantity suggested for frying the onion.

BAKED RISSOLES

The rissoles can be baked quite successfully. Beat 15 ml (1 tbsp) oil with the egg used for coating as this helps to give the breadcrumbs a crisp finish. Place the rissoles on a greased baking sheet and cook for about 30 minutes at 200°C (400°F/gas 6) until the coating is lightly browned.

SEASONING POTATO RISSOLES

Fresh herbs, such as chives, tarragon and thyme, are excellent ingredients for varying the precise flavour of the rissoles; if you use chives you can leave out the onion.

For a less traditional, but equally delicious, flavour, try adding crushed garlic and chopped black olives.

POTATO SALAD

SERVES 6

10–12 potatoes

salt and pepper

60 ml (4 tbsp) tarragon vinegar, cider
  vinegar or wine vinegar

90 ml (6 tbsp) salad oil

15 ml (1 tbsp) finely chopped parsley

Boil the potatoes in their skins, in salted water, for about 20 minutes or until just tender. Then drain and peel them, removing the skin as thinly as possible. Cover the potatoes and set them aside to cool.

Whisk a little seasoning with the vinegar, then whisk in the oil and parsley. Cut the potatoes into slices, about 1 cm (½ inch) thick, and layer them in a serving bowl, sprinkling each layer with some of the dressing. Pour the remaining dressing over the top to ensure that all the potato slices are coated.

Cover the dish and set the salad aside for 2–3 hours so that the dressing flavours the potatoes well before the salad is served.

VARIATIONS

Chopped, drained canned anchovies, sliced black or green olives and sliced or chopped pickled gherkins can be added to the salad. For a luncheon salad, layer sliced cooked beef, chicken or turkey with the potatoes.

COOK'S NOTES

It is important to select a firm or waxy variety of potato to make a good salad. Check the information provided beside the potatoes in most supermarkets, looking for vegetables recommended for boiling rather than baking. Baking potatoes are unsuitable as their floury texture, while deliciously fluffy when a baked potato is cut open, makes them break up or fall easily during boiling.

King Edwards, Maris Piper and Romano are traditional varieties for general cooking, including boiling and baking.

The microwave is useful for cooking a small number of potatoes in their skins for a salad or similar recipe. Four to six potatoes cook well but cook double this number in two batches, otherwise they take far too long. Follow the manufacturer's instructions and timing, but check the potatoes before the time recommended for baked potatoes as they should not be as floury.

NEW POTATO SALAD

Jersey Royals are the early, full-flavoured traditional British treat. For a simple salad, choose young new potatoes or any of the varieties sold as salad potatoes. Scrub them and boil them in their skins, allowing 10–15 minutes for small potatoes. Drain the potatoes and let them cool. Small potatoes can be served whole; slightly larger ones should be halved or sliced before being mixed with salad dressing.

Mayonnaise, thinned with a little single cream (or plain yogurt if preferred), is the popular dressing for cold potatoes. Snipped fresh chives, chopped parsley, fresh dill or tarragon can be added. Alternatively, an oil and vinegar dressing can be poured over the hot potatoes and the vegetables allowed to stand, uncovered, until cold. Crumbled crisply grilled bacon is a good addition, with thinly sliced spring onions.

SPINACH WITH CREAM

SERVES 4

1 kg (2¼ lb) spinach

50 g (2 oz) butter

salt and pepper

pinch of sugar

grated nutmeg

90 ml (6 tbsp) single cream

sippets of toasted bread* or fleurons*

    to garnish

Trim the stalks off the spinach leaves and wash them well. Shake off excess water, then pack the wet leaves into a large saucepan and cover it tightly. Cook the spinach over a moderate to high heat, shaking the pan often at first and adjusting the heat to avoid burning the leaves. (The heat should be high to start, then reduced as the pan heats up and the spinach begins to cook.) After 3–5 minutes, the spinach will be greatly reduced and tender. Drain it well in a colander or sieve.

Squeeze excess water from handfuls of spinach and chop the bundles – the easiest way to do this is to cut them in half or quarters lengthways, then shred them while still holding the spinach firmly together.

Melt the butter and stir in the spinach. Add seasoning, the sugar and nutmeg. Stir over gentle heat for a minute or so, until the spinach is hot, then stir in the cream and heat it through without allowing it to boil. Serve at once, garnished with sippets of toasted bread or fleurons.

COOK'S NOTES

This classic recipe remains one of the finest ways of preparing spinach.

Spinach is a versatile vegetable, much appreciated now for its potential as the focus in meat-free dishes, for example in stuffings for pasta or pancakes or as a filling for pies and quiches. Widely used in Indian, Middle Eastern and Mediterranean dishes, spinach has an affinity for sweet spices, such as cumin and nutmeg. Small young leaves are also a popular salad ingredient, whether fresh or wilted by the addition of a hot dressing or hot ingredients.

Mrs Beeton described spinach as a Persian plant, probably because the Persians pioneered its cultivation for widespread culinary use some two centuries before its popularity spread through Europe to reach Britain.

Mrs Beeton accurately wrote of spinach as 'an excellent vegetable and very beneficial to health'. She suggested that, 'Plainly dressed, it is a resource for the poor; prepared luxuriantly, it is a choice dish for the rich'. In her day, spinach was not considered to be particularly nutritious, but was valued for its laxative properties.

VARIETIES

Mrs Beeton mentioned Good King Henry as a variety of spinach, but this pointed-leafed plant is not one which we now think of as spinach. It is an old-fashioned garden vegetable which is also known as Mercury or Lincolnshire asparagus. It is, however, used in much the same way as spinach.

As with most other young vegetables, the flavour of freshly harvested spinach straight from the vegetable patch is unbeatable. In the supermarket, spinach has usually been carefully selected and is easy to clean; the ready washed baby spinach which can be cooked in the pierced packet in the microwave is an excellent speedy convenience vegetable.

Swiss chard can be cooked and used in the same way as spinach.

EXCELLENT BAKED TOMATOES

SERVES 4

8–10 large, firm ripe tomatoes

salt and pepper

50 g (2 oz) fresh white breadcrumbs

50 g (2 oz) butter, melted (preferably clarified*)

Set the oven at 200°C (400°F/gas 6). Peel the tomatoes and cut out their stalks, then cut them into thick slices. Lay the tomato slices in an ovenproof dish, overlapping them neatly, and season them to taste.

Sprinkle the breadcrumbs over the tomatoes and trickle the butter evenly over the top. Bake the tomatoes for 20–30 minutes, until the breadcrumbs are lightly browned. Serve at once.

COOK'S NOTES

This simple dish is the ideal accompaniment for grilled fish or meat, or any fairly dry main dish.

TO PEEL TOMATOES

The tomatoes were not peeled in Mrs Beeton's original recipe, but they do taste far better without their peel.

1 Pour boiling water over the tomatoes and leave them to stand for 30–60 seconds. The riper the fruit, the quicker the skins loosen.

2 To remove the peel, make a small slit in the tomato and the peel will come away easily.

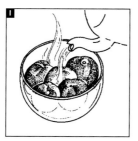 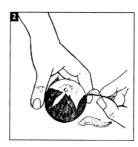

SEASONING, HERBS AND SPICES

Sun-ripened tomatoes have by far the best flavour and this recipe makes a tasty lunch or supper when you have a glut of home-grown produce. Acidic tomatoes or those with a rather insipid flavour benefit from being sprinkled with a pinch of caster sugar as well as salt and pepper.

Chopped parsley, chives, tarragon or marjoram can be sprinkled over the tomatoes before they are topped with breadcrumbs. Fresh basil is a favourite herb for enhancing tomatoes, but its flavour dwindles disappointingly during cooking; for best results use scissors to shred the leaves directly over the baked tomatoes immediately before they are served.

For a hint of exotic seasoning, dust some freshly ground coriander over the tomatoes with the salt and pepper or roast some cumin seeds in a small, heavy-bottomed pan until they are aromatic, then sprinkle them over the slices. Alternatively, take a tip from the Italians and mix Parmesan cheese with the breadcrumbs.

TURNIPS IN WHITE SAUCE

SERVES 4

8 small turnips

salt and pepper

50 g (2 oz) butter

I small onion, finely chopped

I small carrot or ½ medium carrot,
  finely diced

strip of pared lemon rind (optional)

45 ml (3 tbsp) plain flour

300 ml (½ pint) milk

pinch of ground mace

pinch of sugar

Cook the turnips in a saucepan of boiling salted water for about 20 minutes, until they are tender.

Meanwhile, melt half the butter in a small saucepan and cook the onion, carrot and lemon rind (if used) for about 10 minutes, or until the onion has softened but not browned. Stir in the flour, then gradually pour in the milk and bring the sauce to the boil, stirring continuously. Reduce the heat and simmer the sauce for about 3 minutes. Discard the lemon rind and season the sauce to taste, adding a pinch of ground mace and sugar. Beat in the remaining butter.

Drain the turnips and turn them into a serving dish. Coat the turnips with the sauce and serve them at once.

COOK'S NOTES

If you have dismissed turnips as only fit for soups and casseroles, try this recipe and discover how superb they are as a side dish for roast and grilled meats, and for splendid main dishes like beef Wellington.

PREPARATION NOTES

Mrs Beeton suggested turning the vegetables, paring them into small balls or oval shapes, but this elaborate and rather old-fashioned style of preparation is generally avoided today. Of course, if you want to prepare a grand dish, and can use all the discarded pieces of turnip in soup, then buy double the quantity and pare the turnips down into small pear shapes.

Alternatively, the turnips can be cut into neat cubes before being boiled. Small pieces of vegetable cook more quickly, so reduce the cooking time.

MUSTARD SAUCE OR GRATIN TOPPING

A little mustard can be added to the sauce, to emphasise the slightly hot edge to the turnip flavour.

If you are serving the dish for a dinner party and do not want to prepare the sauce at the last minute, the turnips can be cooked and coated in advance, then sprinkled with a few fresh white breadcrumbs mixed with a little grated Emmental or Gruyère cheese. Bake this gratin for about 20 minutes at 200°C (400°F/gas 6), or until the vegetables are hot and the topping is lightly browned.

BOILED SALAD

SERVES   6

salt and pepper ·

1 head of celery, sliced

1 small onion, chopped

½ small cauliflower, broken into

   small florets

225 g (8 oz) French beans, cut into

   2.5 cm (1 inch) lengths

250 ml (8 fl oz) mayonnaise

15 ml (1 tbsp) chopped tarragon,

   chervil, burnet or parsley

1 lettuce heart, shredded, or a little

   curly endive (optional)

Bring a large saucepan of lightly salted water to the boil. Add the celery and onion, bring the water back to the boil and cook the vegetables for 1 minute. Add the cauliflower and French beans, bring the water back to the boil and cook the vegetables for a further 2 minutes.

Drain the vegetables and set them aside to cool until they are just warm. Mix the mayonnaise and tarragon, chervil, burnet or parsley with the vegetables and season the warm salad to taste.

Arrange the lettuce or curly endive (if using) in a salad bowl. Pile the dressed vegetables into the bowl and serve at once.

COOK'S NOTES

This cooked vegetable salad is extremely tasty and makes an ideal buffet dish, particularly when served with cold meats, such as turkey and ham on occasions such as Boxing Day. It is also the ideal accompaniment for grills at barbecue parties. It can be served alongside the potato salad on page 128 – both are winning party dishes.

WINTER SALAD

SERVES 6

1 head of endive, washed and
   shredded
1 punnet of mustard and cress
2 celery sticks, cut into short
   fine shreds
4 hard-boiled eggs, sliced
225 g (8 oz) cooked beetroot, sliced

DRESSING
4 hard-boiled egg yolks
5 ml (1 tsp) prepared English mustard
salt and pepper
60 ml (4 tbsp) single cream
a little white wine vinegar (optional)

Mix the endive, mustard and cress and celery in a shallow bowl. Top with the eggs and beetroot, overlapping the slices or interleaving them with the endive but keeping them separate from each other.

To make the dressing, pound the egg yolks to a paste with the mustard and seasoning; gradually work in the cream. Make sure that each addition of cream is thoroughly incorporated before adding the next. Finally, stir in a little vinegar to taste, adding a few drops at a time. Trickle the creamy egg and mustard dressing over the salad and serve it at once.

COOK'S NOTES

This salad provides a good basic recipe which can be adapted to make a tempting starter or accompaniment for cold meats and cheese. Neatly arranged individual salads, with crusty bread or Granary bread, make an attractive first course. They can be topped with anchovy fillets, strips of Parma ham or crumbled crisp grilled bacon.

ALTERNATIVE DRESSINGS
Mrs Beeton's hard-boiled egg dressing, with cream and mustard, works very well and tastes good with cooked vegetables instead of the usual mayonnaise. However, you can use a modern dressing instead.

Both soured cream and mayonnaise thinned with a little single cream go well with this type of salad. An oil and vinegar dressing could also be served: use walnut or hazelnut oil in combination with olive oil or sunflower oil for a full flavour.

PASTRIES

LAMB PIE

675 g (1½ lb) boneless fillet from

    neck of lamb

2 lamb's kidneys

1 small onion, finely chopped

30 ml (2 tbsp) finely chopped parsley

salt and pepper

about 150–300 ml (¼–½ pint) stock,

    depending on shape of dish

225 g (8 oz) puff pastry★

beaten egg to glaze

Set the oven at 230°C (450°F/gas 8). Slice the lamb evenly into about 1 cm (½ inch) thick pieces. Cut the kidneys in half, then discard their white cores and dice both halves. Layer the lamb in a 1.1 litre (2 pint) pie dish, distributing the kidneys, onion and parsley between the layers. Season the filling as you build up the layers. Pour in enough stock to come just below the rim of the dish.

Roll out the pastry to the same shape as the dish, but about 2.5 cm (1 inch) larger all round. Cut a 1 cm (½ inch) strip from the edge of the pastry. Dampen the rim of the dish and press the pastry strip on to it. Dampen the pastry, then cover the pie with the pastry lid, pressing it around the rim to seal in the filling. Trim off the excess pastry, knock up and scallop the edges.

Make a small hole in the middle of the pie and decorate the top with pastry trimmings. Brush the pie with a little beaten egg and bake it for 15 minutes. Reduce the oven temperature to 180°C (350°F/gas 4) and continue baking the pie for about 1½ hours, or until the lamb is tender. Cover the pie loosely with foil after the first 20–30 minutes to prevent the crust from overbrowning. Pierce the pie with the point of a knife to check whether the meat is cooked and tender.

COOK'S NOTES

This pie has the most wonderful flavour. To make a substantial crust, you can use up to 450 g (1 lb) puff pastry (the actual amount will depend upon the width of the dish) as it will withstand the long cooking time and absorb the flavours of the filling. Be selective if you are buying puff pastry: reject the cheaper brands in favour of a superior-quality brand, preferably chilled (rather than frozen) and made with at least a proportion of butter.

Mrs Beeton suggested using suet pastry★ as an alternative to puff pastry for the crust on this pie. Make the pastry with 75 g (3 oz) shredded suet to 175 g (6 oz) self-raising flour and cook the pie in an oven preheated to the lower temperature of 180°C (350°F/gas 4).

COOKED LAMB AND POTATO PIE

Thinly slice leftover roast lamb and layer it in a pie dish with sliced cooked potato and a finely chopped or grated small onion. Sprinkle the layers with seasoning, a hint of ground mace and chopped herbs, such as parsley, thyme and/or marjoram. Moisten the meat layers with gravy – about 300 ml (½ pint) will be sufficient. Cover the pie with short crust or suet pastry and bake it at 200°C (400°F/gas 6) for 30 minutes, or until the pastry is golden and cooked. If puff pastry is used, cook the pie at the higher temperature of 220°C (425°F/gas 7) for the first 10 minutes, then reduce the temperature to 190°C (375°F/gas 5).

LITTLE RAISED PORK PIES

MAKES   6

450 g (1 lb) plain flour

100 g (4 oz) butter

100 g (4 oz) shredded suet

salt and white pepper

450 g (1 lb) lean boneless pork,
    finely chopped or minced

15 ml (1 tbsp) powdered (rubbed)
    sage

1 egg, beaten, to glaze

Place the flour in a saucepan. Cut the butter into small pieces and add them to the flour with the suet and a good sprinkling of salt. Heat the mixture gently, stirring it occasionally at first, then more often as the flour heats and the fats begin to melt. When the fats are melted, sprinkle in 60 ml (4 tbsp) boiling water and work the mixture together into a ball of pastry. Transfer the pastry to a bowl, cover it with cling film and place it over a saucepan of hot water to keep it warm and pliable.

Season the pork well and mix the sage into it. Divide the meat into six portions. Take a portion of meat and shape it into a neat ball, pressing it between the palms of your hands and kneading it together firmly. Repeat with the remaining portions of meat.

Keep your hands warm while handling the pastry. Cut the pastry into six neat portions. Take one portion and cut off about a quarter, reserving it for a lid. Mould the main piece into a ball. Flatten the ball on the palm of one hand, then gradually thin the middle and cup the edges. Place a ball of meat on the pastry, then smooth the dough around it, gradually flattening the base of the meat and pastry together. When the pastry is evenly thinned around the sides, gently flatten the meat down into it and pinch up the edge to make a neat rim. Place the pie on a lightly floured surface and turn it between your hands so that it becomes neat and round and stands flat and level. Flatten the reserved pastry into a lid and lay it over the meat, then gently pinch the edges together to seal the pie.

Place the pie on a greased baking sheet, neaten its shape, if necessary, and make a small hole in the top. Raise five more pies, then chill all the pies for at least 30 minutes, or until the pastry is firmly set. Set the oven at 220°C (425°F/gas 7).

Brush the pies with beaten egg and bake them for 10 minutes, then reduce the oven temperature to 180°C (350°F/gas 4). Bake the pies for a further 45 minutes, until they are cooked through and well browned. Slide a palette knife under the pies to loosen them, then leave them to cool on the baking sheet until they are firm, when they can be transferred to a wire rack.

COOK'S NOTES

Butchers in the Midlands and North are renowned for producing the most succulent, full-flavoured pork pies. A slice of pork pie was once the traditional treat for breakfast on Christmas morning.

VEAL AND HAM PIE

SERVES 6

30 ml (2 tbsp) chopped mixed fresh
herbs, such as thyme, sage and
parsley

1.25 ml (¼ tsp) grated nutmeg

2.5 ml (½ tsp) ground mace

grated rind of ½ lemon

675 g (1½ lb) diced veal for pies (pie
veal)

salt and pepper

225 g (8 oz) boiled ham, thinly sliced

225 g (8 oz) puff pastry★

1 egg, beaten, to glaze

300 ml (½ pint) good jellied stock or
aspic

Set the oven at 220°C (425°F/gas 7). Mix the herbs, nutmeg, mace and lemon rind. Place a layer of veal in the bottom of a deep pie dish and sprinkle it with seasoning and some of the herb mixture. Add a layer of ham. Continue layering the veal and ham, seasoning each layer and ending with ham on top. Pour about 300 ml (½ pint) water into the dish, or enough to come about halfway up the filling.

Roll out the pastry to the same shape as the dish, but about 2.5 cm (1 inch) larger all around, then cut off a 1 cm (½ inch) strip from the edge. Dampen the rim of the dish and press the strip of pastry on to it. Dampen the pastry edge, then cover the pie with the pastry lid. Trim off the excess pastry, knock up and flute the edges of the pie, then cut a small hole in the top. Roll out the pastry trimmings and use to decorate the top of the pie.

Glaze the pie with beaten egg and bake it for 10 minutes. Reduce the oven temperature to 180°C (350°F/gas 4) and bake the pie for 1½ hours more. Cover the top of the pie loosely with foil after the first hour, if necessary to prevent the pastry from overbrowning.

Heat the jellied stock and bring it to the boil. Taste it for seasoning. Use a small funnel to pour stock into the middle of the cooked pie, adding a little at a time and allowing it to run to the base of the filling before topping it up, until the pie is full to the crust. Leave the pie to cool completely, then chill it for several hours or overnight. Serve the pie cold.

COOK'S NOTES

Mrs Beeton's veal and ham pie is cooked in a deep pie dish and only has a crust on top so it has all the full flavour of raised pie, but is not too heavy. The herbs, spices, lemon rind and cooked ham give the veal an excellent flavour. If you do not eat veal, make the pie with pork instead.

A straight-sided ovenproof glass dish with a slight lip or a deep straight-sided rimmed dish is ideal for making this pie. A glass dish shows off the attractive layers of filling in the cold pie.

Alternatively, the pie can be made as a raised pie, using hot water crust pastry★, in a pie mould or loose-bottomed cake tin. Short crust pastry can also be used to line a plain cake tin or loaf tin. Line the base of the chosen tin with non-stick baking parchment so that the pie can be turned out easily when it is chilled.

PIES IN PARLIAMENT

John Bellamy, the first caterer at the House of Commons, was known for the high quality of his veal pies. He took up the role in 1776 and spent sixty years providing meals at the house. His pies were probably raised pies, whereas this recipe taken from Mrs Beeton's first edition was more suitable for the home cook as it was made in a pie dish, rather than in a raised crust.

MEAT OLIVE PIE

50 g (2 oz) lean gammon or rindless
    bacon, chopped or minced

100 g (4 oz) shredded suet

1 small onion or shallot, finely
    chopped

grated rind of ½ lemon

15 ml (1 tbsp) finely chopped parsley

15 ml (1 tbsp) finely chopped fresh
    sage or thyme

175 g (6 oz) fresh white breadcrumbs

2.5 ml (½ tsp) ground mace

salt

cayenne pepper

2 eggs, beaten

6 thin slices of cold roast veal, beef
    or pork

250 ml (8 fl oz) good stock

60 ml (4 tbsp) double cream

225 g (8 oz) puff pastry★

Mix the gammon or bacon, suet, onion or shallot, lemon rind, herbs, breadcrumbs and mace. Add salt to taste and a pinch of cayenne. Mix in most of the beaten egg to bind the forcemeat, reserving some for glazing the pie.

Set the oven at 200°C (400°F/gas 6). Divide the forcemeat into six equal portions. Shape one portion of forcemeat into an oval and place it on one end of a slice of meat. Roll up the meat around the forcemeat to make a neat olive, or roll. Place the filled meat in a pie dish and repeat with the remaining meat and forcemeat.

Stir the stock and cream together and pour the mixture over the meat, taking care not to overfill the dish. Roll out the pastry to the same shape as the dish, but about 2.5 cm (1 inch) larger all round. Cut a 1 cm (½ inch) strip from around the edge of the pastry. Dampen the rim of the dish and press the pastry on to it. Dampen the pastry, then lay the lid on the pie. Trim off the excess pastry, knock up, seal and flute the edges and use any pastry trimmings to roll out leaves or decorations for the top of the pie.

Make a small hole in the middle of the pie to allow steam to escape. Glaze the pastry with the reserved beaten egg and bake the pie for 30 minutes. Reduce the oven temperature to 180°C (350°F/gas 4) and continue to cook the pie for a further 20 minutes. Serve piping hot.

COOK'S NOTES

This recipe reveals Mrs Beeton's proficiency as a pastrycook and her knowledge of pie-making. The combination of meat, stuffing, stock and cream make a moist pie with a satisfying, well-flavoured, creamy filling. The great thing about this pie is that you can use bought roast meat if you do not have any leftovers from a joint. It would also work well with cooked ham, when chopped mushrooms might be a better addition to the forcemeat than gammon or bacon. Try it – the result is well worth the small effort involved.

STEAK AND KIDNEY PUDDING

100 g (4 oz) shredded beef suet

salt and pepper

275 g (10 oz) self-raising flour

175–200 ml (6–7 fl oz) milk

150 g (5 oz) lamb's kidneys

575 g (1¼ lb) lean rump steak, cut

    into 2.5 cm (1 inch) cubes

30–45 ml (2–3 tbsp) plain flour

    (optional)

Grease a 1.1 litre (2 pint) pudding basin and have a pudding cloth ready for tying around it. Bring a large saucepan of water to the boil, for cooking the pudding.

Stir the suet and 2.5 ml (½ tsp) salt into the flour. When the ingredients are well mixed, gradually stir in the milk. The mixture should bind together well without being sticky. Use three-quarters of the pastry to line the basin, easing it in and making sure that it overlaps the rim of the basin by about 1 cm (½ inch).

Cut the kidneys in half, then discard their white cores and dice the halves. Layer the steak and kidney in the pastry-lined basin, seasoning each layer well and sprinkling the plain flour over the layers if you want the cooking juices to be thickened. Pour in enough cold water to three-quarters fill the basin.

Roll out the remaining pastry to cover the pudding. Dampen the edge of the pastry lining and place the lid on top. Pinch the pastry edges together to seal them well, then dampen the top edge and fold the overhanging pastry neatly on to the top of the pudding, pressing it in place.

Rinse the pudding cloth in very hot water – as hot as your hands can stand – then wring it out tightly. Open the cloth out on a clean surface or board and dredge it well with flour. Place the pudding basin in the middle of the cloth and tie both sets of opposing corners together over the middle of the pudding. Tie a piece of string through the knots in the cloth if the ends are too short to allow you to lower the pudding into the saucepan. Lower the pudding into the pan and bring the water back to the boil.

Boil the pudding for 4 hours, keeping the water bubbling steadily, but not too rapidly. Top up the water with fresh boiling water from the kettle as necessary to keep the pudding covered.

Use a spoon handle to pull up the string or cloth ends and lift the pudding from the pan. Open the cloth and stand the pudding on a plate or shallow dish or surround it with a clean napkin. Cut a round of pastry from the middle of the pudding to prevent it from bursting and serve it at once, cutting portions out of the basin. If you prefer to turn the pudding out before serving it, loosen the pastry around the rim carefully with a heatproof plastic spatula, then invert the pudding on a shallow dish, leaving the pudding basin in place while you carry the dish to the table. Lift off the basin at the last minute or the pudding may collapse.

COOK'S NOTES

The inimitable, rich flavour of a proper, long-cooked meat pudding is more than ample reward for every minute of the boiling or steaming time involved. Suet pastry is very easy to make and preparing the filling takes only a little time and effort. Once the heat is regulated, all you have to do is remember to check the water level occasionally to ensure the success of what is little more than a 'throw-it-all-in' meal.

STEAK PIE

SERVES 4

225 g (8 oz) plain flour

75 g (3 oz) beef dripping

900 g (2 lb) rump steak

salt and pepper

1 egg yolk

Mix the flour with about 150 ml (¼ pint) cold water, gradually stirring it in to make a soft but not too sticky dough. Roll out the dough into a rectangle and dot a third of the dripping over the top two-thirds of the dough. Fold the bottom third of the dough over the middle portion of fat, then fold the top third over that. Give the dough a quarter turn to the right, roll it out and repeat the process twice more to incorporate all the fat. Roll and fold the dough a fourth time without fat. Wrap the pastry in polythene and chill it for 30 minutes.

Set the oven at 180°C (350°F/gas 4). Cut the steak into thin slices measuring about 7.5 x 5 cm (3 x 2 inches). Layer the steak in a 1.1 litre (2 pint) pie dish, mounding it up in the middle and pressing it down neatly. Season each layer very generously. Slowly pour in enough water to come to just below the rim of the dish.

Roll out the dough thickly so that it is large enough to cover the pie with an extra 2.5 cm (1 inch) all round. Cut a 1 cm (½ inch) strip from around the edge of the dough, dampen the rim of the dish and press the strip of dough on to it. Dampen the dough rim, then cover the pie with the lid and seal the edge well. Decorate the top with pastry trimmings.

Beat the egg yolk with 5 ml (1 tsp) water and use this to glaze the pastry. Bake the pie for 1¼ hours, then cover it loosely with a piece of foil to prevent it from becoming too brown. Continue baking the pie for a further 1¼ hours, or until the steak feels tender when the centre of the pie is pierced with a pointed knife.

COOK'S NOTES

The combination of old-fashioned pastry made with beef dripping and succulent steak make a delicious pie. The pastry consists of crisp layers and the underside of the crust is richly flavoured with the cooking juices from the meat. If you like plenty of gravy, make a good beef gravy (separately) to serve with the pie.

MAKING MEAT PIES

Home-made meat pies can be prepared using ready cooked filling, reducing their baking time considerably. Try cooking a large batch of stewing steak with mushrooms or steak and kidney and freezing it in quantities suitable for filling a pie dish. Braised chicken, lamb or pork and sauces of minced meat all make excellent pie fillings. The thawed filling will reheat in the time it takes to cook the pastry crust – about 30 minutes.

PASTRY CRUSTS

Short crust and puff pastries are usually used for meat pies; although bought puff pastry is popular, it is worth making light short crust or even a special, buttery puff pastry for special occasions. Remember flaky and rough puff pastries, too, as both are excellent on pies. Suet crust is often dismissed as suitable only for steamed and boiled dishes but it bakes very well, rising and turning golden to make a light, spongy crust.

SUET PUDDING

350 g (12 oz) self-raising flour

salt and pepper

175 g (6 oz) shredded suet

about 300 ml (½ pint) milk

meat juices or melted butter to serve

Grease a large, double-thick sheet of foil. Sift the flour and stir in 2.5 ml (½ tsp) salt with the suet. Gradually stir in enough milk to make a soft, but not sticky, dough. Gently knead the dough and shape it into a roll, about 25 cm (10 inches) long. Wrap the suet roll in the foil, twisting the ends firmly and sealing the edges of the foil, but leaving the wrapping loose enough to allow room for the pastry to rise.

Bring a large saucepan or deep roasting tin of water to the boil and boil the suet pudding for 2½ hours, topping up the water with fresh boiling water as necessary. If using a roasting tin, tent foil over the top of it, sealing it on the rim to keep in the steam, and top up the water frequently. Alternatively, the pudding can be cooked in a steamer or steamed over a wok, which is ideal as it will accommodate the long shape. Serve the pudding cut into thick slices, dressed with hot meat juices or melted butter.

COOK'S NOTES

This pudding can be cooked in a greased basin and served cut into wedges. Traditionally, it was served in the same way as Yorkshire pudding. The slices of cooked pudding might be laid in the roasting tin around a joint for a few minutes before being served with the roast meat. To stretch a small roast, the pudding would be served coated in gravy, before the meat and vegetables.

BAKED SUET PUDDING

Pour a little dripping from a roast joint into a roasting tin or dish. Shape the suet pastry to fit the tin or dish and trickle extra meat juices over the top. Bake the pudding for about 45 minutes at 180°C (350°F/gas 4), until it has risen and is golden and crisp on top. If it is more convenient to

cook the pudding at a slightly higher temperature, perhaps because a joint is being roasted in the oven at the same time, flatten the pastry and make it thinner, so that it will rise and cook through easily. Reduce the cooking time.

In Mrs Beeton's day, various types of puddings were popular, including a leek pudding based on a suet pudding but filled with cut leeks. Shaped into a roll, this was boiled and served with meat and gravy.

Some puddings included a proportion of oatmeal and breadcrumbs as well as flour, and others were made with grain, such as barley. Barley, spinach and wild leaves, such as nettles and dandelion, were included in the Westmorland speciality pudding, which was boiled and served either hot or cold.

APPLE DUMPLINGS

MAKES 4

225 g (8 oz) self-raising flour

100 g (4 oz) shredded suet

salt

4 cooking apples

90–120 ml (6–8 tbsp) sugar

caster sugar to serve

If you intend to bake the dumplings, grease a baking sheet and set the oven at 200°C (400°F/gas 6). If the dumplings are to be boiled, you will need double-thick foil to enclose them and a large saucepan of boiling water or a steamer in which to cook them.

Mix the flour and suet, adding a generous pinch of salt, then gradually stir in about 175 ml (6 fl oz) cold water to make a soft, but not sticky, dough. Knead the dough gently for a few seconds and cut it into quarters.

Core and peel the apples, placing them in a bowl of cold water as they are prepared. Roll out a portion of pastry to a circle measuring 18 cm (7 inches) in diameter. Drain an apple and place it in the centre of the pastry; fill the core cavity with sugar. Fold and ease the pastry evenly around the apple to enclose it completely, pinching the edges together well to seal them. Roll the apples lightly on a floured surface to make the pastry covering neat and even.

Wrap the dumpling in double-thick greased foil, leaving enough space in the foil for the pastry to rise, but sealing the edges thoroughly to prevent water from entering. Alternatively, place the pastry-covered apples on the greased baking sheet. Make the remaining dumplings in the same way.

Boil or steam the dumplings for 40 minutes or bake them for 30–35 minutes. Serve them as soon as they are cooked, dredged with caster sugar.

COOK'S NOTES

At one time, boiling was the easiest and most economical method of cooking dumplings. They would be wrapped in a floured, damp pudding cloth or simply lowered into steadily simmering water. Country cooks, who were not concerned about keeping the flavour of the main dish separate from the pudding, would often boil apple dumplings in a large pot of broth or alongside a joint of meat.

Baking is an equally traditional method, for which short crust or puff pastry would sometimes have been used instead of suet pastry. Long strips of puff pastry can be wound around the apples, starting at the base and overlapping to seal in the fruit. If this technique is used, the apple is filled with sugar just before the top is covered with pastry. Short crust and puff pastry should be glazed with milk before baking. Caster sugar can be sprinkled over short crust pastry before cooking.

FILLINGS AND ACCOMPANIMENTS FOR APPLE DUMPLINGS

A little ground mixed spice or ground cinnamon can be added to the sugar. Raisins, currants, chopped dried apricots or other dried fruit can be mixed with sugar, then pressed into the cavities in the apples.

Marmalade, jam or mincemeat can replace the sugar or marzipan used to plug the core cavity.

Custard or cream can be poured over the dumplings. Alternatively, a little golden syrup, runny honey or maple syrup can be trickled over. Traditionalists may be delighted at the idea of a jam sauce (warmed jam, sieved and boiled with just a little water) with steamed apple dumplings.

CURRANT DUMPLINGS

225 g (8 oz) self-raising flour

75 g (3 oz) shredded suet

100 g (4 oz) currants

about 175 ml (6 fl oz) milk

TO SERVE

50 g (2 oz) unsalted butter, melted

caster sugar

1–2 lemons, cut into wedges

Bring a large saucepan of water to the boil. Mix the flour, suet and currants. Gradually stir in the milk to make a soft, but not sticky, dough. Knead the dough together lightly, then cut it in half.

Cut each dough half into four portions and roll each into a dumpling. Drop the dumplings into the boiling water, then bring the water back just to a gentle boil, carefully stirring the dumplings to prevent them from sticking together as they start to cook.

Reduce the heat and simmer the dumplings for 20 minutes or until they are well risen. Lift the dumplings out with a slotted spoon and serve them in warmed dishes, with melted butter poured over and a generous sprinkling of caster sugar on top. Serve lemon wedges with the dumplings, so that the juice can be squeezed over them just before they are eaten.

COOK'S NOTES

These dumplings sound and look rather boring, but they taste terrific! The sugar and lemon juice are the magic ingredients that transform the flavour of the fluffy, unsweetened suet pastry. Don't hold back when it comes to sprinkling on the caster sugar – it melts on to the hot, moist suet pastry and makes a delicious syrupy topping when the lemon juice is squeezed over. For comparison, the flavour is similar to that of pancakes, sprinkled with currants, sugar and lemon juice, and eaten piping hot.

If you want to make the dumplings look as appealing as they taste, serve them on individual hot plates and add two or three lemon wedges. Sprinkle over a little caster sugar. Take the bowl of caster sugar and the melted butter to the table. The dumplings must be eaten piping hot.

FREEZER TIP

Cooked suet pastry dumplings freeze well. Drain and cool the dumplings, then wrap them individually in cling film and place them on a baking sheet in the freezer. When the dumplings are hard, pack them in a freezer bag or container. Thaw and reheat the dumplings singly or in pairs in the microwave.

BLACKCURRANT PUDDING

SERVES 6

350 g (12 oz) self-raising flour

salt

150 g (5 oz) shredded beef suet

450 g (1 lb) blackcurrants

150 g (5 oz) sugar

Prepare a steamer and grease a 900 ml (1½ pint) pudding basin. Mix the flour with a pinch of salt and the suet, then gradually mix in about 250 ml (8 fl oz) water to make a soft, but not sticky, dough.

Knead the suet pastry lightly, then cut off and reserve about a quarter of the dough. Roll out the remaining pastry and use to line the basin, leaving the excess pastry hanging over the edge.

Place the blackcurrants in the lined basin, sprinkling a little sugar over each layer of fruit. Roll out the remaining pastry to cover the pudding. Dampen the edge of the pastry lining and place the lid on top. Pinch the pastry edges together to seal them well, then dampen the top edge and fold the overhanging pastry neatly over on to the top of the pudding.

Cover the pudding with greased double-thick foil, making a pleat in the foil to allow room for the pastry to rise during cooking. Crumple or tie the edge of the foil securely on to the rim of the basin to exclude moisture. Steam the pudding for 2½ hours, topping up the water occasionally, as necessary.

Use a palette knife to loosen the pastry carefully from the rim and side of the basin. Cover the pudding with an upside-down dish and invert both, then lift off the basin carefully. Serve the pudding at once.

VARIATIONS

Redcurrants can be used instead of blackcurrants. A mixture of raspberries and redcurrants makes a tempting pudding. Other tart fruit also go well in a suet pudding – plums, gooseberries, damsons, apples and rhubarb are good examples.

COOK'S NOTES

If you prefer lighter desserts during the summer months, freeze some blackcurrants to make this irresistible suet pudding when the weather is cooler. Pour plenty of steaming hot custard over each portion or spoon generous dollops of clotted cream on to the plate beside a wedge of blackcurrant pudding.

DELHI PUDDING

SERVES 4

3 small cooking apples, peeled, cored
   and sliced

45 ml (3 tbsp) sugar

grated rind of ½ lemon

1.25 ml (¼ tsp) grated nutmeg

salt

225 g (8 oz) self-raising flour

100 g (4 oz) shredded suet

50 g (2 oz) currants

a little butter for greasing

caster sugar to serve

Cook the apples with the sugar, lemon rind and nutmeg, stirring them until they are soft and pulpy. Transfer the cooked apples to a bowl and leave them to cool. Prepare a large saucepan of boiling water for cooking the pudding.

Stir a generous pinch of salt into the flour, then stir in the suet and gradually mix in about 175 ml (6 fl oz) water to make a soft, but not sticky, dough. Roll out the dough into a rectangle measuring about 20 cm (8 inches) wide and about 30 cm (12 inches) long: the pastry must not be too wide to fit into the saucepan.

Spread the cooked apple over the pastry, leaving a small gap around the edge, and sprinkle the currants over the top. Roll up the pastry from the narrow side. Pinch the pastry edges and ends together to seal them. Grease a double-thick sheet of foil large enough to enclose the pudding. Wrap the pudding, allowing space for it to rise. Fold the edges of the foil over to seal them well and keep the water out.

Boil the pudding for 2 hours, topping up the water as necessary to keep the pudding covered. Serve the pudding dredged with caster sugar.

COOK'S NOTES

Various roly-poly puddings can be made in the same way: spread jam over the pastry instead of apple and currants to make a jam roly-poly, or use marmalade or mincemeat. However, in the main recipe, the flavour of the spicy apple filling spiked with grated lemon rind is the perfect foil for suet pastry, making second helpings inevitable.

CONTAINERS FOR BOILING ROLY-POLY

If you do not have a saucepan or stockpot which is large enough to hold a roly-poly, try using a deep roasting tin instead. A large, deep wok is ideal. Remember to check the level of the boiling water and add more, if necessary, during cooking.

BAKED ROLY-POLY

Another way of cooking roly-poly is to bake it, sealed in a loose wrapping of greased foil on a baking sheet. Allow 45 minutes at 180°C (350°F/gas 4). The foil can be opened for the final 15 minutes, to brown the pudding.

ROLLING SUET PASTRY

1 Spread the filling evenly over the pastry. Always leave a narrow gap around the edge so that the pastry can be pinched together to seal in the filling. Roll up the pastry very loosely to avoid squeezing out the filling.

2 When the pastry and filling are rolled up by about two-thirds of the total length, fold the opposite end up over the top of the roll. This ensures that the filling is not squeezed out at the end.

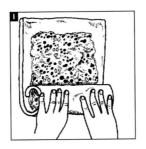
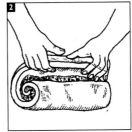

FRUIT TURNOVERS

MAKES 4–8

900 g (2 lb) cooking apples, peeled,
    cored and sliced

100 g (4 oz) sugar

4 cloves (optional)

350 g (12 oz) puff pastry*

1 egg white

a little caster sugar

Cook the apples with the sugar and cloves (if liked), adding 15 ml (1 tbsp) water to prevent them from burning at first, until they are soft and pulpy. Stir the fruit often during cooking, then leave it to cool. Remove the cloves, if used.

Set the oven at 220°C (425°F/gas 7). Cut the pastry into quarters. Roll out one portion into a round measuring roughly 23 cm (9 inches). Trim the pastry into a neat 20 cm (8 inch) circle, using a plate or saucer as a guide if necessary. Spoon a quarter of the cooked apple on one side of the pastry, leaving a clear gap around the edge. Dampen the edge of the pastry, then fold the uncovered side over the filling.

Press the pastry edges together to seal in the apples. Knock up the edges and flute them, then place the turnover on a baking sheet. Repeat with the remaining pastry and apple. Lightly whisk the egg white to break it up until it is slightly frothy, then brush this over the turnovers. Sprinkle a little caster sugar over and bake the turnovers for 15–20 minutes, until well puffed and golden.

Serve the turnovers freshly cooked or transfer them to a wire rack to cool. The turnovers are large, with plenty of filling, so one will provide two average portions.

COOK'S NOTES

Using cooked fruit is far more successful in turnovers than raw filling, which tends to shrink, produce too much syrup and leak.

OTHER FRUIT FILLINGS

Blackcurrants Cook these with sugar until soft. Drain and allow them to cool before filling the turnovers.

Blackberries or Raspberries Use these raw, piling them on one side of the pastry and sprinkling them with a little sugar.

Gooseberries Cook these with sugar and allow them to cool before filling the turnovers. Very juicy cooked fruit can be thickened with cornflour.

Rhubarb Slice the rhubarb into small pieces and cook the fruit with sugar. If liked, the fruit juices can be thickened with a little cornflour so that they can be added to the filling.

Apricots or Plums Halve and stone the fruit, then slice the halves and use them raw. Pile the slices on half the pastry and sprinkle them with a little sugar.

Jam or Mincemeat Both make delicious turnovers; use good-quality fruit jam.

SERVING SUGGESTIONS

Fruit turnovers are just as acceptable as a tea-time treat as they are for dessert. Whipped or clotted cream can be served. A hot custard goes well with apple, rhubarb or jam turnovers.

CREAMED APPLE TART

SERVES 6

225 g (8 oz) puff pastry*

450 g (1 lb) cooking apples, quartered, peeled, cored and thinly sliced

50 g (2 oz) sugar

grated rind of ½ lemon

15 ml (1 tbsp) lemon juice

300 ml (½ pint) milk, plus extra for glazing

15 ml (1 tbsp) cornflour

1 bay leaf

5 egg yolks

25 g (1 oz) caster sugar

2.5 ml (½ tsp) natural vanilla essence

15 ml (1 tbsp) brandy

Set the oven at 220°C (425°F/gas 7). Roll out the pastry to the shape of a pie dish, but about 2.5 cm (1 inch) larger than the top, then cut a 1 cm (½ inch) strip from around the edge. Dampen the rim of the dish and press the pastry strip on to it. Use a fluted cutter to stamp a hole in the middle of the rolled pastry lid – it should be about 3.5 cm (1½ inches) across or slightly smaller. Roll out the cut-out circle so that it becomes slightly larger without losing its shape.

Place the apples in the pie dish, sprinkling the sugar, lemon rind and juice over them as you layer the slices in the dish. Dampen the pastry rim and cover the pie. Trim, knock up and decorate the pastry edge. Brush the pastry with a little milk, including the circle cut from the middle. Replace the circle on top of the pie to cover the hole, but do not press it firmly in place.

Bake the pie for 10 minutes. Reduce the temperature to 190°C (375°F/gas 5) and cook the pie for a further 25–30 minutes.

Meanwhile, blend the cornflour with a little of the measured milk. Bring the remaining milk to the boil with the bay leaf, then remove it from the heat and set it aside until just hot. In a large bowl, whisk the egg yolks with the caster sugar and vanilla essence until they are pale and creamy. Discard the bay leaf and whisk the milk and brandy into the yolks. Stir in the cornflour mixture and pour the custard back into the saucepan. Heat, stirring continuously, until boiling. Remove the pan from the heat and beat the custard well.

Use a sharp pointed knife to remove the circle of pastry from the top of the pie. Carefully spoon the custard into the pie, teasing it down under the crust with the point of a knife. Allow the custard to seep down into the pie between additions. When the pie has been filled with custard, replace the pastry circle and allow the pie to cool completely before serving it.

COOK'S NOTES

In the above recipe, a little cornflour has been used to thicken the custard as a thin sauce does not complement the cooked apple and it tends to make the underside of the pastry soggy. The idea of pouring custard into the pie is both clever and successful. It can be eaten hot or warm, but is most impressive cool, when the custard has thickened slightly. The custard filling is equally delicious if pears are used instead of apples.

The basic recipe can be used for apple pie, without adding custard. Mrs Beeton added an 'icing' to her basic pie three-quarters of the way through cooking. For this, she whisked the white of an egg until it was frothy, but not stiff, and brushed it over the pastry. Then she dredged caster sugar over the top and sprinkled the pie with a little water. After being glazed, the pie was baked carefully to ensure that the sugar topping did not burn.

CHRISTMAS APPLE PIE

In Bedfordshire, a special apple pie was baked at Christmas. When cooked, the crust was removed and heated spiced ale was added to the cooked apple filling. The crust was cut into sections and replaced on the pie, which was served at once before the pastry had time to soften.

BAKEWELL PUDDING

100 g (4 oz) puff pastry★

about 60 ml (4 tbsp) jam

1 egg

4 egg yolks

100 g (4 oz) caster sugar

100 g (4 oz) butter, melted

25 g (1 oz) ground almonds

Set the oven at 180°C (350°F/gas 4). Roll out the pastry thinly and use to line a 23 cm (9 inch) tart plate, flan dish or shallow pie dish. Spread a layer of jam over the pastry.

Whisk the egg with the yolks and caster sugar until pale, thick and creamy. Gradually whisk in the melted butter, then stir in the ground almonds. Pour the mixture into the pastry case to cover the jam completely.

Bake the pudding for about 30–35 minutes. The pastry case should have risen and the filling should be set and golden brown. Serve the pudding hot, warm or cold.

COOK'S NOTES

This version of the recipe is slightly less sweet than the original, which used 175 g (6 oz) sugar, but it is still quite sweet. You may like to add a few drops of natural almond essence or oil of bitter almonds to the mixture as this gives the pudding a more definite flavour. A tangy fruit jam will provide much needed flavour contrast.

A fruit jelly or marmalade can be used instead of jam, if you like. Orange marmalade works particularly well.

Serve clotted, whipped or pouring cream with the pudding. Fromage frais, slightly tangy yogurt or soured cream would be the perfect foil for the sweetness of the pudding.

LEMON TART

SERVES 6-8

4 egg yolks

100 g (4 oz) caster sugar

grated rind and juice of 1 lemon

100 g (4 oz) unsalted butter, melted

175 g (6 oz) puff pastry* (see Cook's Notes)

Set the oven at 190°C (375°F/gas 5). Whisk the egg yolks with the sugar, lemon rind and juice until the mixture is pale, thick and creamy. Gradually whisk in all the melted butter, adding it at a steady trickle.

Line a 20 cm (8 in) flan dish or slightly larger tart plate with the pastry and prick it all over. Pour the lemon mixture into the pastry case.

Bake the lemon tart for 40 minutes, or until the lemon filling is set and lightly browned and the pastry case has risen and is cooked through. Serve the lemon tart hot or cold.

COOK'S NOTES

This is a type of lemon curd or cheese tart. The filling is smooth, full-flavoured and tangy. It is splendid hot, with scoops of really good vanilla ice cream served beside each portion. Cream, fromage frais or yogurt also go well with the tart.

VARYING THE CITRUS FRUIT
Lime or orange can be used instead of lemon. Use the juice of 2 limes and add only the rind of the orange, retaining the lemon juice to give the filling its characteristic tangy flavour.

ALTERNATIVE PASTRY
Mrs Beeton suggested puff pastry, but even if you make your own, this pastry is not the best choice to complement the smooth, light filling. A rich, lightly sweetened short crust pastry, made entirely from butter, does justice to the lemon mixture.

FOLKSTONE PUDDING PIES

MAKES 12

300 ml (½ pint) milk

1 bay leaf

strip of pared lemon rind

40 g (1½ oz) ground rice

50 g (2 oz) sugar

40 g (1½ oz) butter

3 eggs, beaten

225 g (8 oz) puff pastry*

50 g (2 oz) currants

Heat the milk with the bay leaf and lemon rind to just below boiling point, then set it aside to infuse for 15 minutes. Reheat the milk, remove the bay leaf and lemon rind, then sprinkle in the ground rice, stirring continuously. Bring the milk to the boil, stirring, then reduce the heat and simmer the mixture gently for 5 minutes, stirring occasionally.

Remove the pan from the heat and stir in the sugar and butter. When both have melted into the rice and the mixture has cooled slightly, strain the beaten eggs over the top, then stir them in until they are thoroughly incorporated.

Set the oven at 190°C (375°F/gas 5). Roll out the pastry thinly, cut out circles and use them to line 12 fairly deep patty tins. Spoon the ground rice mixture into the lined tins and sprinkle the currants over the top. Bake the pudding pies for 25 minutes, until the filling is cooked and lightly browned. Serve the pudding pies hot or transfer them to a wire rack and leave them to cool before serving them cold.

COOK'S NOTES

These little pies fill with air and puff up beautifully as they cook. The puff pastry works well, making a crisp base for the incredibly light filling, which is distinctly – and deliciously – flavoured with bay leaf.

Mrs Beeton frequently used bay leaves in sweet dishes, but it is a herb that has been overlooked in this context by many generations of cooks. If you particularly like the taste of bay in savoury dishes – soups, sauces and the like – you may be taken by surprise when you first taste it in sweet food, but your palate will soon become accustomed to it.

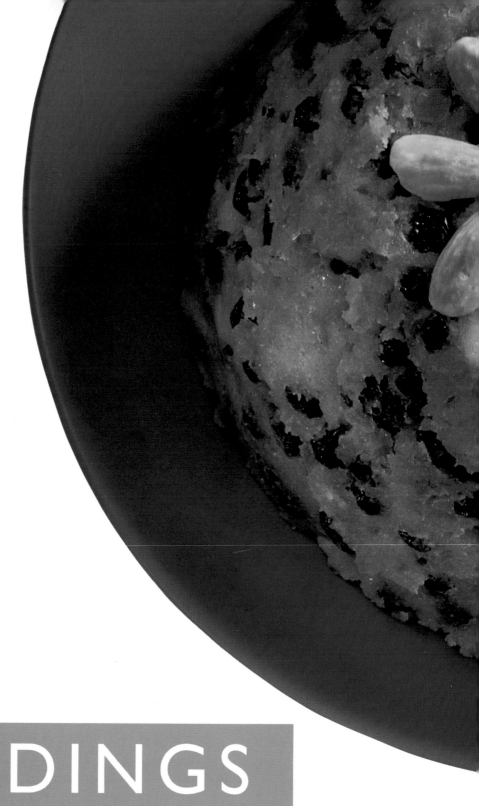

PUDDINGS

& DESSERTS

STEAMED SPONGE PUDDING

100 g (4 oz) unsalted butter

100 g (4 oz) caster sugar

2 eggs

100 g (4 oz) self-raising flour

50 g (2 oz) currants

Grease a 1.1 litre (2 pint) pudding basin and prepare a steamer over a saucepan of boiling water. Cream the butter with the sugar until pale and soft. Beat in the eggs, adding a little of the flour to prevent the mixture from curdling. Lightly fold in the remaining flour and the currants.

Turn the mixture into the prepared basin. Cover the pudding with greased double-thick foil, making a pleat in the foil to allow space for the pudding to rise during cooking. Crumple the foil firmly around the rim of the basin or tie it in place with string to exclude moisture.

Steam the pudding for 2 hours, topping up the boiling water in the saucepan as necessary. Turn the pudding out and serve it piping hot.

COOK'S NOTES

In the original recipe (entitled Alma Pudding), the flour and currants were mixed into the creamed ingredients before the eggs; however, the more familiar method of folding in the dry ingredients gives a lighter pudding, more in keeping with modern tastes.

This is an excellent basic recipe, which can be used to make a variety of favourite steamed puddings. For example, leave out the currants and place a few spoonfuls of jam or orange marmalade in the bottom of the basin before adding the mixture.

STEAMING PUDDINGS
Traditionally, a steamed pudding is cooked in a perforated steamer placed over a saucepan of boiling water.

An oriental bamboo steamer which is deep enough to hold a pudding basin can also be used. This type of steamer is placed in a wok and usually used for steaming foods which cook quickly. When steaming puddings for hours, check the water frequently as it may well evaporate and the wok will burn dry.

Electric steamers are also available. These worktop appliances include a heating element in the base with several perforated layers on top. Integral timers will remind you to top up the water level.

A pudding can be steamed directly over boiling water in a saucepan. Place a cereal bowl upside down in the bottom of the saucepan and stand the pudding basin on it. Pour in boiling water, making sure that it does not rise any more than a quarter of the way up the outside of the basin. Regulate the heat so that the water boils steadily, but not too rapidly, and cover the pan. Top up the water frequently.

HALF-PAY PUDDING

SERVES 4–6

100 g (4 oz) currants

100 g (4 oz) raisins

100 g (4 oz) shredded suet

100 g (4 oz) self-raising flour

100 g (4 oz) fresh white breadcrumbs

30 ml (2 tbsp) treacle

300 ml (½ pint) milk

Grease a 1.1 litre (2 pint) pudding basin and prepare a steamer over a saucepan of boiling water. Mix the currants and raisins with the suet, flour and breadcrumbs.

Warm the treacle with a little of the milk to make it more runny, then stir in the rest of the milk and pour the mixture over the dry ingredients. Mix the pudding well, beating the mixture to ensure that all the ingredients are thoroughly combined. It should be quite wet, rather like a thin cake mixture.

Turn the mixture into the prepared basin. Cover the pudding with greased double-thick foil, making a pleat in the foil to allow space for the pudding to rise during cooking. Crumple the foil firmly around the rim of the basin or tie it in place with string to exclude moisture.

Steam the pudding for 2 hours, topping up the boiling water in the saucepan as necessary. Turn the pudding out and serve it piping hot.

COOK'S NOTES

Where steamed sweet puddings were concerned, Mrs Beeton seldom messed about with small proportions. Once the pan was boiling on the stove, it was an ideal opportunity for the efficient cook to boil up a sensible quantity. A good pudding would be the highlight of many everyday meals and any leftovers could successfully be reheated in a steamer or over a saucepan of hot water. Among the many recipes for steamed fruit puddings, this stands out as having modest proportions.

Tracing the exact origin of the name of this pudding is difficult, but it was obviously related to the necessity for economy.

It is fascinating to note that the pudding is devoid of sugar, spice and eggs, all ingredients that would have been used with discretion when money was short. The result is a plain pudding, perfectly acceptable to our tastes, but not oversweet. Steaming hot custard is the ideal accompaniment, especially when made slightly sweeter than usual.

BARONESS PUDDING

SERVES 6–8

175 g (6 oz) shredded suet

175 g (6 oz) raisins

175 g (6 oz) self-raising flour, plus
   extra for dusting

pinch of salt

150 ml (¼ pint) milk

caster sugar to serve

Mix the suet, raisins, flour and salt. Stir in the milk to make a fairly stiff mixture (not as loose as cake mixture). Continue to mix the ingredients for a few minutes to make sure that all the flour is thoroughly incorporated and moistened.

Rinse a pudding cloth in water as hot as you can stand; wring it out firmly. Open out the cloth on a clean surface or board and dust it evenly with flour. Pile the mixture in the middle of the cloth and bring both sets of opposing corners together over the top. Bind the ends of the cloth with string and tie it securely. The cloth should be slightly loose around the pudding to allow it to expand during cooking.

Lower the pudding into a saucepan of boiling water. Bring the water back to the boil, then regulate the heat so that the pudding cooks steadily, but not too fast. Boil the pudding for 3 hours, topping up the water to keep the pudding covered.

Drain the pudding, transfer it to a serving plate and sift a little caster sugar over it. Offer extra caster sugar which can be sprinkled over individual portions to taste.

COOK'S NOTES

Mrs Beeton's recipe used double the quantities given above and the pudding was quite spectacular, but not very practical. A large stockpot was essential for boiling it and there was enough to feed several families by today's standards.

If you have never tried boiling a pudding, do have a go at this one. The result is succulent, fruity and a wonderful reward for experimenting with an unfamiliar technique. Serve plenty of caster sugar dredged over portions of the pudding to sweeten it and form a moist, syrupy coating.

PUDDING CLOTHS
Pudding cloths were familiar in the Victorian kitchen, either cut from cotton fabric or hand-knitted from dishcloth cotton. After use, they were soaked in cold or warm water, then washed and scalded in a pan of boiling water. Clean, dry cloths were folded and kept ready for use in a kitchen

drawer or cupboard. Today, it makes sense to keep pudding cloths in a tied polythene bag so that they stay perfectly clean.

1 A long, slightly narrow piece of muslin or fine cotton can be used. Fold it in half on a flat surface, placing the top layer at an angle to partially cover the bottom half of the cloth. This gives a wider area on which to pile the pudding mixture.

2 Tying the corners of the cloth with string is safer than relying on knotting them, and ensures that they do not come apart during boiling.

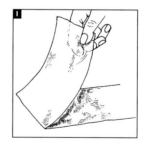
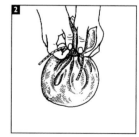

A BATCHELOR'S PUDDING

SERVES 4-6

1 small cooking apple (see method)

100 g (4 oz) currants

100 g (4 oz) fresh white breadcrumbs

50 g (2 oz) sugar

1.25 ml (¼ tsp) grated nutmeg

grated rind of ½ lemon

2 eggs, beaten

Grease a 600 ml (1 pint) pudding basin and prepare a steamer over a saucepan of boiling water.

Peel and core the apple, then weigh 100 g (4 oz) of the peeled apple. Grate it into a bowl and add the currants, breadcrumbs, sugar, nutmeg and lemon rind. Beat in the eggs.

Turn the mixture into the prepared basin and cover the pudding with greased double-thick foil, making a pleat in the foil to allow space for the pudding to rise during cooking. Crumple the foil firmly around the rim of the basin or tie it in place with string to exclude moisture.

Steam the pudding for 2 hours, topping up the boiling water in the saucepan as necessary. Turn the pudding out and serve it freshly cooked.

COOK'S NOTES

This is a sensible, everyday pudding. It is not too sweet, not too extravagant and not at all sophisticated. The tangy apple and lemon are well married with currants and nutmeg, and a steaming hot jug of custard will match the texture and flavour of the pudding.

Alternatively, a fruit sauce can be served; try heating apricot jam with a little dry sherry or a stewing fruit, then thickening it with arrowroot and sweetening it with sugar.

When preparing this pudding, it is important to peel and core the apples before weighing and grating them. Sultanas or raisins could be used instead of currants. Make the most of this light and tempting pudding when it is freshly cooked as it does not reheat well, so is not a suitable candidate for freezing.

CARROT PUDDING

350 g (12 oz) carrots, sliced

75 g (3 oz) sugar

100 g (4 oz) raisins

100 g (4 oz) currants

225 g (8 oz) fresh white breadcrumbs

100 g (4 oz) shredded suet

2.5 ml (½ tsp) grated nutmeg

2 eggs

Grease a 1.1 litre (2 pint) pudding basin. Prepare a steamer over a saucepan of boiling water.

Cook the carrots in boiling water for 15 minutes, then drain and purée them. Add the sugar, raisins, currants and breadcrumbs to the carrot purée. Stir in the suet and nutmeg, then beat in the eggs. The eggs are added last to allow time for the hot carrots to cool.

Turn the mixture into the basin and cover the top with greased double-thick foil, making a pleat in the foil to allow space for the pudding to rise during cooking. Crumple the foil firmly around the rim of the basin or tie it to prevent steam from entering. Steam the pudding for 2½ hours, keeping the water boiling steadily throughout and topping it up regularly with boiling water from a kettle.

TO BAKE THE PUDDING

Butter a pie dish instead of a pudding basin; set the oven at 160°C (325°F/gas 3). Turn the prepared mixture into the dish and smooth the top, then bake the pudding for 1–1¼ hours, until it is firm and lightly browned. Sprinkle a little caster sugar over the top of the baked pudding before serving it.

COOK'S NOTES

Mrs Beeton's carrot pudding proves to be a versatile recipe when put through its paces in today's kitchen! The mixture responds well to being baked in a 1 kg (2 lb) loaf tin instead of a pie dish. It turns out neatly to look quite impressive when topped with a decoration of chopped glacé fruits and toasted flaked almonds. Individual slices also look appetizing when served on generous puddles of hot custard sauce*.

Leftover pudding tastes irresistible when cold – rather like a moist carrot cake – and it can be served lightly chilled, decorated with piped whipped cream.

CARROT PUREE

A food processor or blender makes short work of puréeing vegetables; however, a purée can be made by first mashing and then sieving the cooked carrots for this pudding. Other useful utensils for the purpose include a ricer – a fine mesh sieve with a plunger or pestle-like hand pusher – and a food mill, which is a type of mechanical sieve with blades of varying fineness, depending on the consistency required.

GINGER CARROT PUDDING

Substitute 100 g (4 oz) chopped candied ginger and the grated rind of 1 lemon for the currants. Line the base of a soufflé dish with non-stick baking parchment and grease the sides with butter. Bake the pudding in this dish, then turn it out on to a flat platter and remove the lining paper. Pipe a border of whipped cream on the platter – at a slight distance from the pudding to avoid melting the cream – and decorate the cream with slices of preserved stem ginger.

AN UNRIVALLED
PLUM PUDDING

SERVES 6–8

100 g (4 oz) raisins

150 g (5 oz) currants

75 g (3 oz) sultanas

25 g (1 oz) chopped mixed candied
 peel

150 g (5 oz) dark soft brown sugar

175 g (6 oz) fresh white breadcrumbs

150 g (5 oz) shredded suet

grated rind of 1 lemon

7.5 ml (1½ tsp) grated nutmeg

10 ml (2 tsp) ground cinnamon

3 eggs

a few drops of oil of bitter almonds
 or natural almond essence

30 ml (2 tbsp) brandy

Grease a 1.1 litre (2 pint) pudding basin and prepare a steamer over a saucepan of boiling water.

Mix the raisins, currants, sultanas, candied peel, sugar, breadcrumbs, suet, lemon rind, nutmeg and cinnamon until all these ingredients are thoroughly combined. Beat the eggs with the almond oil or essence and brandy, then mix them into the pudding.

Turn the mixture into the prepared basin. Cover the top with greased double-thick foil, making a pleat in the foil for the pudding to rise during cooking. Crumple the foil firmly around the rim of the basin or tie it in place with string. Steam the pudding for 5–6 hours, topping up the boiling water as necessary.

To store the cooked and cooled pudding, remove the foil and cover it with a clean dry cloth or double-thick greaseproof paper. Then cover the basin with foil or put it in a polythene bag. Do not place foil directly over the pudding without a layer of greaseproof paper underneath as the natural acid in the fruit will react with the foil, causing it to disintegrate. Store the pudding in a cool, dry place.

To serve the pudding, unwrap it, cover it with fresh foil and steam it for a further 1½–2 hours.

COOK'S NOTES

The pudding should be made at least one, and preferably two, months before Christmas so that it matures well and is richly flavoured when served. If it is well wrapped with a clean covering and stored in a cool place, the pudding will keep for several months or up to a year. Check the pudding occasionally during long storage to make sure that it is neither drying out and shrinking nor sweating, when it may become mouldy. Pierce the pudding with a metal skewer and trickle a little brandy into it occasionally to keep it moist, well-flavoured and preserved.

BAKED BREAD AND
BUTTER PUDDING

SERVES 6

9 thin slices of bread and butter,
    crusts cut off

75 g (3 oz) currants

grated rind of 1 lemon

grated nutmeg

40–50 g (1½–2 oz) caster sugar, plus
    extra for sifting

4 eggs

900 ml (1½ pints) milk

Butter a large ovenproof dish. Cut the slices of bread and butter in half or into quarters, then layer them in the dish. Sprinkle each layer with a few currants, a little lemon rind and grated nutmeg, and caster sugar.

Beat the eggs with the milk, then strain the mixture through a sieve over the pudding. For best results, leave the pudding to stand for about 2 hours, so that the bread is well soaked. At least allow the pudding to stand for 30 minutes.

Set the oven at 180°C (350°F/gas 4). Bake the pudding for about 1 hour, until it has risen and is golden and set. Sift a little caster sugar over the top and serve the pudding freshly baked.

RICH BREAD AND BUTTER PUDDING

The pudding will be much richer if single cream is used instead of milk. Replacing a third of the milk with cream enriches it slightly. An additional 2–4 egg yolks can be added and a little chopped candied peel layered with the currants. The custard mixture can be flavoured with a little natural vanilla essence – about 2.5 ml (½ tsp) or less if it is highly concentrated. There is no need to add lemon rind with the vanilla essence.

COOK'S NOTES

The poor impression so many people have of bread pudding can only come from chunks of cold, leaden leftover bakes which bear absolutely no resemblance to the risen, light and caramel crusted puddings that emerged steaming from Mrs Beeton's oven.

Mrs Beeton offered several different recipes for bread puddings, some baked, others steamed. Brown breadcrumbs were used in one recipe and flavourings included chopped candied peel, bitter almonds and brandy.

MINIATURE BREAD PUDDINGS

Soak 225 g (8 oz) breadcrumbs for 30 minutes in 600 ml (1 pint) boiling milk. Beat 4 eggs with 30 ml (2 tbsp)

brandy, 5 ml (1 tsp) grated lemon rind and 40 g (1½ oz) caster sugar, then stir this mixture into the soaked bread. Divide the mixture between well-buttered custard cups, dariole moulds, ramekins or individual soufflé dishes. Bake the puddings as in the main recipe, but for only 20 minutes, until set and browned.

FRUIT SAUCES

A tangy fruit sauce alters the image of this type of pudding. A lightly sweetened purée of fresh raspberries or lightly cooked apricots goes well; alternatively, try a zesty jam sauce made of plum or damson preserve warmed with a little dry sherry and a dash of lemon juice.

BAKED APPLE PUDDING

SERVES 6

50 g (2 oz) butter

600 ml (1 pint) milk

60 ml (4 tbsp) plain flour

3 eggs

3 small to medium cooking apples,
    peeled, cored and halved

grated nutmeg

caster sugar to serve

Set the oven at 180°C (350°F/gas 4). Use about a third of the butter to grease a shallow ovenproof dish.

Gradually whisk a little of the milk into the flour to make a smooth paste, then beat in the eggs before whisking in the remaining milk. Pour the custard mixture into the dish, then arrange the apple halves in it, placing them cut sides down.

Sprinkle a little nutmeg over the pudding and dot the remaining butter on top of the apples. Bake the pudding for about 1–1¼ hours, until the mixture is risen and lightly browned, and the apples are cooked. Dredge caster sugar thickly over the top of the pudding and serve it at once.

NOTE

The pudding is also good when made with thickly sliced apples added to the batter instead of the halved fruit.

COOK'S NOTES

At first glance this appears to be a batter pudding, but when the ingredients are assembled it soon becomes clear that it is based on a custard, with just a little flour, rather than a heavier batter. It is soft, light and tempting, with the smooth custard complementing the tart apples. Originally, the apples were cored and cooked with their peel on. This kept them in shape but made them less appetizing. Sugar is not added to the mixture, so it is important to dredge the top of the cooked pudding quite generously with caster sugar. Pears, halved peaches or plums can be cooked in the same way as the apples, as can halved apricots or stoned cherries.

BAKED ORANGE PUDDING

SERVES 6–8

100 g (4 oz) butter

175 g (6 oz) plain flour

90 ml (6 tbsp) caster sugar

175 g (6 oz) plain cake (see Cook's Notes)

grated rind of 1 orange and juice of 2 oranges

3 eggs

450 ml (¾ pint) milk

Set the oven at 180°C (350°F/gas 4). Rub the butter into the flour, then stir in 30 ml (2 tbsp) of the caster sugar. Sprinkle in 45-60 ml (3-4 tbsp) cold water and mix lightly to bind the ingredients into a sweet short pastry. Press the pastry together, then roll it out and use it to line a 20 cm (8 inch) round flan dish. Prick the base all over with a fork.

Crumble the cake into the pastry case, breaking it up evenly. Sprinkle the orange juice over the crumbs. Whisk the orange rind and remaining caster sugar with the eggs, then gradually whisk in the milk. Pour the egg and milk mixture over the crumbs, adding it slowly to allow time for each addition to be absorbed by the crumbs (otherwise it may overflow around the sides of the pastry case).

Bake the pudding for about 1¼ hours, until the filling is set, risen and golden brown. Leave the pudding to cool for 10 minutes before serving or allow it to cool completely and serve cold.

COOK'S NOTES

Good-quality plain cake is important for this recipe. Either a whisked sponge or a cake based on a creamed mixture (Victoria sandwich or Madeira) would be ideal, but any cake that is strongly flavoured would be unsuitable.

A flan dish is a better choice then the pie dish originally used, to ensure that the crust cooks well. Since the pudding requires lengthy cooking, there is no need to bake the pastry case separately before filling it. However, the pastry case can be dispensed with, and the filling cooked on its own in a suitable dish to make a lighter pudding. In this case, the cooking time should be reduced by 10-15 minutes.

Serve custard or a jam sauce with the hot pudding, or flavour some whipped cream with a little sweet orange liqueur to complement the cold pudding. If it is served cold, the pudding is best at room temperature, rather than chilled, when the texture can become rather dense.

JAM SAUCE
This is one of those simple, classic sweet sauces that goes well with all sorts of plain puddings, whether steamed or baked. Heat about 225 g (8 oz) good-quality fruit jam with 30-45 ml (2-3 tbsp) water, stirring until the jam has melted and has combined well with the liquid. This can be done in a small, heavy-bottomed saucepan or in a suitable jug in the microwave. A little dry sherry or white wine can be used instead of the water. Try apricot, raspberry or strawberry jam; marmalade also makes a versatile sauce.

BAKED APPLE CUSTARD

SERVES 6

450 g (I lb) cooking apples,
    quartered, peeled, cored and sliced

40 g (I ½ oz) light soft brown sugar

2 eggs

30 ml (2 tbsp) caster sugar

grated rind of I lemon

300 ml (½ pint) milk

grated nutmeg

Cook the apples with the soft brown sugar, adding 30 ml (2 tbsp) water to prevent the fruit from burning in the first stage of cooking before it softens and becomes juicy. Stir the apples occasionally to break them down, and continue cooking until they are pulpy. Turn the cooked apple into an ovenproof dish and smooth the top.

Set the oven at 160°C (325°F/gas 3). Beat the eggs with the caster sugar and lemon rind. Heat the milk until hand hot, then stir it into the eggs and strain the custard over the apples. Sprinkle the custard with a little nutmeg. Bake the pudding for about 45 minutes, or until the custard is set and lightly browned on top.

Allow the pudding to stand for about 1 hour before serving, or allow it to cool completely, then chill it before serving.

COOK'S NOTES

This is one of those simple, nutritious, traditional puddings that is quite light and easy to prepare – particularly if you have a stock of apple purée in the freezer.

It is surprising how sophisticated a simple dessert can be when it is dressed up slightly. For example, if the pudding is cooled and chilled, it can be topped with swirls of whipped cream, sprinkled with toasted flaked almonds.

Alternatively, the apple, with its custard topping, can be cooked in a pastry flan case to make a tempting tart. It is also a good idea to include a little fruit purée under the custard filling for individual custard tarts, particularly if they are cooked in deep muffin tins instead of patty tins.

To vary the flavour, but retain the consistency of the purée, cooking other types of fruit with the apple. Rhubarb, blackberries or blackcurrants would all be suitable.

BAKED RICE PUDDING

SERVES 6

1.1 litres (2 pints) milk

strip of pared lemon rind

100 g (4 oz) pudding rice

30 ml (2 tbsp) sugar

15 g (½ oz) butter

2.5 ml (½ tsp) grated nutmeg

Heat the milk with the lemon rind until almost boiling, then set it aside to cool. Set the oven at 160°C (325°F/gas 3).

Place the rice in a sieve. Wash it under cold running water, then tip it into an ovenproof dish. Sprinkle the sugar over the rice and stir in the milk, discarding the lemon rind. Float the butter on the pudding and sprinkle the nutmeg over the top.

Bake the pudding for about 2 hours. Stir the pudding after 20 minutes' cooking and at intervals of about 20 minutes for the first hour, then leave the pudding to develop a deep golden crust.

COOK'S NOTES

This is Mrs Beeton's plain and economical rice pudding. It is a nursery version of a far richer recipe made with eggs, beef marrow, butter, currants and brandy, which was baked in a pastry case.

Candied peel, sultanas, raisins or currants can be added to the pudding; 50–100 g (2–4 oz) is about the right amount. A beaten egg (or 2–4 lightly whisked egg yolks) can be stirred into the pudding 40 minutes before the end of cooking. Allow the rice pudding to cool for 2–3 minutes before stirring in the eggs or yolks.

Traditionally, baked seasonal fruit, such as apples or plums, would have been prepared at the same time as a rice pudding and served as a tangy accompaniment.

RICE PUDDING REVISITED

Leftover rice pudding can be used to make various dessert treats. Creamy rice pudding is delicious when layered with stewed fruit and chilled. Stewed apples, blackcurrants or rhubarb can be used. For an extra rich dessert, fold some whipped cream into the pudding and spoon it into ramekins or individual soufflé dishes that can safely be used under the grill. Top each pudding with a layer of soft brown sugar and chill well. Caramelize the sugar topping under a hot grill before serving.

One of the quickest desserts consists of individual dishes of rice pudding, each topped with a fruity dollop of excellent preserve, such as cherry or raspberry jam.

SMALL ALMOND PUDDINGS

SERVES 4–6

225 g (8 oz) ground almonds

30 ml (2 tbsp) caster sugar

30 ml (2 tbsp) single cream

100 g (4 oz) unsalted butter, melted,

    plus extra for greasing

a few drops of oil of bitter almonds

    or natural almond essence

2 eggs plus 2 egg yolks, beaten

    together

custard sauce★ to serve

Set the oven at 180°C (350°F/gas 4). Butter six dariole moulds or four slightly larger ramekins (small individual soufflé dishes). Mix the ground almonds and caster sugar, then stir in the cream and measured melted butter. Add the oil of bitter almonds or almond essence. Beat in the eggs.

Divide the mixture between the buttered dishes or dariole moulds and bake the puddings for 25–30 minutes, until they are risen, set and lightly browned. Turn the puddings out on to plates or a serving dish and offer custard sauce with them.

COOK'S NOTES

These are simple to prepare and look very impressive. Line the base of each mould or ramekin with a little circle of non-stick baking parchment to make certain that the puddings will turn out easily, especially if you know from previous experience that your moulds have a tendency to stick. The mixture puffs up into light domes when first cooked, then sinks back slightly. This is normal, and does not affect the flavour or texture, which is like that of a close, fine, moist almond sponge. The puddings are just as good warm as they are when freshly cooked.

As alternatives to custard with the puddings, try serving a fairly thin chocolate sauce, smooth fruit sauce or whipped cream flavoured with kirsch and sweetened to taste.

STEWED PEARS

SERVES 6

100 g (4 oz) sugar

6 cloves

6 whole allspice berries

150 ml (¼ pint) port

6 large firm pears

Heat the sugar, cloves and allspice with 250 ml (8 fl oz) water in a saucepan large enough to hold the whole pears in one layer. Stir until the sugar has dissolved, then add the port. Take the pan off the heat.

Peel the pears, leaving their stalks in place, and core them from underneath. As each pear is prepared, add it to the pan, turning to coat it in syrup and prevent it from discolouring.

Bring the pears to the boil and reduce the heat immediately so that the syrup is barely simmers. Cover the pan and poach the pears gently for about 2 hours, or until they are tender. Watch them closely, turning them occasionally, and make sure the syrup stays at the right temperature to cook the pears slowly and steadily.

Use a slotted spoon to transfer the pears to a serving dish. Boil the syrup hard until it is reduced by about a third or slightly more, then strain it over the pears. Leave the pears to cool, then chill them for several hours before serving.

COOK'S NOTES

This classic dessert never fails to please. The water and port can be replaced by the same volume of full-bodied red wine if you do not have a bottle of port handy or if the one available is too good for cooking.

MOULDED PEARS
Mrs Beeton also included a recipe for quartered pears, cooked with spices and lemon rind, then set in a jelly of raisin wine. To make a similar moulded dish, quarter the pears and reduce the cooking time by half or more. The syrup does not have to be reduced to the same extent,

but it should be boiled briefly to concentrate the flavours. Dissolve a sachet of gelatine in the syrup and pour it over the pear quarters, having arranged them in a suitable mould. Remember to rinse the mould with cold water first if you intend turning out the dessert.

A SAINT-DAY DESSERT
In Bedfordshire, stewed pears were traditionally served on October 28th, the feast of St. Simon and St. Jude. The pears were cooked in red wine, flavoured with cloves and cinnamon.

TRIFLE

SERVES 6

4 slices of plain cake, such as Madeira
  cake, or 1 layer of a whisked
  sponge cake
6 almond macaroons
12 ratafias
175 ml (6 fl oz) sherry
30–45 ml (2–3 tbsp) brandy
60–90 ml (4–6 tbsp) raspberry or
  strawberry jam
grated rind of ½ lemon
25 g (1 oz) flaked almonds
25 g (1 oz) cornflour
25 g (1 oz) caster sugar
4 egg yolks
5 ml (1 tsp) natural vanilla essence
600 ml (1 pint) milk
300 ml (½ pint) double cream
30 ml (2 tbsp) icing sugar
candied and crystallized fruit and peel
  to decorate

Arrange the cake, macaroons and ratafias in a trifle bowl, pressing the mixture down gently. Reserve about 50 ml (2 fl oz) of the sherry, then pour the rest over the biscuits and cake, with the brandy. Warm the jam, then pour it over the trifle base and spread it lightly. Sprinkle the lemon rind and almonds over the jam.

Mix the cornflour, caster sugar, egg yolks and vanilla to a smooth cream with a little of the milk. Heat the remaining milk in a pan, then stir some of it into the egg mixture. Pour the mixture back into the saucepan to join the rest of the milk. Bring to the boil, stirring continuously, then reduce the heat. Simmer the custard for 3 minutes.

Cool the custard slightly before pouring it over the trifle base. Cover the surface with a piece of dampened greaseproof paper or cling film. Leave the custard to cool completely.

Whip the cream and icing sugar with the reserved sherry until the mixture stands in soft peaks. Swirl the whipped cream over the custard and chill the trifle thoroughly. Decorate with pieces of candied and crystallized fruit and peel.

COOK'S NOTES

The original custard topping, made with 8 eggs to 600 ml (½ pint) milk and cooked slowly over hot water, rather spoilt this magnificent trifle as it tasted very 'eggy'. Making a custard with all yolks is another alternative, but the result is usually very thin. Crème pâtissière, or pastry cream, thickened with flour and egg yolks, then enriched with cream, is another good topping for trifle, but in this recipe it does not set off Mrs Beeton's wonderful syllabub topping to best advantage.

The syllabub topping was a key feature in the original recipe, when it was made with 600 ml (1 pint) cream whisked with 2 egg whites. It was prepared the day before it was swirled on to the trifle.

FRUIT TRIFLES
Fresh fruit brightens and lightens a trifle for a summer dessert. Raspberries are the perfect foil for sweet jams and rich creams: add a layer on top of the sponge cake and coat them with the warmed jam.

Mrs Beeton made an extremely good apple trifle by covering a purée of lemon-flavoured cooked apples with custard and whipped cream. Spreading the apple purée over cake moistened with a little sherry or ginger wine would make the trifle more interesting.

GINGER CREAM

SERVES 6

15 ml (1 tbsp) gelatine

4 egg yolks

75 g (3 oz) preserved stem ginger, very thinly sliced

30 ml (2 tbsp) syrup from the ginger jar

600 ml (1 pint) double cream

slices of preserved ginger or citron peel to decorate

Sprinkle the gelatine over 45 ml (3 tbsp) cold water in a small heatproof bowl and set it aside. Beat the egg yolks in a heatproof bowl, then stir in the ginger, syrup and cream. Set the bowl over a saucepan of hot water and stir the cream with a hand whisk until the yolks cook and the cream thickens very slightly – enough to coat the back of a spoon. Remove the bowl from the pan and continue stirring the cream frequently until it cools.

Meanwhile, dissolve the gelatine over hot, not boiling, water. When the cream is barely warm, stir in the gelatine and whisk the cream until it forms soft peaks. Spoon the cream into six glasses or dishes, then chill the ginger cream for several hours. Decorate with slices of preserved ginger or candied citron peel.

COOK'S NOTES

Creams, whips and syllabubs were popular desserts in Mrs Beeton's day. For this recipe, she used isinglass as a setting agent. This was a product derived from the swim bladder of fish. Similar to gelatine, it was used as a clearing agent for wine or beer. The original setting agent may be out of favour for modern cooks but the cream has a pleasing flavour as ginger is a popular modern ingredient. As usual, Mrs Beeton included notes relating to the preserved ginger she would have purchased. Her comments make fascinating reading today.

'PRESERVED GINGER comes to us from the West Indies. It is made by scalding the roots when they are green and full of sap, then peeling them in cold water, and putting them into jars, with a rich syrup; in which state we receive them. It should be chosen of a bright-yellow colour with a little transparency: what is dark-coloured, fibrous, and stringy, is not good. Ginger roots, fit for preserving, and in size equal to West Indian, have been produced in the Royal Agricultural Garden in Edinburgh.'

Happily, selecting preserved ginger today involves nothing more arduous than buying a high-quality product, whether this be a jar containing ginger preserved in syrup or a pot of candied ginger. The latter is very similar to preserved ginger, but because it is chopped and is packaged without the syrup it is more economical. Ginger root can be grown easily in a greenhouse in summer, or in a heated conservatory, to form a house plant that resembles bamboo.

WHIPPED SYLLABUB

SERVES 4 – 6

75 ml (3 fl oz) sherry

30 ml (2 tbsp) brandy

juice of 1 small lemon

40 g (1½ oz) caster sugar

grated nutmeg

300 ml (½ pint) double cream

Whisk the sherry, brandy, lemon juice, sugar and a little grated nutmeg together lightly until the sugar dissolves. Stir in the cream, then whip the mixture until it is thick, light and slightly frothy.

Pour the syllabub into tall glasses or dishes and chill it for 30 minutes before serving. The syllabub can be prepared 2–3 hours before it is served.

COOK'S NOTES

Syllabub is an old Elizabethan creation based on cream thickened or curdled with wine or cider. The thin version was consumed as a drink, the thicker one, as here, eaten for dessert. There are many versions, including a light dessert syllabub with whisked egg whites folded in. In the first edition of her book, Mrs Beeton also included the thin version of syllabub served as a drink. For this she combined 600 ml (1 pint) sherry or wine with half a grated nutmeg and 900 ml (1½ pints) milk. Sugar was added to taste. Her suggestions for enriching the mixture were as follows: 'Clouted (clotted) cream may be laid on the top, with pounded cinnamon or nutmeg and sugar; and a little brandy may be added to the wine before the milk is put in. In some counties, cider is substituted for the wine: when this is used, brandy must always be added. Warm milk may be poured on from a spouted jug or teapot; but it must be held very high.'

Mrs Beeton made two suggestions for this syllabub: it could either be served as suggested above, or the ingredients could simply be mixed together without being whipped, then poured into glasses and topped with the same whipped cream covering the trifle (page 170).

BLANCMANGE

SERVES 6

600 ml (1 pint) creamy milk

pared rind of 1 lemon

100 g (4 oz) sugar

30 ml (2 tbsp) gelatine

25 g (1 oz) almonds

a few drops of oil of bitter almonds
 or natural almond essence

600 ml (1 pint) single cream

sweet almond oil or other light oil
 for greasing

Stir the milk, lemon rind and sugar over low heat until the sugar dissolves, then sprinkle in the gelatine and leave the mixture over low heat, without stirring, for 15 minutes. Stir the milk well to ensure that the gelatine has dissolved, increase the heat until the milk is just about to simmer, then take the pan off the hob and set it aside until the milk mixture has cooled.

Meanwhile, cover the almonds with boiling water, leave them to stand for 1–2 minutes, then drain and skin them. Purée them with a little of the milk, then add them to the remaining milk with the oil of bitter almonds or essence.

Strain the milk and stir in the cream. Lightly grease a mould with oil and pour in the blancmange mixture. Chill for several hours, until the blancmange is set. Invert the mould on a wetted plate or serving dish and slide it into the middle before lifting it off the blancmange.

COOK'S NOTES

There were many suggestions for blancmange in the first edition of Mrs Beeton's work. Flavourings which could be added to the above recipe included bay leaf, vanilla, brandy, noyeau, Curaçao or any favourite liqueur.

Although the above recipe is possibly the most interesting, the following are just as relevant for today's cook and certainly worth sampling.

ARROWROOT BLANCMANGE
An inexpensive recipe. Heat 600 ml (1 pint) milk with 3 bay leaves or the pared rind of ½ lemon; set this mixture aside to infuse for at least 30 minutes.

Strain the milk into a clean pan and bring it to the boil. Mix 75 ml (5 tbsp) arrowroot with 300 ml (½ pint) milk

until it forms a thin cream, then stir in the boiling milk and sugar to taste. Pour the mixture back into the pan and bring it to the boil, then immediately remove the pan from the heat and pour the mixture into an oiled mould. Cover the surface of the blancmange with wetted greaseproof paper or cling film to prevent a skin from forming. Cool and chill the blancmange until it is set.

MRS BEETON'S CHEAP BLANCMANGE
Heat 1.1 litres (2 pints) milk with 100 g (4 oz) sugar, the rind of ½ lemon and 4 bay leaves. Leave the milk to infuse, then heat it again until almost boiling and dissolve 30 ml (2 tbsp) gelatine in it. Strain the milk into an oiled mould, leave it to cool, then chill until set.

FRESH ORANGE JELLY

SERVES 6–8

14 oranges

1 lemon

175 g (6 oz) sugar

1 Seville or bitter orange

25 g (1 oz) gelatine

Rinse a jelly mould with cold water. Chill it while you make the jelly. Pare the rind from 1 orange and half the lemon. Heat the fruit rind with the sugar and 600 ml (1 pint) water, stirring until the sugar dissolves. Skim off any scum which rises to the surface of the syrup.

Squeeze the juice from 9 oranges, the lemon and the Seville orange. Add this to the syrup and heat the mixture, stirring occasionally, until it comes to the boil. Remove the pan from the heat and stir in the gelatine. When the gelatine has dissolved completely, strain the syrup through a jelly bag, muslin-lined sieve or paper coffee filter. Leave the jelly to cool.

Peel the remaining oranges, removing all the pith. To do this, slice off the top and bottom of each fruit, then slice off the peel from top to bottom, working around the fruit. Remove any stray bits of pith. Slice the fruit, discarding any pips.

Pour a thin layer of jelly into the base of the chilled mould; chill until set. Arrange a layer of orange slices on the jelly and pour in enough jelly to cover them. Chill the jelly until it sets to hold the oranges in place. Continue adding layers of orange and jelly, setting each layer before adding the next to prevent the fruit from floating.

When all the oranges have been added, chill the mould for several hours before turning it out. Any leftover jelly can be chilled separately, then chopped and used to decorate the dessert.

COOK'S NOTES

Plastic moulds with a small lid on the base are excellent, ensuring success every time when turning out jellied desserts. Removing the lid on the inverted base breaks the vacuum and the dessert slides out of the mould.

The traditional method of loosening jelly from a mould is to dip the mould into hot water for a few seconds. Take care with traditional thick glass moulds – if the water is too hot, the glass will crack. Mrs Beeton gave first-edition readers a useful tip: rinse a tea-towel in boiling water, wring it out thoroughly, then wrap it around the outside of the mould for a minute or two before unmoulding the jelly. (You will have to protect your hands with rubber gloves to wring out the very hot water from the cloth.)

CHOICE OF MOULDS

A plain mould or dish works well for fruit in jelly, showing off the pieces to best advantage. A loaf tin, charlotte mould or straight-sided dish will do. Individual dishes also work well – ramekins, for example – but you may have to halve or quarter the orange slices in order to arrange them neatly.

ORANGE SALAD

S E R V E S   4

5 oranges

50 g (2 oz) caster sugar

2.5 ml (½ tsp) ground mixed spice

100 g (4 oz) raisins

60 ml (4 tbsp) brandy

Peel 4 oranges, removing all the pith, and slice them, discarding any pips. Layer the oranges in a small dish, sprinkling the sugar, spice and raisins over them.

Squeeze the juice from the remaining orange and trickle it over the fruit with the brandy. Cover the dish with cling film and chill the oranges for a day before serving them.

COOK'S NOTES

This is a superb fruit salad – aromatic with spice and brandy, and bursting with citrus flavour. It makes an ideal dessert for the Christmas season, when everyone feels rather weighed down by rich meals.

Mrs Beeton suggested using muscatel raisins. Most supermarkets offer high-quality fruit these days, but it is worth looking in healthfood shops for large succulent raisins. Taste them before use as some can be very seedy, which spoils the salad. Sultanas can be used instead of raisins, but the colour contrast will not be as marked.

FRUIT ICE CREAM

600 ml (1 pint) fruit purée, such as
    raspberry, redcurrant, blackcurrant
    or strawberry
icing sugar to taste
600 ml (1 pint) double cream

Rub the fruit purée through a sieve to remove any seeds. Sweeten it with icing sugar, adding sufficient to make the fruit taste just too sweet for your liking. Cream will dilute the flavour and freezing dulls both flavour and sweetness.

Whip the cream lightly to thicken it to the same consistency as the fruit purée, then fold both together. Freeze the mixture, whisking it two or three times as it solidifies and a ring of ice forms around the edge of the container.

With each whisking, the ice crystals are broken down and the mixture should become smooth and thick. A food processor is ideal for this – chill the bowl and blade beforehand for best results.

Finally, freeze the ice cream for several hours, until it is firm. Leave it at room temperature for about 15 minutes to soften it for serving.

COOK'S NOTES

Charles I introduced ice cream to Britain on his marriage to Princess Henrietta Maria of France. In an attempt to keep his dessert discovery a uniquely royal treat, the king paid his chef £500 a year to keep the recipe a secret.

USING AN ICE CREAM MAKER

An ice cream maker can, of course, be used for this recipe, but is by no means essential. A food processor will whiz the ice crystals quickly into a smooth, pale cream. Alternatively, use an electric beater.

FRUIT PUREES

Stone fruit, such as plums, damsons, peaches or apricots, make good ice cream. Add a little lemon juice to enhance the flavour of peaches or apricots; a squeeze of lemon also improves the balance if the fruit is very ripe.

SPEEDY ICES

Mrs Beeton very sensibly suggested using jam to make ice cream. One of her home-made fruit preserves would have provided a wonderful flavour. High-quality conserves, packed with fruit and without too much added sugar are available from most larger supermarkets and can be used to make an excellent quick ice cream. Whip cream with a little icing sugar to sweeten it to taste, then fold in the preserve. Add enough to slightly oversweeten the mixture, then fold it through the cream so that it is about three-quarters mixed in. Freeze this mixture until firm, without whisking it partway through.

BAKING

EXCELLENT ROLLS

MAKES 12

450 g (1 lb) strong plain flour

5 ml (1 tsp) salt

5 ml (1 tsp) sugar

1 sachet fast-action easy-blend
    dried yeast

150 ml (¼ pint) milk

75 g (3 oz) butter, cut into pieces

2 eggs, beaten

Grease two baking sheets. Mix the flour, salt, sugar and yeast. Make a well in the middle of the dry ingredients. Heat the milk until it is hand hot, add the butter and stir until the butter has melted. Do not allow the mixture to become too hot – if necessary, let it cool so that it is once more hand hot.

Pour the milk mixture into the well in the flour and add three-quarters of the beaten egg. Reserve the remaining egg for glazing the rolls. Gradually beat the dry ingredients into the egg and milk mixture to make a soft dough that is not too sticky.

Knead the dough thoroughly on a well-floured surface until it is smooth and elastic. Shape into twelve oval rolls and place these on the baking sheets. Cover the rolls loosely with cling film or polythene and leave them in a warm place until they have doubled in size.

Meanwhile, set the oven at 220°C (425°F/gas 7). Beat a little water and a pinch of salt into the reserved egg, then brush this over the risen rolls just before placing them in the oven. Bake the rolls for about 20 minutes, until they are golden brown. Turn one of the rolls over and tap the base to check if it is cooked: if the bread sounds hollow, it is ready; if it sounds solid and damp, bake the rolls for a few minutes more before checking them again. Transfer the rolls to a wire rack to cool.

COOK'S NOTES

Yeast cookery, as it was referred to by previous generations of cooks, has changed more in the last fifty years than any other basic technique. Dried yeast first revolutionized dough making by virtue of its long shelf life and the fact that it was less temperamental in use than fresh yeast.

Easy-blend dried yeast is stirred into dry ingredients rather than being moistened and sponged. Fast-action easy-blend dried yeast cuts out the need for more than one rising. The dried yeast is mixed with the dry ingredients and a liquid – which should be hand hot – is added. When adding eggs, it is important to strike a balance between using hand-hot liquid to activate the yeast and making sure that the liquid is not so hot that it begins to set the egg.

FRESH YEAST

Fresh yeast is available from bakers where the bread is baked on the premises; some supermarkets also sell fresh yeast from their bakeshops. Fresh yeast is beige in colour and moist, with a slightly crumbly or flaky texture when

cut. It should have a 'fresh' clean smell. Tied in a polythene bag, it will keep in the refrigerator for up to a week or can be frozen for up to a year.

Blend fresh yeast to a thin paste with a little lukewarm water. Hand-hot water would be too hot for fresh yeast which is not protected by the additional ingredients used in the manufacture of dried yeast. Sprinkle a little flour over the surface of the yeast liquid, cover the bowl and leave in a warm place until frothy. A little sugar can be mixed with the yeast, but this can make the mixture overwork, giving the baked goods a yeasty flavour.

Mix the frothy yeast and additional liquid with the dry ingredients, following the recipe instructions. Fresh yeast mixtures should be allowed to rise twice: after the first rising, the mixture is 'knocked back' by kneading it quickly and fairly lightly, or by beating a softer mixture to knock out the bubbles. Then the dough or mixture is shaped or placed in a container and allowed to rise, or prove, until doubled in volume before baking. The longer process involved when using fresh yeast gives a good flavour and texture.

MUFFINS

MAKES 20

450 g (1 lb) strong white flour, plus extra for dredging

300 ml (½ pint) milk

5 ml (1 tsp) salt

1 sachet fast-action easy-blend dried yeast

lard or oil for cooking

Dredge a baking sheet or dish with an even layer of flour about 5 mm (¼ inch) thick. Heat the milk until hand hot.

Mix the measured flour, salt and yeast, then stir in the milk to make a soft dough. Knead the dough thoroughly on a well floured surface, keeping it moving to prevent it from sticking. When the dough is smooth and elastic, mark it into 20 portions. Using the marks as a guide, break off a piece of dough and knead it quickly into a round, flat cake. Place this on the floured baking sheet. Repeat with the remaining dough.

Cover the batch of muffins loosely with cling film or polythene and leave them in a warm place until doubled in size.

Heat a griddle or heavy-bottomed frying pan, then grease it lightly. Cook the muffins on both sides for about 8 minutes until golden. Transfer the cooked muffins to a wire rack to cool.

TO TOAST MUFFINS

Hold a muffin between your hands and use both thumbs to split the crust all around the edge, dividing the dough slightly without actually pulling the muffin apart. This ensures that the muffin will heat right through to the middle when toasted. Toast the muffin fairly slowly on both sides, until well browned. Pull the muffin open and butter it lightly on both sides, then put the halves back together again. Cut the muffin in half and serve at once.

COOK'S NOTES

The muffin man was once a familiar figure on British streets. In the words of the well-known nursery rhyme:

> 'Polly put the kettle on,
> Sally blow the bellows strong,
> Molly call the muffin man,
> We'll all have tea.'

It is difficult to interpret Mrs Beeton's original recipe exactly as she made a very soft muffin dough, starting with a quart of milk and then mixing in the yeast and flour. The soft muffins were broken off and set to rise on wooden trays coated with a 5 cm (2 inch) bed of flour

In her introduction to bread-making, Mrs Beeton commented that 'Hot rolls, swimming in melted butter, and new bread, ought to be carefully shunned by everybody who has the slightest respect for that much-injured individual – the stomach'. However, the thought of Mrs Beeton's breads, muffins and crumpets, freshly baked and served with lashings of butter is sufficient to send any enthusiastic cook racing to the kitchen with total disregard for the consequences, real or imaginary.

CRUMPETS

MAKES 10–12

200 g (7 oz) strong white flour

2.5 ml (½ tsp) salt

2.5 ml (½ tsp) sugar

1 sachet fast-action easy-blend
   dried yeast

100 ml (3½ fl oz) hand-hot milk

pinch of bicarbonate of soda

lard or oil for frying

Mix the flour, salt, sugar and yeast, then make a well in the middle. Add the milk and 125 ml (4 fl oz) hand-hot water, then gradually stir in the surrounding dry ingredients to make a thick batter. Beat this thoroughly until smooth and elastic.

Cover the bowl with cling film and leave it in a warm place for 45 minutes or until the batter has doubled in bulk.

Dissolve the bicarbonate of soda in 15 ml (1 tbsp) warm water and beat it into the batter. Heat a griddle or heavy-bottomed frying pan over medium heat, then grease it. Also grease metal crumpet rings, poaching rings or large plain biscuit cutters about 7.5 cm (3 inches) in diameter.

Place the rings on the hot griddle, pour some batter into each to cover the base thinly and cook until the top is set and the bubbles have burst. Remove the rings and turn the crumpets over. Cook the other side for just 2–3 minutes, until the batter is firm but barely coloured. Cool the crumpets on a wire rack.

To serve the crumpets, toast them under a hot grill, starting with the browned side, then toasting the pale, bubbly side. Spread the bubbly side of each crumpet with butter, cut the crumpet in half and serve it at once.

COOK'S NOTES

CRUMPETS AND PIKELETS

What someone living in the south of England or Wales would call a crumpet would be a pikelet in Scotland or on the tea tables in the north of England. Meanwhile, a Welsh pikelet would be a drop scone to a southerner. To add to the confusion, a Scotch crumpet is another name for a Scotch pancake – or drop scone.

The most difficult thing about making crumpets is the fact that the batter is so elastic that it tends to trickle beyond the boundaries within which you try to keep it.

The hob usually needs a thorough scrub after a crumpet-making session

The plus points far outweigh the mess though, as home-made crumpets are moist, crisp, hot and yeasty compared to their flavourless, commercial distant cousins.

Home-made crumpets are excellent freezer candidates, keeping successfully for months – indeed, from one winter right through to the next – but a very large batch indeed would have to be cooked if any are to make it into cold storage!

RICE BREAD

100 g (4 oz) long-grain rice

450 ml (¾ pint) milk

450 g (1 lb) strong plain flour

10 ml (2 tsp) salt

2.5 ml (½ tsp) sugar

1 sachet fast-action easy-blend
    dried yeast

beaten egg to glaze

Place the rice in a saucepan of water, bring to the boil, then drain the rice and put it back in the pan. Add the milk. Bring to the boil, stirring occasionally, then reduce the heat and partially cover the pan. Simmer the rice for 15 minutes.

Grease a baking sheet. Mix the flour, salt, sugar and yeast in a bowl. Make a well in the middle and pour in the rice with the hot milk and 50 ml (2 fl oz) cold water. Mix in the flour using a cutting action – the cold water should cool the rice sufficiently to prevent it from killing the yeast.

Turn the dough out on a well-floured surface and knead until it is smooth and elastic, sprinkling a little flour over to prevent the dough from sticking. Shape the dough into two long oval loaves and place these on the baking sheet. Cover loosely with oiled polythene and leave in a warm place until the dough has risen well and spread into slightly flattened loaves.

Meanwhile, set the oven at 220°C (425°F/gas 7). Brush the risen loaves with beaten egg and bake them for 35–45 minutes, until well browned and firm. The loaves should sound hollow when tapped on the bottom. Cool on a wire rack.

COOK'S NOTES

When the recipe was included in the first edition of her work, Mrs Beeton did not comment upon it, despite stating at the beginning of the bread, biscuits and cakes chapter that 'Rice cannot be made into bread'.

The bread is unusual, with a close, slightly elastic, texture. Cut into thick slices and served warm, it is moist and delicious – the ideal accompaniment for buttery grilled mushrooms or a steaming hot bowl of soup.

Easy-cook varieties of rice are not suitable for this recipe. Use long-grain white rice or pudding rice.

TEACAKES

MAKES 8

450 g (1 lb) strong plain flour

2.5 ml (½ tsp) salt

100 g (4 oz) butter

1 sachet fast-action easy-blend
    dried yeast

100 g (4 oz) currants

25 g (1 oz) sugar

250 ml (8 fl oz) hand-hot milk, plus
    extra for glazing

Grease two baking sheets. Mix the flour and salt, then rub in the butter. Stir in the yeast, currants and sugar. Mix in the milk to make a pliable dough. Knead the dough on a well-floured work surface until it is springy and elastic.

Divide the dough into eight portions and shape each into a ball, then flatten or roll these into large teacakes. Place the teacakes on the baking sheets as they are shaped. Cover the teacakes loosely with cling film or polythene and leave them to rise in a warm place until doubled in size.

Meanwhile, set the oven at 220°C (425°F/gas 7). Brush the teacakes with a little milk and bake them for about 20 minutes. Cool them on a wire rack.

TOASTED TEACAKES

Slice the teacakes in half and toast each half on both sides, starting with the crust side. Butter the cut sides and sandwich the teacakes back together. Serve the toasted teacakes immediately.

COOK'S NOTES

In spite of her general advice that her readers should avoid eating newly baked breads at all costs, Mrs Beeton did admit that 'These cakes should be buttered and eaten hot as soon as they are baked; but when stale, they are very nice split and toasted'.

If you have an open fire, buy yourself a toasting fork and discover the wonderful flavour of toasted teacakes, quickly browned over hot coals, buttered as soon as they are ready and eaten promptly, without ceremony.

FLAVOURING TEACAKES

A little chopped candied peel and a good pinch of ground mixed spice are traditional flavourings for teacake dough. Chopped candied ginger is a contemporary but quite delicious addition, especially if the sugar is left out of the dough and the teacakes are served buttered and spread with a hint of honey.

YORKSHIRE TEACAKES

Yorkshire is the home of large flat teacakes, plain or fruited with currants and candied peel, and sometimes spiced. The teacakes are split, toasted, dotted with knobs of butter and quickly reassembled. The butter then melts evenly to coat the toasted surfaces.

Teacakes are said to have evolved from manchets, hand-shaped rolls made for the aristocracy in medieval times. The flour for the dough was sifted to remove the bran and make the rolls finer in texture.

A NICE YEAST CAKE

350 g (12 oz) strong plain flour

1 sachet fast-action easy-blend
    dried yeast

175 g (6 oz) currants

25 g (1 oz) chopped candied peel

100 g (4 oz) sugar

grated nutmeg (optional)

150 ml (¼ pint) milk

100 g (4 oz) butter

2 eggs, beaten

Base-line and grease a deep 18–20 cm (7–8 inch) round tin. Mix the flour, yeast, currants, candied peel and sugar. Add a little grated nutmeg (if liked). Make a well in the middle of the dry ingredients.

Heat the milk and butter together gently until the butter melts and the mixture is hand hot. Pour the milk mixture into the well in the dry ingredients and stir in some of the flour mixture. Then stir in the beaten eggs and gradually work in the rest of the dry mixture. Beat the mixture thoroughly for 1–2 minutes, so that it becomes quite smooth and elastic, then turn it into the tin. Cover the top loosely with polythene and leave the cake to rise in a warm place until it has domed above the top of the tin and doubled its original volume.

Set the oven at 200°C (400°F/gas 6). Bake the cake for 20 minutes. Cover loosely with foil and bake for 20–25 minutes more, until it is cooked through and is well browned on top. Insert a clean metal skewer into the middle of the cake to check if the centre is cooked. If the skewer comes out without any sticky mixture on it, the cake is cooked. If there are thick smears of mixture on the skewer, cook for a further 5–10 minutes before checking the cake again.

Turn the cake out on to a wire rack and leave it to cool completely. It will keep well for up to 2 weeks in an airtight container in a cool place.

COOK'S NOTES

This is indeed a very 'nice' cake, with a good texture and excellent flavour. It is not unlike Italian panettone or the many Eastern European cakes that are baked for Christmas or Easter. Whereas Continental recipes are strongly flavoured with vanilla, Mrs Beeton relied on fruit, with a little nutmeg in her recipe.

Yeast was commonly used as a raising agent in Mrs Beeton's day. The yeast liquid was fermented at home from hops and malt, then stored in ginger-beer bottles. The brewed liquid was mixed with mashed potatoes and flour, then proved before being used to ferment the flour dough.

The other popular raising agent was bicarbonate of soda, combined with tartaric acid or cream of tartar. Baking powder was listed in one or two of the first-edition recipes.

Self-raising flour is a comparatively modern ingredient. It was not introduced until 1910 and it was another decade before it was widely available. By the sixties self-raising flour was used for the majority of cake-making and it remains an exremely popular ingredient today.

IRISH SODA BREAD

575 g (1¼ lb) plain flour

5 ml (1 tsp) bicarbonate of soda

5 ml (1 tsp) salt

5 ml (1 tsp) cream of tartar

300 ml (½ pint) milk

Lightly grease a baking sheet. Set the oven at 190°C (375°F/gas 5). Mix all the dry ingredients, then make a well in the centre. Add the milk and mix it in lightly and quickly.

On a lightly floured surface, flatten the dough into a round loaf about 2.5 cm (1 inch) thick. Turn the loaf on to the prepared baking sheet and cut a large cross in the surface with a floured knife so that it will heat through evenly.

Bake the soda bread for 40 minutes. Pierce the centre with a thin skewer to check that it is cooked through – the skewer should come out clean. Wrap the loaf in a clean tea-towel to keep it soft until required.

COOK'S NOTES

Buttermilk or sour milk can be used and since both of these are acidic, the cream of tartar can be reduced or left out completely.

WHOLEMEAL AND GRAINY SODA BREAD
Wholemeal or Granary flour can be used instead of plain; a good mixture can be prepared by using half wholemeal and half white flour with a generous sprinkling of mixed seeds, such as sesame, basil seeds (if available), cumin or caraway and poppy seeds. These give the soda bread a superb flavour and pleasing, crunchy texture.

FREEZING SODA BREAD
Soda bread should be eaten on the day it is baked as it rapidly becomes somewhat dry and stale. Freezing the bread avoids this problem, so it is worthwhile wrapping any leftovers in cling film and packing them in polythene to be frozen for another occasion.

PLAIN BUNS

MAKES 12

450 g (1 lb) plain flour

2.5 ml (½ tsp) bicarbonate of soda

2.5 ml (½ tsp) cream of tartar

50 g (2 oz) butter

50 g (2 oz) sugar

100 g (4 oz) currants

5 ml (1 tsp) caraway seeds (optional)

1 egg

300 ml (½ pint) milk

Set the oven at 200°C (400°F/gas 6). Grease two baking sheets. Sift the flour, bicarbonate of soda and cream of tartar together. Rub the butter into the flour mixture, then stir in the sugar, currants and caraway seeds (if used).

Make a well in the middle of the dry ingredients. Beat the egg with the milk and pour the mixture into the middle of the ingredients. Gradually mix the dry ingredients into the liquid and stir until evenly combined.

Use a fork or spoon and fork to shape the mixture into buns on the prepared baking sheets. Bake the plain buns for about 20–25 minutes, until they are risen and lightly browned. Cool the buns on a wire rack.

COOK'S NOTES

These buns are a type of rock cake and the mixture can be baked in paper cake cases supported in patty tins, if preferred. The buns should be eaten on the day they are baked as they quickly become stale. However, once cooled, they freeze well.

Mrs Beeton entitled her recipe 'Light Buns' and she used it as a basic mixture for small and large cakes. She noted that, 'This mixture makes a very good cake, and if put in a tin should be baked 1½ hour. The same quantity of flour, soda and tartaric acid, with ½ pint of milk and a little salt, will make either bread or teacakes, if wanted quickly'.

CAKES FOR SHARING

These versatile little cakes would have been ideal for all manner of ancient festivities. For example, they were ideal for picnics. In old England, Whitsun was a holiday and an occasion for feasting, when parishioners would gather for a Whitsuntide supper, taking along whatever they could to make up a sort of picnic, usually held in a barn or hall. Ale was an important feature, so much so that the suppers became rather rowdy and the idea of Whitsun-ale was gradually dropped.

New Year Greetings and November Soul Cakes

Giving cakes at the door is a tradition that has survived to recent generations. In Welsh villages, on New Year's day, pennies or cake were handed out to well-wishers calling before noon. In Lancashire, on November 1st, All Saint's Day, spiced cakes were marked with a cross and baked as Soul Cakes. These were given out to visitors on All Soul's Day, November 2nd, and children would knock on doors asking for 'A soul, soul, a soul cake'.

St Clement's Cakes

St Clement was the patron saint of blacksmiths and on November 23rd they set their bellows aside to celebrate the saint's day. Spiced St Clement's cakes or tarts were baked, the tarts with a lemon or orange filling, and children went 'clementing', asking for cakes or apples. The day was also known as Bite Apple Day, as the apples were as popular with children as St Clement's cakes.

SPONGE CAKE

MAKES A

23 CM (9 INCH) CAKE

175 g (6 oz) sugar

3 eggs

grated rind of 1 lemon

175 g (6 oz) plain flour

Set the oven at 160°C (325°F/gas 3). Base-line a 23 cm (9 inch) round deep cake tin. Grease the base but not the sides of the tin.

Heat the sugar and 75 ml (3 fl oz) water gently, stirring continuously until the sugar dissolves. Stop stirring and bring the syrup to the boil. Boil the syrup hard for 2 minutes; set it aside to cool slightly for about 2 minutes. Use an electric beater to beat the eggs. Pour the syrup into the eggs in a thin steady stream, beating hard until it has all been incorporated. Continue beating until the mixture is pale and thick, then beat in the lemon rind.

Fold in the flour. Turn the mixture into the prepared tin. Bake the cake for about 1 hour, until it has risen well and is golden brown and springy to the touch. Leave the cake in the tin for 2 minutes, then turn it out on to a wire rack and remove the lining paper. Leave the cake to cool completely.

COOK'S NOTES

This makes a splendid sponge cake with a fine, moist texture. Do not line the sides of the tin as the light mixture needs to adhere lightly to the tin as it rises and sets.

The cooled sponge can be sliced into two or three layers and sandwiched together with jam or a sweet preserve, such as lemon curd. Fill with whipped cream as well as jam, if you like. Sift a little caster or icing sugar over the top of the cake.

SPONGE FOR DESSERT

This plain sponge makes the perfect base for trifles and charlottes. It can also be transformed into a luscious gâteau, with fresh fruit and lightly sweetened whipped cream sandwiched between the layers. A filling of coffee or chocolate cream also goes well with plain cake.

VICTORIA SANDWICHES

MAKES 27

4 eggs

about 225 g (8 oz) each of butter,
caster sugar and self-raising flour
(see method)

about 375 g (12 oz) jam or
marmalade

Set the oven at 160°C (325°F/gas 3). Base line and grease two 23 cm (9 inch) square sandwich cake tins. Weigh the eggs in the shell and measure out an equal weight of butter, caster sugar and self-raising flour.

Cream the butter with the caster sugar until pale and soft. Beat in the eggs, adding a little of the flour to prevent the mixture from curdling. Fold in the rest of the flour, then divide the mixture equally between the prepared tins and spread it out evenly.

Bake the cakes for 25–30 minutes, until risen, golden and springy to the touch. Turn the cakes out on to wire racks and remove the lining papers, then invert the cakes and leave them to cool completely.

Warm the jam slightly and spread a layer over one cake. Place the other cake on top. Press the layers together lightly, then cut the cake into three strips. Cut the strips into fingers, each measuring about 2.5 cm (1 inch) wide and 7.5 cm (3 inches) long. Serve the Victoria sandwiches piled in a criss-cross pattern on a glass dish.

COOK'S NOTES

The Victoria sandwich was originally baked in a large Yorkshire pudding tin, then layered and cut into fingers.

The cake evolved into the round, light, perfectly level butter sponge. The perfect Victoria sandwich should have a smooth golden crust lightly dusted with caster sugar. Neither a blister nor a white speckling of sugar spots should blemish the surface, and peaks or hollows are definitely undesirable. Layered with a full-flavoured fruity,

home-made raspberry jam, this really is an extremely good cake. It is tempting to cut the cake into two strips rather than three, but this would result in rather large portions – perfect for a hungry teenager but hardly elegant enough for Aunt Agatha.

The quantities given in the main recipe can be baked in two 20 cm (8 inch) round sandwich cake tins. Sandwich the layers together with jam or marmalade.

QUEEN CAKES

100 g (4 oz) butter

100 g (4 oz) caster sugar

225 g (8 oz) self-raising flour

225 g (8 oz) currants

2 eggs

150 ml (¼ pint) single cream

1.25 ml (¼ tsp) natural almond
essence

COOK'S NOTES

These are good, everyday cakes. They keep well in an
airtight container for 4–5 days or they may be frozen. The
almond essence can be left out, if preferred, as it does
rather dominate the flavour of the cakes. The grated rind
of I lemon or orange can be added to vary the mixture,
and raisins or sultanas can be used instead of currants.

Set the oven at 200°C (400°F/gas 6). Grease 24 patty tins or stand paper cake cases
in them.

Cream the butter and sugar together until pale and soft. Sift the flour over the
creamed mixture, then sprinkle the currants on top. Beat the eggs with the cream
and almond essence. Pour this over the other ingredients and stir until thoroughly
combined.

Fill the patty tins or paper cases, allowing room for the mixture to rise. Bake the
cakes for 15–20 minutes, or until they have risen and browned, and are springy to
the touch. Cool the cakes on a wire rack.

GOOD HOLIDAY CAKE

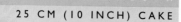
75 g (3 oz) butter

50 g (2 oz) lard

450 g (1 lb) self-raising flour

225 g (8 oz) currants

100 g (4 oz) raisins

50 g (2 oz) chopped candied peel

100 g (4 oz) soft light brown sugar

2 eggs

250 ml (8 fl oz) milk

Set the oven at 160°C (325°F/gas 3). Line and grease an 18 cm (7 inch) round deep cake tin.

Rub the butter and lard into the flour, then stir in the currants, raisins, candied peel and sugar. Make a well in the middle of the dry ingredients. Beat the eggs with the milk, pour the mixture into the dry ingredients and gradually stir until thoroughly combined.

Turn the mixture into the prepared tin and smooth the top. Bake the cake for about 1½ hours, until it has risen and browned and is cooked through. Insert a clean metal skewer into the middle of the cake to check if the centre is cooked. If the skewer comes out without any sticky mixture on it, the cake is cooked. If there are thick smears of mixture on the skewer, cook the cake for a further 5–10 minutes before checking it again.

If necessary, cover the top of the cake loosely with foil to prevent it from overbrowning during cooking. Turn the cake out on to a wire rack. Remove the lining paper, then leave it to cool completely. Once cold, store the cake in an airtight container. It tastes best when allowed to mature for 2–3 days, and it will keep for 2 weeks in a cool place.

COOK'S NOTES

The idea of a holiday cake sounds particularly appealing in today's busy world, where we may not have regular baking sessions, but might enjoy spending the occasional Saturday morning beating up a cake. Making a cake for bank holiday weekends, half term or family holidays is an excellent idea. This no-nonsense recipe is easy to prepare and tastes so good that it will probably become as important a feature of holidays at home as a passport is for excursions abroad!

Equally, the cake may well prove so popular that holidays will be held to be far too infrequent for it to be limited to them. You could easily end up making it every weekend.

midbaking

VERY GOOD SEED CAKE

MAKES A
20 CM (8 INCH) CAKE

225 g (8 oz) butter

175 g (6 oz) caster sugar

3 eggs

225 g (8 oz) self-raising flour

2.5 ml (½ tsp) ground mace

5 ml (1 tsp) grated nutmeg

15 ml (1 tbsp) caraway seeds

45 ml (3 tbsp) brandy

Line and grease a 20 cm (8 inch) round deep cake tin. Set the oven at 160°C (325°F/gas 3).

Cream the butter with the sugar until pale and soft. Beat in the eggs, one at a time, adding a little of the flour to prevent the mixture from curdling. Fold in the remaining flour, adding the mace, nutmeg and caraway seeds at the same time. Finally, fold in the brandy.

Turn the mixture into the tin and smooth the top. Bake the cake for about 1½ hours, until it has risen, browned lightly and is cooked through. Insert a clean metal skewer into the middle of the cake to check if the centre is cooked. If the skewer comes out without any sticky mixture on it, the cake is cooked. If there are thick smears of mixture on the skewer, cook the cake for a further 5–10 minutes before checking it again.

If necessary, cover the top of the seed cake loosely with foil to prevent it from overbrowning during cooking. Turn the cake out on to a wire rack and remove the lining paper, then leave it to cool completely. Once cold, store the seed cake in an airtight container.

COOK'S NOTES

Mrs Beeton was absolutely right in her choice of title for this delectable cake. Mace and nutmeg contribute a warm, full flavour which perfectly balances the somewhat refreshing flavour of caraway seeds. The brandy also enriches the mixture.

If you have previously sampled dry-textured seed cake, dominated by caraway, with little depth of flavour, bake this recipe to discover how the spicy seeds can be used to great effect. Even if you really do not like the taste of caraway seeds, the cake is worth making with mace and nutmeg alone.

SIMPLE BAKING FOR COUNTRY FESTIVALS
Seed cake was traditionally baked to celebrate the end of the spring wheat sowing season. There are many different recipes as this was a popular cake, both among country folk and the ladies who took tea in their elegant drawing rooms.

Similar cakes made for hungry farm workers included shearing cake and harvest cake, along with a variety of light fruit cakes that were ideal for carrying out to the fields in chunky baskets.

THICK GINGERBREAD

350 g (12 oz) black treacle

75 g (3 oz) butter

450 g (1 lb) plain flour

75 g (3 oz) demerara sugar

45 ml (3 tbsp) ground ginger

15 ml (1 tbsp) ground allspice

50 ml (2 fl oz) milk

3.75 ml (¾ tsp) bicarbonate of soda

2 eggs, beaten

Set the oven at 160°C (325°F/gas 3). Line and a grease a 20 cm (8 inch) square deep cake tin.

Heat the treacle and butter together gently, stirring occasionally, until they have melted and combined. Mix the flour, sugar, ginger and allspice, then make a well in the middle of these dry ingredients.

Pour the treacle and butter into the middle of the dry ingredients, then warm the milk in the pan. Take the pan off the heat and stir in the bicarbonate of soda, then pour this mixture on to the treacle and butter. Stir the liquids together, add the beaten eggs, then gradually mix in the dry ingredients to form a thick batter. Beat the batter until it is smooth.

Turn the batter into the tin and bake the gingerbread for 1 hour 20 minutes, or until it has risen and browned and is springy to the touch. Leave the gingerbread to set in the tin for 15 minutes, then turn it out on to a wire rack to cool.

COOK'S NOTES

This is a strongly flavoured, dark gingerbread which will be appreciated by connoisseurs of the speciality. For a lighter version, replace a third of the black treacle with an equal quantity of golden syrup. The amount of allspice can be reduced to 10 ml (2 tsp) for a less intense flavour.

Gingerbread is one of those cakes which improves with keeping. It should be allowed to mature for 2–3 days (at least) before being eaten and will keep in an airtight container in a cool place for up to a month. Gingerbread should be served sliced and can be spread with butter.

LIGHT GINGERBREADS

225 g (8 oz) butter

450 g (1 lb) plain flour

225 g (8 oz) caster sugar

35 ml (7 tsp) ground ginger

15 ml (1 tbsp) grated nutmeg

grated rind of 1 lemon

150 ml (¼ pint) milk

2.5 ml (½ tsp) bicarbonate of soda

Set the oven at 220°C (425°F/gas 7). Grease two baking sheets. Rub the butter into the flour, then stir in the sugar, ginger, nutmeg and lemon rind.

Warm the milk until it is just lukewarm, then stir in the bicarbonate of soda and stir this liquid into the mixture. Stir to make a dough; knead very lightly on a floured surface until just smooth.

Roll out the dough to about 1 cm (½ inch) thick and use a 5 cm (2 inch) round cutter to stamp out circles. Place the circles of dough on the baking sheets and bake them for about 15 minutes, or until risen, browned and cooked.

Cool the gingerbreads on a wire rack. Serve the gingerbreads plain, or split them horizontally and spread them with butter.

COOK'S NOTES

These were a fascinating discovery – they resemble light, sweet, slightly crisp scones with a mild yet distinctive gingerbread flavour.

The gingerbreads soften and mature in flavour if stored for a couple of days in an airtight container. They are extremely good split and buttered, especially when fresh, but perfectly tasty eaten entirely plain, as a sort of cross between a biscuit and a scone.

Do set them well apart on the baking sheets, as the mixture flattens, cracks and spreads as it cooks.

SCOTCH SHORTBREAD

225 g (8 oz) butter

50 g (2 oz) caster sugar

450 g (1 lb) plain flour

15 ml (1 tbsp) caraway seeds

25 g (1 oz) blanched almonds,
  chopped

100 g (4 oz) candied orange peel,
  finely chopped

Set the oven at 160°C (325°F/gas 3). Cut three pieces of non-stick baking parchment large enough to line three baking sheets. Warm the butter in a bowl over hot water (or on a plate in the microwave) until it is very soft, but not oily. Add the caster sugar and beat the mixture to a pale, very soft cream. Gradually stir in the flour, caraway seeds and almonds. Use your hands to bring the mixture together and knead it into a dough.

Cut the dough into three equal portions. Press one portion together into a smooth ball. Working on a piece of non-stick baking parchment, flatten the dough into a rough square shape, then continue to flatten it until it is about 2.5 cm (1 inch) thick, or slightly less. Lift the dough, on the paper, on to a baking sheet. Pinch the edges neatly and prick the dough all over. Cut the shortbread diagonally into four triangles, but do not separate them. Press a third of the candied orange peel into the top of the biscuits. Shape the remaining pieces in the same way, then chill the shortbread for at least 15 minutes.

Bake the shortbread for about 50 minutes, until pale golden and cooked. Run a knife along the cuts while the shortbread is still warm and soft, then leave the pieces on the baking sheets for a few minutes to firm up. As soon as it is firm enough, transfer the shortbread to a wire rack to cool.

COOK'S NOTES

In her recipe, Mrs Beeton did not cut the shortbread into triangles. She used double the quantities suggested above, and made six large biscuits, each 2.5 cm (1 inch) thick. These were pricked, then baked. It appears to have been left to the good sense of the cook as to whether the dough was cut up before being baked or the biscuits randomly broken before being eaten.

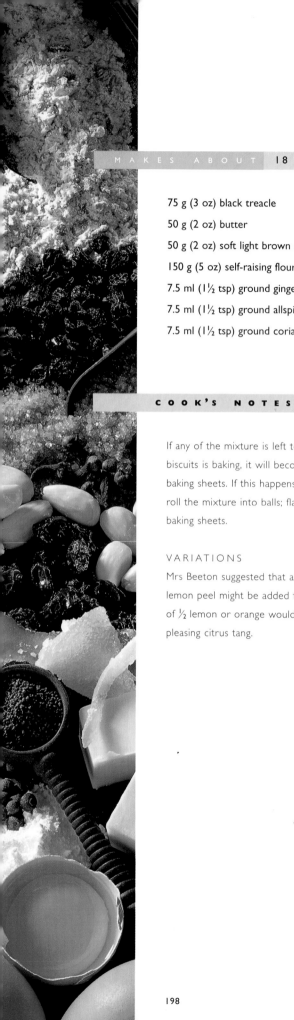

SUNDERLAND
GINGERBREAD NUTS

75 g (3 oz) black treacle

50 g (2 oz) butter

50 g (2 oz) soft light brown sugar

150 g (5 oz) self-raising flour

7.5 ml (1½ tsp) ground ginger

7.5 ml (1½ tsp) ground allspice

7.5 ml (1½ tsp) ground coriander

Set the oven at 160°C (325°F/gas 3). Line several baking sheets with non-stick baking parchment.

Melt the treacle with the butter and sugar until thoroughly combined. Sift the flour, ginger, allspice and coriander together, then stir in the melted mixture to make a smooth paste.

Drop spoonfuls of the mixture well apart on the prepared baking sheets, allowing plenty of room for spreading. Bake the biscuits for about 15 minutes, until they are set and very lightly browned. Leave them to cool on the baking sheets until they begin to firm up, then transfer them to a wire rack to cool completely.

COOK'S NOTES

If any of the mixture is left to stand while a batch of biscuits is baking, it will become too firm to drop on to the baking sheets. If this happens, simply wet your hands and roll the mixture into balls; flatten them thinly on to the baking sheets.

VARIATIONS

Mrs Beeton suggested that a little finely chopped candied lemon peel might be added to the mixture; the grated rind of ½ lemon or orange would also give the biscuits a pleasing citrus tang.

Another comment from the original recipe was that some culinary authorities liked to add a little cayenne pepper to the mixture. Mrs Beeton left the decision to her readers but there is scant merit in the suggestion as the mixture is already extremely well spiced; introducing even a hint of chilli heat would detract attention from the true flavour, in which black treacle dominates. If preferred, the amount of treacle could be reduced to 25 g (1 oz) and 50 g (2 oz) golden syrup added. The biscuits keep well in an airtight tin or jar for several weeks, becoming characteristically hard and crunchy.

MACAROONS

2 egg whites

100 g (4 oz) caster sugar

100 g (4 oz) ground almonds

5 ml (1 tsp) orange flower water or
    rose water

about 10 blanched almonds, split

rice paper

Set the oven at 160°C (325°F/gas 3). Cover two or three baking sheets with rice paper. Whisk the egg whites until they stand in stiff peaks, then whisk in the sugar and continue whisking until the mixture is very glossy. Stir in the ground almonds and orange flower water or rose water.

Spoon the mixture into a piping back fitted with a large plain nozzle. Pipe smooth rounds of the mixture well apart on the rice paper and top each one with a piece of split almond.

Bake the macaroons for 15–20 minutes, until they are set and pale golden brown. Leave the macaroons on the baking sheets for a few minutes, so that they become firm, then transfer them to a wire rack to cool. Trim off the excess rice paper from around the edge of each macaroon.

COOK'S NOTES

These biscuits are very difficult to resist. From the almond topping to the soft, slightly chewy centres, they are so delicious that one is never enough.

RATAFIAS
The same basic mixture is used to make ratafias. Mrs Beeton added bitter almonds, but a little natural almond essence or oil of bitter almonds can be used instead. Ratafias should be piped on to non-stick baking parchment or a reliably non-stick baking sheet to avoid the need for a rice-paper base. Use a piping bag and pipe the mixture so the biscuits are the size of small buttons. Do not add an almond to the top. Bake ratafias for about 10 minutes then cool on wire racks.

PRESERVES

BENTON SAUCE

30 ml (2 tbsp) freshly grated
    horseradish

10 ml (2 tsp) prepared mustard

10 ml (2 tsp) caster sugar

125 ml (4 fl oz) malt vinegar

The horseradish should be finely grated. Mix it with the other ingredients, stirring until the sugar has dissolved completely. Serve the sauce with hot or cold roast beef.

COOK'S NOTES

This is a piquant, spicy sauce which can be used to season any savoury dish which needs a lift without the complicated flavours of a highly spiced chutney or fruit sauce.

   The result can be refined by using a different type of vinegar; malt vinegar would probably have been used in the Victorian kitchen, but the flavour is harsh and quite crude. For a lighter flavour, try cider vinegar. Balsamic vinegar greatly improves the sauce, making it richer and deeper in flavour.

   If you grow your own horseradish, make a large jar of this sauce as it will keep well.

PREPARING HORSERADISH

Preparing fresh horseradish can be quite a painful process, causing the eyes to stream and any cuts or nicks in the fingers to sting. Wear rubber gloves to avoid getting any juices under your nails and scrub the root thoroughly in a bowl of water. Having done this, rinse the root, then peel it under cold running water. If you have a food processor, use it to chop the horseradish finely – it will be much kinder to your eyes than grating it by hand.

HORSERADISH SAUCE

60 ml (4 tbsp) grated horseradish

5 ml (1 tsp) caster sugar

5 ml (1 tsp) salt

2.5 ml (½ tsp) pepper

10 ml (2 tsp) prepared mustard

30 ml (2 tbsp) vinegar

60 ml (4 tbsp) single or double cream

Mix the horseradish, sugar, salt, pepper and mustard in a heatproof basin. Stir in the vinegar and cream. If the sauce is to be served with hot roast beef, warm it through by standing the bowl over a saucepan of hot water. Do not allow the water to boil or the sauce will curdle.

If the sauce is to be served with cold meat or another cold dish, there is no need to warm it.

COOK'S NOTES

Mrs Beeton strongly favoured serving a warm horseradish sauce with roast beef. 'This sauce is a great improvement on the old-fashioned way of serving cold-scraped horseradish with hot roast beef. The mixing of the cold vinegar with the warm gravy cools and spoils everything on the plate.'

In the original recipe, the quantity of vinegar was left to the discretion of the reader, with the instruction to add enough for the sauce to have the consistency of cream. This is difficult to interpret, but the above amount is sufficient to moisten the mixture. The cream was optional, but it does enrich the sauce, particularly when double cream is used.

Again, the choice of vinegar greatly affects the flavour and acidity of the sauce. Malt vinegar really makes it quite harsh; cider vinegar gives a mild result; and wine vinegars vary in their acidity.

PROPERTIES OF HORSERADISH

Like many condiments, herbs and spices, horseradish was put to medicinal use long before it graduated to the kitchen. Being a strong diuretic, horseradish was used by ancient herbalists to treat water-retentive conditions, such as dropsy, and it was also used as an antiseptic. Horseradish was used instead of mustard to make a poultice and the grated root was applied to chilblains. The very thought of horseradish being applied to any area of tender skin brings tears to the eyes – presumably the pain inflicted by the application was so great that the previous suffering was comparatively minor.

Among its other uses, the root was given as a cure for coughs and recommended as a dose for children who had worms. Infused with wine, horseradish was used as a stimulant; infused with milk it was an ingredient for certain skin preparations.

CHRISTOPHER NORTH'S SAUCE

175 ml (6 fl oz) port

30 ml (2 tbsp) Worcestershire sauce

10 ml (2 tsp) mushroom ketchup

10 ml (2 tsp) caster sugar

15 ml (1 tbsp) lemon juice

1.25 ml (¼ tsp) cayenne pepper

2.5 ml (¼ tsp) salt

Mix all the ingredients in the top of a double saucepan or a heatproof bowl set over simmering water. Heat gently, without boiling, then serve.

Alternatively, pour the sauce into an airtight jar or bottle and store it in a cool place. It will keep indefinitely.

COOK'S NOTES

This sauce is a type of potent, runny relish. It is an extremely good condiment for grilled steak or other meats but its real value in today's cooking is as an ingredient for enriching sauces and gravies. It also makes an excellent addition to a small quantity of wine, stock or water used for deglazing a pan after frying game or meat, either in the first stages of cooking, as when making a casserole, or to complement pan-fried meats. Keep a bottle alongside your favourite seasonings and you will find yourself adding a dash of the sauce to all sorts of dishes, from a simple cottage pie to a salad dressing for roasted peppers!

WALNUT KETCHUP

MAKES ABOUT
1.75 LITRES (3 PINTS)

100 tender green walnuts

handful of salt

1.1 litres (2 pints) vinegar

10 g (¼ oz) each of whole mace,
cloves and black peppercorns

10 g (¼ oz) each of ground nutmeg
and ginger

small piece of horseradish, finely
grated

20 shallots, peeled and finely chopped

2 × 50 g (2 oz) cans anchovy fillets,
drained and finely chopped

600 ml (1 pint) port

Layer the green walnuts in a large bowl, glazed earthenware jar or glass container, bruising them slightly and sprinkling them with the salt. Pour in the vinegar, cover the container and leave the nuts in a cool place for 8 days, stirring them daily and crushing them to release their flavour.

Tie the whole spices in a piece of thin muslin. Strain all the liquor from the nuts through muslin and boil it with the bag of spices and remaining ingredients for 30 minutes. Remove the whole spices and pour the ketchup into sterilized clean bottles. Cover with airtight lids.

COOK'S NOTES

The walnuts must be picked before their shells have formed, towards the end of June and beginning of July. Check the tree frequently as the period between the formation of the fruit and the hardening of the shells is short; test the nuts by piercing them with a needle. The whole spices do not have to be tied in muslin before boiling if the cooked ketchup is strained.

MRS BEETON'S ALTERNATIVE RECIPE
For this 'half a sieve' of green walnut shells were soaked for 10 days in 1.1 litres (2 pints) water and 'a large quantity of salt'. The strained brine was boiled with 225 g (8 oz) shallots, 25 g (1 oz) garlic and 25 g (1 oz) each of

mace, cloves and peppercorns until the shallots sank. The cold bottled ketchup was allowed to mature for 6 months before use, during which time it was boiled again if it began to ferment.

STORING SAUCES
Store sauces in a cool, dry place out of direct sunlight. Mrs Beeton had strong views when it came to labelling sauces clearly and storing them systematically: 'Nothing shows more, perhaps, the difference between a tidy thrifty housewife and a lady to whom these desirable epithets may not honestly be applied, than the appearance of their respective store-closets'.

PICKLED ONIONS

MAKES ABOUT

1.4 KG (3 LB)

1.4 kg (3 lb) pickling onions

675 g (1½ lb) salt, plus extra for

  blanching

2.25 litres (4 pints) distilled white

  vinegar

25 g (1 oz) fresh root ginger

2 dried red chillies

25 g (1 oz) whole allspice

25 g (1 oz) black peppercorns

1 small nutmeg

8 cloves

2 blades of mace

milk (see method)

olive oil (see method)

The onions should be whole, with the peel, but rinsed free of dirt or loose pieces of skin, root and stalk.

Dissolve a third of the salt in 2 litres (3½ pints) water in a large bowl. Add the onions, turning them in the brine, then lay a plate on top to keep the onions submerged. Cover the bowl and leave the onions to soak for 24 hours.

Meanwhile, heat the vinegar with all the spices. When the mixture is about to boil, take the pan off the heat and pour the vinegar into a bowl or large container. Cover the container and leave the spices to infuse in the vinegar until you are ready to use it again.

Drain the onions and rinse the bowl. Dissolve half of the remaining salt in 2 litres (3½ pints) water and soak the onions as before. After 24 hours, drain the onions and repeat the soaking process with the remaining salt.

At the end of the third soaking time, put a colander in the sink, ready to drain the onions. Place a thick layer of old towels on the work surface. A blanket or several thick towels should be ready for covering the onions.

Pour half the brine into a large saucepan. Add an equal quantity of milk and a further 30 ml (2 tbsp) salt. Drain the onions, discarding the remaining brine, and add them to the pan. Cook over moderate heat, stirring continuously with a slotted spoon to blanch the onions evenly, but taking care not to break them. Take the pan off the heat just before the liquid boils.

Drain the onions and turn them on to the thick layer of towels. Cover them quickly with towels and/or a blanket to keep in the steam and leave them to stand overnight.

Next day, the onions will be yellow and shrivelled. Peel them and place them in a saucepan. Add the vinegar and spices. Bring the liquid to the boil, then pour the mixture into a bowl and cover it closely. Leave to stand until next day, then pack the onions into sterilized jars.

Strain the vinegar and pour it into the jars to cover the onions. Float a layer of olive oil on top of each jar of pickles and cover with an airtight lid. Leave the onions to mature for 4–6 weeks before sampling them.

COOK'S NOTES

This is the original recipe for making pickled onions 'as white as snow'. Mrs Beeton finished by reminding her readers that the onions 'should be beautifully white, and eat crisp, without the least softness, and will keep good many months'.

Mrs Beeton also provided a quick recipe for onions which were simply peeled and pickled in spiced vinegar, without being salted or blanched. They were intended for use within 6–8 months, before they softened.

Onion skins contain a potent dye, so use old towels or cloths, or cover them with paper. The towels will need a very hot wash after use to get rid of the smell.

A PAIR OF
FLAVOURED VINEGARS

MAKES ABOUT
600 ML (1 PINT) OF EACH TYPE

1 head of garlic, separated into cloves,
    peeled and sliced

15 ml (1 tbsp) cayenne pepper

10 ml (2 tsp) soy sauce

10 ml (2 tsp) Walnut Ketchup (page
    205) or 1 pickled walnut, chopped

600 ml (1 pint) malt vinegar (see
    Cook's Notes)

CAMP VINEGAR

Mix all the ingredients in an airtight jar and leave them to infuse for a month. Strain the vinegar and store it in clean airtight bottles.

2 cucumbers or 5 ridge cucumbers,
    peeled and sliced

1 onion, sliced

7.5 ml (1½ tsp) salt

15 ml (1 tbsp) pepper

generous pinch of cayenne pepper

600–750 ml (1–1¼ pints) distilled
    white vinegar (see Cook's Notes)

CUCUMBER VINEGAR

Layer the cucumbers and onion with the salt, pepper and cayenne in a bowl. Pour in enough vinegar to cover. Cover the bowl and leave the mixture to stand for 4–5 days. Strain the vinegar and store it in clean, airtight bottles.

COOK'S NOTES

These vinegars are useful for flavouring salad dressings, marinades and sauces. Although malt vinegar was originally used for both recipes, it is extremely harsh and you may prefer to try any one of the many different types of vinegar available today, such as wine, sherry, balsamic or cider vinegar.

Camp vinegar is hot and fiery – great for barbecue sauces or marinades for spicy grills. The cucumber vinegar is also hot, but can be tamed if the cayenne pepper is left out. Without the cayenne, the vinegar is versatile for salad dressings to go with fish and seafood as well as poultry and vegetables.

RHUBARB AND ORANGE JAM

6 oranges

I lemon

900 g (2 lb) rhubarb, sliced

900 g (2 lb) sugar

Wash, dry and peel the oranges, removing all the pith. Discard half the orange peel; cut the rest into fine strips and place these in a large saucepan. Roughly chop all the orange flesh, discarding the pips, and add it to the peel.

Squeeze the lemon and add the juice to the pan. Finely chop the lemon shell, tie it in scalded muslin and add it to the pan with the rhubarb. Pour in 300 ml (½ pint) water and heat gently, stirring often, until the juice runs from the rhubarb.

Bring the mixture to the boil, lower the heat and simmer, covered, for about 1¼ hours, or until the orange peel is tender. Remove the muslin bag, squeezing the juice from it into the pan. Stir in the sugar and heat gently, stirring until it has dissolved completely.

Boil the jam rapidly until setting point is reached (see page 212). Remove from the heat, skim, pot, cover and label.

COOK'S NOTES

Lemon has been added to increase the pectin content as sweet oranges will not provide the best set. Mrs Beeton contended that this jam would 'resemble Scotch marmalade'. It is a shining example of the inventiveness of inspired British home cooks, who were always ready to improvise when exotic ingredients were unavailable or when money was short. It is also a good recipe for using a glut of rhubarb.

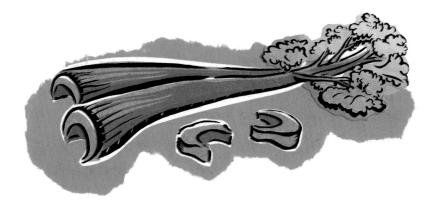

ORANGE MARMALADE

MAKES ABOUT
4 KG (9 LB)

1 kg (2¼ lb) Seville or bitter oranges

1 kg (2¼ lb) preserving sugar

Wash and thinly peel the oranges. Cut the peel into fine shreds. Halve the fruit and squeeze out the juice, reserving the pulp which remains and tying it in a piece of muslin with any pips.

Place the peel, juice and muslin bag of trimmings in a large saucepan. Add 2.25 litres (4 pints) water and bring the mixture to the boil. Reduce the heat, cover the pan and simmer the fruit for 2 hours, or until the rind is completely tender.

Remove the muslin bag of trimmings, allow it to cool until it can be handled, then squeeze all the juice from it back into the pan. Add the sugar and heat the mixture gently until it has dissolved, stirring often.

Bring the marmalade to a full boil and boil it fast until setting point is reached. Test for setting using a sugar thermometer or the saucer test (see page 212). Remove the pan from the heat and skim the marmalade.

Leave the marmalade to cool slightly, until a skin begins to form on the surface, then stir it well to distribute the shreds of peel. Pot the marmalade in warmed, sterilized pots and cover the surface of the preserve with waxed paper discs. Leave the marmalade until it is completely cold, then cover and label the pots.

COOK'S NOTES

Many people shy away from making marmalade because they believe it requires much experience and secret knowledge passed down through generations of cooks. This is, of course, nonsense and it is necessary only to remember two key points.

Firstly, don't be tempted to skimp on the cooking time for the fruit rind. It is absolutely essential that it is completely tender before any sugar is added.

The other point which it is easy to overlook when the preserve is cooked is the short standing time after skimming and before potting. Even if the marmalade looks as though there is not the slightest danger of the rind floating, let it stand because if you pot the preserve straight away, the rind will definitely rise to the surface, leaving a clear bottom and a shred-packed layer at the top.

STERILIZING JARS

It is a good idea to get into the habit of sterilizing jars for all types of preserves, even very acidic mixtures like pickles and flavoured vinegars, and it is particularly important for jams and marmalades. Use a sterilizing solution of the type recommended for washing baby-feeding equipment and follow the instructions on the bottle, which usually involve soaking the clean jars in a sink of water with the sterilizing solution added.

Do not dry them conventionally, but rinse the jars with very hot water (protecting your hands with rubber gloves), then stand them upside down on a folded tea-towel in a flat roasting tin. Stand them in a cool oven until you are ready to pot the preserve, by which time they will be dry, clean and hot.

EXCELLENT MINCEMEAT

MAKES ABOUT

4 KG (9 LB)

3 large cooking apples, cored

3 large lemons

450 g (1 lb) raisins

450 g (1 lb) currants

450 g (1 lb) suet

900 g (2 lb) soft light brown sugar

25 g (1 oz) candied orange peel,
    chopped

25 g (1 oz) candied citron or lemon
    peel, chopped

30 ml (2 tbsp) orange marmalade

250 ml (8 fl oz) brandy

Set the oven at 200°C (400°F/gas 6). Bake the apples in a covered ovenproof dish for 50–60 minutes, until they are thoroughly tender. Leave to cool.

Grate the lemon rind and squeeze out their juice. Set both rind and juice aside. Chop the lemon shells and simmer them, in just enough water to cover, for about 1 hour, or until the shells are soft enough to chop very finely. Drain, cool and chop the shells.

Scoop the apple flesh from the skins and mix it with the reserved lemon rind and juice, then stir in all the remaining ingredients, including the chopped lemon shells. Cover the bowl and leave the mincemeat to stand for 2 days, stirring it occasionally.

Press the mincemeat down well into sterilized pots and cover them with airtight lids. Label the mincemeat and allow it to mature for at least 2 months.

COOK'S NOTES

Adding cooked lemon shells to this mincemeat makes it refreshingly different as the tart flavour contrasts sharply with the dried fruit and sugar.

Mrs Beeton did not mention mincing the dried fruit – perhaps she took it for granted that everyone would automatically do so or perhaps she strayed from tradition and did not consider it essential in this particular recipe. Certainly, the succulence of the whole currants and raisins makes for wonderfully moist and juicy mince pies so perhaps this is a convention worth reinstating.

CARROT PRESERVE

MAKES ABOUT
1.4 KG (3 LB)

2 large lemons

900 g (2 lb) carrots, sliced

5 ml (1 tsp) oil of bitter almonds or
   natural almond essence

25 g (1 oz) blanched almonds,
   chopped

675 g (1½ lb) sugar

60 ml (4 tbsp) brandy

Wash, dry and grate the lemons. Squeeze out the juice and reserve with the rind. Finely chop the lemon shells and place them in a small saucepan with just enough water to cover. Bring the water to the boil, cover the pan tightly, lower the heat and simmer the lemons for about 1 hour or until the pulp is soft. Strain the cooking liquid through a fine sieve into a jug and set it aside.

Cook the carrots in boiling water until tender, then drain and mash them. Place the mashed carrots in a preserving pan. Add the grated lemon rind and juice, the strained cooking liquid, the almond oil or flavouring and the nuts. Add the sugar and heat the mixture gently, stirring all the time until all the sugar has dissolved.

Bring the preserve to the boil and boil it rapidly until setting point is reached. Remove from the heat and skim off any scum from the surface. Quickly stir in the brandy. Pot, cover and label the jam.

COOK'S NOTES

Mrs Beeton's carrot jam was intended to imitate apricot preserve. In this recipe, whole lemons have been added to improve the consistency of the jam. The result is surprisingly good and certainly not immediately identifiable as carrot preserve. In fact, carrots have featured in sweet preserves since Mrs Beeton's day, notably during the war years when imported fruit was not available.

TESTING FOR SETTING

The following are standard techniques for testing whether any sweet preserve has boiled long enough.

Temperature Test Use a sugar thermometer. The preserve should reach 105°C (220°F) when the concentration of sugar is right for setting.

Saucer Test Drop a little preserve on to a cold saucer and leave it for a few minutes. The preserve should form a distinct skin, which wrinkles when it is gently pushed with the fingertip. While you conduct the saucer test, take the pan off the heat or turn the heat off to prevent the preserve from overcooking.

A–Z OF BASIC RECIPES

APPLE SAUCE

Peel, core and slice 3 large cooking apples, placing them in a bowl of cold water to prevent them from turning brown. Drain the sliced apples and cook them with a sprinkling of water (just enough to prevent them from burning) until they are soft and pulpy. Beat until smooth, then stir in the butter and 50-75 g (2-3 oz) sugar, to taste. Transfer the sauce to a serving dish.

BASIC BREAD DOUGH

MAKES TWO LOAVES	

25 g (1 oz) butter or lard
450 g (1 lb) strong white flour
5 ml (1 tsp) salt

1 sachet fast-action, easy-blend
  dried yeast

Rub the butter or lard into the flour. Stir in the yeast and salt. Gradually mix in about 250 ml (8 fl oz) hand-hot water to make a firm dough. Use your hand to roll the mixture around the bowl to gather up any remaining dry ingredients. On a lightly floured surface, knead the dough thoroughly for about 10 minutes, or until it is smooth and elastic. The dough should spring back when depressed with a fingertip. Shape the dough as required and cover loosely with oiled polythene. Leave the dough to rise in a warm place until doubled in volume. Bake according to the recipe instructions.

Using Fresh Yeast *Notes on using fresh yeast are given on page 180.*

BÉCHAMEL SAUCE

MAKES ABOUT 600 ML (1 PINT)	

Marquis Louis de Béchameil is credited with inventing this French foundation sauce.

1 small onion, thickly sliced
1 small carrot, sliced
1 small celery stick, sliced
600 ml (1 pint) milk
1 bay leaf
a few parsley stalks
1 fresh thyme sprig

1 clove
6 white peppercorns
1 blade of mace
salt
40 g (1½ oz) butter
40 g (1½ oz) plain flour
60 ml (4 tbsp) single cream (optional)

Mix the onion, carrot, celery, milk, herbs and spices in a saucepan. Add salt to taste and heat until simmering. Take off the heat and allow to stand for 30 minutes, then strain into a jug.

Melt the butter. Stir in the flour and cook gently for 2-3 minutes. Gradually stir in the milk and bring to the boil, stirring continuously. Beat briskly for about 30 seconds to give the sauce a gloss. Stir in the cream, if used, and take the sauce off the heat at once. Do not allow the sauce to come to the boil again.

BEEF STOCK

This is a simple recipe which gives a reasonably good stock.

a little beef dripping or lard

1 kg (2¼ lb) shin of beef, stewing or braising beef, in one piece

2 large onions, sliced

2 large carrots

4 celery sticks

1 bouquet garni

1 blade of mace

12 black peppercorns

salt

Set the oven at 230°C (450°F/gas 8). Use the dripping or lard to lightly grease a heavy-bottomed, flameproof casserole which can be placed in the oven. Place the beef in the casserole and roast it, uncovered, for 20 minutes. Turn the meat over and continue roasting it for a further 20 minutes, by which time it should be well sealed and lightly browned outside.

Remove the meat from the casserole, add the onions, carrots and celery, then replace the meat on top. Pour 300 ml (½ pint) water over the vegetables around the meat. Place the casserole on the hob and bring the liquid to simmering point. Add the bouquet garni, mace and peppercorns, then cover the casserole tightly. Simmer the ingredients over very low heat for 15 minutes.

Pour 600 ml (1 pint) water into the casserole. Add salt to taste. Heat until simmering, cover and simmer gently for 30 minutes. Add 1.4 litres (2½ pints) extra water in two or three batches, simmering for 15 minutes between each addition. Each time water is added, the cooking juices from the pan should be stirred in. When all the water has been added, bring the water to simmering point and cover the pan tightly. Cook the stock over very low heat, so the liquid barely simmers, for about 4 hours.

When the meat is completely tender and the stock has a good flavour, remove the pan from the heat. Leave the meat to cool in the stock for 2-3 hours. Remove the meat and strain the stock. Skim any fat from the surface.

Note: The best stock is made with meat on the bone, including cuts such as knuckle of veal. For a rich, strong stock, Mrs Beeton used shin of beef, knuckle of veal, lean ham, poultry trimmings and vegetables. It may be difficult to locate veal on the bone – some good butchers will supply it, but small, local establishments simply do not have the demand for such cuts and few supermarkets sell it.

The stock can be left unsalted, allowing the seasoning to be added according to the requirements of the dish in which the stock is used; however, if the stock is salted, the cooked piece of beef will have more flavour and can be minced or finely chopped for making rissoles or similar dishes.

BREAD SAUCE

MAKES ABOUT 600 ML (1 PINT)

600 ml (1 pint) milk
1 large onion studded with 6 cloves
1 blade of mace
4 peppercorns
1 allspice berry
1 bay leaf

100 g (4 oz) fine fresh white
  breadcrumbs
15 g (½ oz) butter
salt and pepper
freshly grated nutmeg
30 ml (2 tbsp) single cream (optional)

Put the milk in a small saucepan with the studded onion, mace, peppercorns, allspice and bay leaf. Bring very slowly to boiling point, then remove from the heat, cover the pan and set it aside for 30 minutes.

Strain the flavoured milk into a heatproof bowl, pressing the onion against the sides of the strainer to extract as much of the liquid as possible. Stir in the breadcrumbs and butter, with salt, pepper and nutmeg to taste.

Set the bowl over simmering water and cook for about 20 minutes, stirring occasionally until thick and creamy. Stir in the cream, if using, when serving.

CHICKEN STOCK

Make as for White Stock, but leave out the veal and boil a small whole chicken (or 8 chicken drumsticks) instead, reducing the cooking time to 2 hours. The gammon can be omitted or bacon substituted. The meat from the chicken can be added to a well-flavoured Béchamel or mushroom sauce and used as a filling for a pie, savoury pancakes or a similar dish.

CLARIFIED BUTTER

Melt the butter in a small, clean saucepan: heat it gently (avoid letting it get too hot or it will brown) until it stops bubbling and a white sediment forms on the base of the pan. Gently pour the clear yellow butter into a jug, leaving the sediment behind. The last of the butter can be strained through fine muslin if necessary. Clarified butter will keep for several weeks in an airtight container in the refrigerator or it can be frozen for up to a year.

CROUTONS

Cut the crusts off medium-thick slices of bread and cut the bread into small squares. Fry these in a mixture of butter and olive oil, turning them frequently, until they are golden and crisp. Drain the croûtons on absorbent kitchen paper. Serve them as a garnish for soups and sauced dishes. They are also popular in salads.

CUSTARD SAUCE

MAKES ABOUT 500 ML (17 FL OZ)

This is a classic, thin custard.

500 ml (17 fl oz) milk
2.5 ml (½ tsp) natural vanilla essence
   to taste

6 egg yolks
25-50 g (1-2 oz) caster sugar

Warm the milk with the vanilla. In a heatproof bowl, beat the egg yolks with the sugar until creamy. Add the warm milk to the egg mixture. Stand the bowl over a pan of hot, not simmering, water and stir the custard for 20-30 minutes, until it thickens slightly to coat the back of the spoon. Take care not to let the water boil or overcook the custard or it will curdle. Serve hot or cold.

CUSTARD SAUCE, SIMPLE

MAKES ABOUT 750 ML (1¼ PINTS)

Cornflour stabilizes this custard, which is boiled. It is far thicker than a custard sauce made with yolks alone.

30 ml (2 tbsp) cornflour
30 ml (2 tbsp) caster sugar
600 ml (1 pint) milk

2.5 ml (½ tsp) natural vanilla essence
4 egg yolks

Mix the cornflour and sugar to a smooth paste with a little of the milk. Heat the rest of the milk, then stir it into the cornflour. Return the mixture to the pan, bring to the boil, lower the heat and simmer for 1-2 minutes, stirring all the time. Stir in the vanilla and egg yolks, then immediately take the pan off the heat. Taste the custard for sweetness and flavouring. Serve at once.

FISH STOCK

MAKES ABOUT 1 LITRE (1¾ PINTS)

Do not overcook fish stock or its flavour will be dull or even bitter.

25 g (1 oz) butter
1 onion, sliced
2 carrots, sliced
fish trimmings without gills or 350 g
   (12 oz) white fish fillet, in chunks

strip of pared lemon rind
1 bouquet garni
salt and pepper

Melt the butter in a large saucepan. Fry the onion, carrots and fish trimmings in the butter for 10 minutes. If using fish fillet, fry the vegetables for 5 minutes, then add the fillet and cook for a further 5 minutes.

Add the strip of lemon rind and the bouquet garni, with 1.1 litres (2 pints) water. Stir in a little salt and pepper and bring the stock to the boil. Reduce the heat, cover the pan and simmer the stock for 30 minutes. Strain the stock through a muslin-lined sieve or coffee filter paper.

FLAKY PASTRY

MAKES ABOUT 450 G (1 LB)

Flaky pastry does not have as many layers as puff pastry. It contains less fat to flour and the dough is rolled and folded fewer times.

225 g (8 oz) plain flour
pinch of salt
175 g (6 oz) butter or 75 g (3 oz) each
  butter and lard, chilled
5 ml (1 tsp) lemon juice
flour for rolling out

Sift the plain flour and salt into a bowl. If using butter and lard, mix them together. Rub in a quarter of the fat, keeping the remaining fat chilled. Stir in the lemon juice and enough cold water to mix the ingredients to a soft dough. The mixture should take about 125 ml (4 fl oz) water but this should be added by the spoonful to avoid making the dough too wet.

On a lightly floured surface, roll out the dough into a rectangle measuring about 25 x 15 cm (10 x 6 inches). Mark the dough into thirds. Cut the fat into three equal portions. Dot one portion of fat over the top two-thirds of the dough.

Fold the bottom third of the dough up over the middle portion, then fold the top third down so that the lumps of fat are enclosed completely. Press the edges of the dough together with the rolling pin. Give the dough a quarter turn in a clockwise direction, then roll out as before.

Repeat the process of dotting the dough with fat, folding and rolling it, twice more. Chill the dough briefly between each rolling. Finally, fold and roll the pastry once more, without any fat, then chill again before using it as required.

FLEURONS

These are small shapes cut from puff pastry. They should be brushed with beaten egg and baked at 220°C (425°F/gas 7) for about 10 minutes, until well puffed and golden. Cool on a wire rack. Serve as a garnish for soups and sauced dishes.

HAM STOCK

This is the cooking liquid from boiling a joint of bacon or ham; it is not usually prepared as a stock in its own right. Onions, carrots, a bay leaf, parsley sprigs and black peppercorns are usually added to flavour the cooking liquid. Celery and other vegetables, such as turnips, can be added.

The stock should be strained and excess fat skimmed off; further fat can be removed when the stock is chilled.

Ham stock can be quite salty, even with modern curing methods, so always taste it before use, and do not add seasoning unless required.

HOT WATER CRUST PASTRY

MAKES 350 G (12 OZ)

This pastry is used for pork, veal and ham, and raised game pies. It must be moulded while still warm.

200 g (7 oz) plain flour
2.5 ml (½ tsp) salt

75 g (3 oz) lard
100 ml (3½ fl oz) milk or water

Sift the flour and salt into a warm bowl and make a well in the centre. Keep the bowl in a warm place.

Meanwhile, heat the lard and milk or water until boiling. Add the hot mixture to the flour, mixing well with a wooden spoon. When the pastry comes together, knead it lightly into a smooth ball on a lightly floured surface. Take care not to burn your hands. Mould the pastry as required as soon as it begins to become firm enough to hold its shape. Work quickly; if it cools, it will become crumbly.

MELBA TOAST

This is thin, slightly curled toast. Toast medium-thick slices of white bread on both sides. As soon as the toast is cooked, trim off the crusts and cut each slice horizontally into two thin layers. Turn the thin slices untoasted side up and toast them under the grill, well away from the heat source, until lightly browned and slightly curled. The toast should be crisp. Cool on a wire rack and store in an airtight container. Serve with soups and pâtés.

MINT SAUCE

Mrs Beeton's recipe for mint sauce was simple and involved mixing finely chopped mint with `pounded' sugar, then stirring in vinegar until the sugar had dissolved completely. Mrs Beeton measured her mint and sugar in dessertspoons, but for modern cooks the proportions would be 60 ml (4 tbsp) chopped mint to 30 ml (2 tbsp) caster sugar (or more to taste), mixed with 150 ml (¼ pint) vinegar. It is easier to dissolve the sugar if it is first mixed with 45 ml (3 tbsp) freshly boiled water before the mint is added, and this also makes the sauce taste less harsh if malt vinegar is used. Wine vinegar or cider vinegar can be used, if preferred. Cider vinegar makes a mild sauce which is especially good with grilled lamb.

PUFF PASTRY

MAKES ABOUT 450 G (1 LB)

225 g (8 oz) plain flour
pinch of salt
225 g (8 oz) butter, chilled

5 ml (1 tsp) lemon juice
flour for rolling out

Sift the flour and salt into a bowl. Rub in 50 g (2 oz) of the butter. Add the lemon juice and enough cold water to mix the ingredients to a smooth, fairly soft dough. The mixture should take about 125 ml (4 fl oz) water but this must be added by the spoonful to avoid making the dough too wet. Wrap in cling film and chill briefly.

Shape the remaining butter into a rectangle measuring about 10 x 7.5 cm (4 x 3 inches), then chill again. On a lightly floured surface, roll out the dough into a rectangle measuring about 25 x 15 cm (10 x 6 inches), or slightly smaller. Place the butter in the middle of the dough, then fold the bottom third over it and fold the top third down to enclose the butter completely.

Press the edges of the dough together with the rolling pin. Give the dough a quarter turn in a clockwise direction. Roll out the dough into the same shape as before, fold it again, then wrap in cling film. Chill for 30 minutes. Roll and fold the pastry 6 times in all, chilling it well each time. To remember the number of rollings, mark dents in the dough with your fingertips – one dent after the first rolling, two after the second and so on. After the process of rolling and folding is complete, chill the pastry again before using it.

ROUGH PUFF PASTRY

MAKES ABOUT 450 G (1 LB)

A slightly easier version of puff pastry. All the fat must be well chilled for success. For best results, chill the bowl of flour too and before handling the dough, always make sure your hands are very cold by holding them under cold running water.

225 g (8 oz) plain flour
pinch of salt
175 g (6 oz) butter, cut in chunks
  and chilled

5 ml (1 tsp) lemon juice
flour for rolling out

Sift the flour and salt into a bowl. Add the butter and mix in lightly using a round-bladed knife. Mix in the lemon juice and enough ice-cold water to make a soft dough. The mixture should take about 125 ml (4 fl oz) or very slightly more, but add the water a spoonful at a time to avoid making the dough too wet. The dough should be soft and very lumpy.

On a lightly floured surface, roll out the dough into a rectangle, keeping the corners square. Mark the dough into thirds, then fold and roll it as for flaky pastry. Repeat the process four times in all, chilling the dough between each rolling or as necessary. The rolled dough should be smooth. Wrap it in cling film and chill well before rolling it out.

SHORT CRUST PASTRY

MAKES ABOUT 350 G (12 OZ)

225 g (8 oz) plain flour
pinch of salt

50 g (2 oz) butter, diced
50 g (2 oz) lard, diced

Sift the flour and salt, then rub in the butter and lard until the mixture resembles fine breadcrumbs. Add enough cold water to make a stiff dough. Press the dough together. If time permits, wrap in cling film and rest in the refrigerator for 30 minutes before rolling it out.

SIPPETS OF FRIED OR TOASTED BREAD

Cut the crusts off thin slices of bread, then use cocktail cutters or small biscuit cutters to stamp out shapes from the slices. Alternatively, cut the slices diagonally into quarters and cut each piece in half again to make eight small triangles.

Fry the bread shapes in hot fat until golden, turning once. Traditionally, lard or meat dripping would have been used, but butter or a mixture of olive oil and butter, are equally suitable. Drain the sippets well on absorbent kitchen paper.

For toasted sippets, simply toast the whole slices of bread, then cut off the crusts and cut the toast into the required shapes.

SUET PASTRY

MAKES 350 G (12 OZ) OR 8 DUMPLINGS

225 g (8 oz) self-raising flour
pinch of salt
100 g (4 oz) shredded suet

Sift the flour. Stir in the salt and suet. Gradually stir in about 175 ml (6 fl oz) cold water to make a soft, but not sticky, dough. Gently knead the dough on a lightly floured surface, shape into a ball and use as required.

SWEET WHITE SAUCE

20 ml (4 tsp) cornflour
250 ml (8 fl oz) milk
15-30 ml (1-2 tbsp) sugar

natural vanilla essence or other
*   flavouring*

Blend the cornflour with a little of the milk to form a smooth, thin paste. Heat the remaining milk, stir it into the cornflour paste, then return the mixture to the pan and stir until boiling. Reduce the heat and cook, stirring frequently, for 3 minutes. Stir in sugar to taste and add the chosen flavouring. Serve hot.

VEGETABLE STOCK

MAKES ABOUT 1.1 LITRES (2 PINTS)

2 large onions, sliced

4 carrots, thinly sliced

6 celery sticks, sliced

1 small turnip, diced

4 open cup mushrooms

1 bouquet garni

1 blade of mace

4 black peppercorns

Place all the ingredients in a saucepan and add 1.4 litres (2½ pints) water. Bring to the boil, reduce the heat and cover the pan. Simmer for 1½ hours, then strain.

WHITE SAUCE

MAKES 600 ML (1 PINT)

40 g (1½ oz) butter

40 g (1½ oz) plain flour

600 ml (1 pint) milk

salt and pepper

Melt the butter. Stir in the flour and cook over low heat for 2–3 minutes. Gradually stir in the milk and bring to the boil, stirring continuously. Beat briskly for a few seconds to give the sauce a good gloss. Add seasoning to taste.

WHITE STOCK

MAKES ABOUT 2.25 LITRES (4 PINTS)

The meat and bones are not browned for a white stock; instead, the ingredients are boiled from raw for a lighter flavour.

1 gammon steak, trimmed of rind and fat, cut into pieces

900 g (2 lb) knuckle of veal, on the bone, or stewing veal, cut into pieces

meaty carcass of roast chicken or 4 chicken drumsticks

1 carrot, sliced

1 onion, sliced

6 celery sticks, sliced

6 white peppercorns

1 blade of mace

15 g (½ oz) salt (optional)

Place the gammon, veal and chicken in a large saucepan. Pour in 300 ml (½ pint) water and heat until just simmering. Cover and cook gently for 15 minutes.

Pour in 2 litres (3½ pints) cold water and add the remaining ingredients. Heat until simmering, then skim any scum off the surface of the stock. Continue skimming the stock at intervals for about 5 minutes, until no more scum rises, then cover the pan and simmer for 5 hours. Cool the stock slightly, then strain.

INDEX